A PRIMER OF PSYCHOTHERAPY

Other Books by Robert Langs

LSD: Personality and Experience. 1972.

The Technique of Psychoanalytic Psychotherapy. Vol. 1. 1973.

The Technique of Psychoanalytic Psychotherapy. Vol. 2. 1974.

The Bipersonal Field. 1976.

The Therapeutic Interaction. Vol. 1: Abstracts of the Psychoanalytic Literature. 1976.

The Therapeutic Interaction. Vol. 2: A Critical Overview and Synthesis. 1976.

The Listening Process. 1978.

Technique in Transition. 1978.

The Supervisory Experience. 1979.

The Therapeutic Environment. 1979.

Interactions: The Realm of Transference and Countertransference. 1980.

Intrapsychic and Interpersonal Dimensions of Treatment: A Clinical Dialogue (with Harold F. Searles, M.D.). 1980.

The Therapeutic Experience and Its Setting: A Clinical Dialogue (with Leo Stone, M.D.). 1980.

Resistances and Interventions: The Nature of Therapeutic Work. 1981.

The Psychotherapeutic Conspiracy. 1982.

Psychotherapy: A Basic Text. 1982.

Unconscious Communication in Everyday Life. 1983.

Workbooks for Psychotherapists. Vol. I: Understanding Unconscious Communication. 1985.

Workbooks for Psychotherapists. Vol. II: Listening and Formulating. 1985.

Workbooks for Psychotherapists. Vol. III: Intervening and Validating. 1985.

Madness and Cure. 1985.

The Genius of the Dreamer. (In press).

A PRIMER OF
Psychotherapy

ROBERT LANGS, M.D.

GARDNER PRESS, INC.
New York • London

To the members of the Society for Psychoanalytic Psychotherapy,
in honor of their steadfast dedication to the field
and in appreciation for their support and caring

GARDNER PRESS, INC.
19 UNION SQUARE WEST
NEW YORK, NEW YORK 10003

All foreign orders except Canada and South America to:
Afterhurst Limited
Chancery House
319 City Road
London, N1, England

Printed in the United States of America

Library of Congress Cataloging-in-Publication Data

Langs, Robert, 1928–
Primer of psychotherapy.

Bibliography: p.
Includes index.
1. Psychotherapy. 2. Psychotherapist and patient.
3. Insight in psychotherapy. I. Title. [DNLM:
1. Professional-Patient Relations. 2. Psychotherapy—
methods.   WM 420 L285pb]
RC480.5.L3534 1988   616.89'14   86-22869
ISBN 0-89876-142-5

Design by
Publishers Creative Services, Jamaica, N.Y.

Contents

v

Preface

This primer is distinctive in several ways. It offers the first condensed summary of the communicative approach in psychoanalytic psychotherapy. And it represents an essential distillation of clinical findings developed over 15 years of study in which the patient's unconscious validation of the therapist's interventions has been central to the therapeutic interaction. Such communicative findings have permitted new insights not only into the nature of the therapeutic interaction, but also into the nature of the human mind and its functioning. They have dictated, in particular, a new way of understanding how the mind processes emotionally charged information. Thus, along with summarizing validated technical precepts, this primer serves to introduce fundamental revisions in our understanding of basic mental functioning, with particular focus on Freud's topographic model and his conception of primary and secondary process thinking.

The book also takes a fresh look at the nature and function of the ground rules of psychotherapy, and includes recent studies of the nature of meaning, the role of death anxiety, and the importance of psychotic communications from nonpsychotic patients in the psychotherapeutic experience, all of which have suggested new ways of illuminating the structure and function of madness and its cure.

Because this book is a primer, it contains little in the way of elaborate clinical documentation for its stated positions and principles of technique. Clinical illustrations are plentiful, but brief. Virtually no effort has been made to discuss the literature, either within or outside the communicative approach, that has played a role in the development of a particular clinical precept or idea; however, a reading list is provided for the reader interested in pursuing such references.

THE COMMUNICATIVE APPROACH

The communicative approach began with the development of a listening process that would take into full account the spiraling nature of the conscious and especially unconscious communicative interaction between patient and therapist. This involved a particular way of listening, intervening, and especially of decoding unconscious messages from patients in light of specific events in the therapeutic interaction.

The approach has now broadened to function as a method of understanding the unconscious dimension of communications not only from patients, but from therapists as well. It has become a way of comprehending messages, information, and meaning as they pertain both to the structure of a participant's madness and to the specific transactions of the ongoing therapeutic situation. (The word *madness* is used here, and throughout this book, in its broadest possible sense, to indicate any emotionally founded dysfunction. See "Defining Madness" in Chapter 1.) The communicative approach, then, is both a technique and a point of view. It is a distinctive way of practicing psychotherapy, in which the correct (validated) decoding of unconscious meaning in patients' material has revealed over time a set of effective technical precepts; but the approach has also become a way of understanding the unconscious level of communication in any interaction between patient and therapist, regardless of the extent to which the therapist involved understands and interprets the unconscious dimension. Communicative insights into the process of *cure*—or more accurately, the means by which patients are offered *relief* from expressions of madness (*i.e.*, symptoms)—are both unique and incisive, the result of distinctive realizations available only through the consistent decoding of unconscious expressions.

It is to be stressed, then, that this book offers only those clinical propositions that have been repeatedly validated within the therapeutic interaction by unconscious or derivative (encoded) communication. As such, the book reflects the special and unique appreciation of the communicative approach for the role played by unconscious thinking, meaning, communication, experience, and information processing both in the development and maintenance of emotionally founded dysfunctions (forms of madness) and in their optimal cure. The overall goal of this primer is to succinctly describe the basic premises of the communicative approach, the full range of its fundamental techniques, and the most important aspects of its growing understanding of madness—and, more broadly, of the nature of human psychosocial functioning and adaptation.

Finally, this primer is designed to introduce the reader to an updated model of the mind, based on insights derived from the communicative approach. The mind has two distinct realms of thinking, functioning, and ways of processing emotionally charged information. I have called these realms the *deep unconscious system* and the *conscious system* (which has its own separate unconscious components; see Chapter 9). The deep unconscious system operates according to a distinctive set of premises, and the results of its efforts are known to the conscious system only by way of indirect or *transformed* images—that is, by way of images that have been displaced (from the anxiety-provoking stimuli actually perceived) and transformed into less dangerous symbols of those raw stimuli. The deep unconscious system processes meanings and messages that are sources of inordinate anxiety and terror. As such, its contents evoke profound awe and deep dread. Patients and therapists alike fear to represent, embody, and comprehend the information and meaning existing on this level of experience. Nonetheless, the main clinical-theoretical thrust of the present volume concerns the functioning and contents of this realm.

On the purely clinical level, this primer is designed to present a fundamental way of listening, intervening, and validating based on the various levels of meaning discerned in material from patients in psychotherapy. If the reader is able to grasp, master, and utilize these fundamental tools, he or she will be in a position to discover the insights derived from such efforts through his or her own clinical work. It is only on the basis of clinical experience that a sense of commitment and conviction about the wisdom of the communicative approach is truly possible. It is the goal of this volume to provide a sound basis for this commitment and for the therapeutic work to which it leads.

CHAPTER 1

Basic Premises

The basic premise of the communicative approach is that a patient and therapist are involved in a circular interaction and constitute themselves as a system of two—as two polarities of a bipersonal field. This interaction is transactional. That is, the patient is evoking responses in the therapist, and also reacting to the therapist's inputs as they impinge on the patient's experience; similarly, the therapist is evoking reactions in the patient, and also responding to stimuli emanating from the patient. The context of this interaction is always flowing or spiraling: Each evocation and response changes the context to which both parties are constantly adapting.

There are both *quiet communications* and *noisy communications*. The latter are projective identifications (interactional projections). Quiet communications, from either patient or therapist, are communications that occur without extensive unconscious efforts to arouse or stir up specific introjects and responses in the other participant. In contrast, a projective identification has more interactional power; the mechanism is constituted as an interactional effort to project into the other person aspects of one's own introjects, conflicts, and other disturbing inner contents. As such, interactional projection is designed to agitate and to create introjects and information that can then be metabolized toward insight. (If interactional projection happens without understanding, however, the recipient responds with additional interactional projects.)

The central task in psychotherapy involves an adaptation to the other participant in light of one's own inner needs, conflicts, and assets. For the patient, the therapist becomes an exceedingly meaningful object (person) whose interventions exert extraordinary influence both on the vicissitudes of the patient's madness, and on the communication of narratives and images that illuminate the *unconscious basis* of this madness. And the patient also exerts a special influence on the therapist's inner mental world and inner state, and especially on the nature of his or her interventions.

Nevertheless, even though patient and therapist are under pressures to adapt to each other, the means of this adaptation is—or should be—rather different for each participant. For the therapist, the goal is to respond to the patient by creating as ideal as possible a setting in which the therapeutic work can unfold. In addition, it is the therapist's responsibility to process the information contained in the patient's free associations and behaviors in a way that will lead to sound understanding and intervention—with special consideration given to the unconscious dimension of these messages.

The therapist's means of adaptation, then, is the creation and management of a proper set of ground rules for the psychotherapy, and a processing of information such that projective identifications and other expressions can be metabolized toward understanding and insight. Both of these requisites are anxiety-provoking for therapists and difficult to execute, because the role requirements or rules for adaptation are essentially defined by the patient's derivative or unconscious expressions. Thus, the therapist is far more vulnerable to expressions of madness (as defined by failures to meet one's role requirements) than the patient.

This insight can be better understood by considering the means of adaptation to the therapist and to therapy available to the patient. The patient is offered the opportunity to free associate and to cooperate or resist—oppose—the therapeutic process. The role requirements of the patient dictate only that he or she be capable of finding the therapist's office, sit in the chair or lie on the couch, say whatever comes to mind, listen attentively to the therapist's interventions, leave the session at the appointed moment, pay the therapist's bill when due, and return to the session again at the next appointed hour. There is far less opportunity for expressions of madness in these tasks than in those required of the therapist. Many acute symptoms occur in patients as reactions to the primary madness of the therapist as expressed in errant and frame-deviant interventions.

THE INTERACTION

The therapeutic interaction is well conceptualized as a stimulus–response paradigm, but only so long as the circularity of the interaction is taken into account. It may also be characterized as a spiraling communicative interaction with both conscious and unconscious elements or expressions. This interaction itself, as noted, is the context to which both participants are constantly attempting to adapt, and it is the main stimulus for the patient's mad expressions.

From the patient's vantage point, the stimulus for communication is that of the therapist's interventions. In general, the patient's *conscious expressions* are a reaction to the manifest contents of the therapist's efforts. The patient's *unconscious or derivative communications*, on the other hand, are, as a rule, a response to the *implications* of the therapist's interventions, especially those of which the patient is unaware. The central component of the patient's unconscious communications involves the patient's unconscious perceptions of these implications. That is, the responses of the patient contain in *disguised or encoded* form his or her unconscious perceptions of the meanings implied by the therapist's interventions. These unconsciously perceived meanings are quite literally outside the conscious awareness of the patient (and often of the therapist as well). The patient expresses them only indirectly, in an effort to deal with their ramifications without arousing anxiety. The therapist is, accordingly, able to decode the patient's encoded perceptions only in so far as he or she is aware of the meanings actually implied by the ongoing therapeutic situation.

It must be stressed in this regard that recognition of the immediate therapeutic interaction as central to the patient's unconscious communications does not exclude the genetic dimension of mad expressions. Similarly, we may recognize the validity of the patient's unconscious perceptions of the meanings implied by the therapist's interventions without discounting the intrapsychic dimension of the patient's reactions. Traditional psychoanalytically oriented therapy understands the intrapsychic dimension as an unconscious distorting factor in the patient's conscious perceptions; the communicative approach recognizes the intrapsychic dimension, rather, as an unconscious *selective factor* in the patient's represented unconscious perceptions. That is, the meanings selected by the patient for encoded representation actually have been implied by the therapist's interventions; but the patient has selected only those that are pertinent to his or her own madness.

Genetic elements are continually in operation and do, of course, influence the present state of the patient's madness by contributing to the selectivity of his or her perceptions. It is extremely rare, however, to find a clinical situation in which the genetic influence leads to an actual *distortion* of the patient's view of the therapist. It is mainly when the frame is secure and the therapist's interventions are validated (and therefore correct) that genetic factors lead to a measure of *exaggeration* in the patient's perceptions of the implications of the therapist's interventions. Under all other conditions, this factor of exaggeration is minimal, and the patient's perceptions tend to be veridical, even though they are unconscious and represented by way of derivatives. In fact, the genetic influence is often constituted in terms of the errant therapist's repeating on some level and in some form a version of an earlier traumatic genetic experience and interaction that has contributed to the origins of the patient's psychopathology or madness.

The following brief excerpt will make this point clear.

The patient is a young man in once-weekly therapy because of depression and problems both in leaving home and in establishing a lasting relationship with a woman. The therapy had been arranged by the patient's employer under an Employees' Assistance Program. The therapist, a woman, had agreed to submit quarterly reports to the employer, though they included little in the way of detail.

In the second month of therapy, the patient began an hour by alluding in passing to the report situation. He then went on to say that he hadn't yet straightened out his relationships with women. He had told one woman in particular who "kept coming on to" him that he didn't want to see her anymore. "She has a boyfriend," he explained. "She shouldn't need me." A friend had told the patient that this was the kind of woman who needed to create triangles, which the patient thought was "pretty stupid, if not destructive." This woman had the habit of telephoning her boyfriend in the patient's presence, and she had once called the patient in the boyfriend's presence. Next, the patient recalled a dream about finding his own apartment. He then went on to speak of the intrusiveness of his mother, who, to this day, thought nothing of coming into the bathroom when the patient was on the john.

The *trigger* (or, technically, the *adaptive context*) for this material is revealed in the patient's allusion at the beginning of the session to the report situation. The stimulus, then, is constituted as an intervention by the therapist— or, more accurately, as the patient's expectation that the therapist would soon file a report on his psychotherapy to his employer (she had already completed a preliminary form). Without fully defining the interactional method of decoding as yet, we may simply take the patient's displaced story (narrative) and view it as a vehicle of encoded perceptions concerning the therapeutic interaction— with particular reference to the anticipated intervention of the therapist. The images speak of a stupid and destructive threesome that is so intrusive to the patient that he wishes to be rid of it. In a spirit of rectification (both within therapy and outside it), the patient dreams of having his own apartment—his own space; in particular, he wishes to be rid of his intrusive mother.

It seems reasonable to suggest that the patient has perceived the therapist's contact with his employer as a triangular relation-

ship that reflects both ignorance and destructiveness. Furthermore, the intrusive employer is seen as comparable to the patient's mother—the critical genetic figure for the moment. In
substance, then, it can be proposed that the patient unconsciously perceives the therapist as having created an intrusive
relationship similar to the ones he is describing with his girlfriend and his mother.

All of these images are reasonable, well-stated, and highly
perceptive. They are expressed by way of displacement and disguise, in a narrative with a derivative or transformed meaning.
There is no sign of distortion, but the patient has *selected* a particular set of meanings among the many that are actually implied by the therapist's interventions, and he has experienced
those meanings in terms of his own madness and genetic history. Clearly, the genetic and intrapsychic factors (centering
here on the patient's pathological relationship with an intrusive
mother) are critical in determining the particular meaning of the
third-party situation that the patient has unconsciously chosen
to represent, work over, and attempt to rectify.

For another patient, the same third-party situation might
well be perceived and represented quite differently—in terms of
its other possible meanings. For example, a patient for whom homosexual issues had unconscious and genetic importance might
unconsciously perceive the therapist's report as a way of bringing a man into the treatment situation and of offering him (the
patient) a homosexual object. If the therapist were male, the patient might also perceive the third-party involvement as a way
in which the therapist was attempting to protect himself from
homosexual wishes toward the patient. It is in this manner that
intrapsychic fantasies, memories, and the like influence the specific way in which each patient processes the incoming messages and the information contained in the interventions of the
therapist.

In principle, the unconscious and conscious dimensions of
the ongoing therapeutic interaction are central to the patient's
adaptation and communication and to the vicissitudes of his or
her madness. The patient's narratives and comments about outside events should always be attended to for possible encoded
perceptions concerning the therapeutic interaction. On very rare
occasions, a highly significant outside trauma, such as the death

of an important family member, may evoke a significant measure of derivative expression from the patient. Nonetheless, it is important even in situations of that kind to attend to the means by which the outside experience is, through condensation, also being used unconsciously to represent in derivative fashion issues within the therapeutic interaction.

The communicative approach has identified seven specific dimensions to the therapeutic interaction (Chapter 8)—dynamics and genetics, communication and meaning, ground rules and frame, mode of relatedness, mode of cure, identity and narcissism, and sanity and madness. Issues in each of these seven components of human relatedness are brought into play in the therapeutic context as they are stimulated by the immediate therapeutic experience. Thus, attention to the here-and-now—even as it includes an understanding of unconscious communication from both participants to treatment—is only the starting point for a consideration of the implications of the patient's material. As implications of the therapeutic experience touch on issues in each of the seven dimensions, the patient expresses their meanings unconsciously. The immediate therapeutic interaction becomes a constant reference point for understanding the meaning of these issues and the patient's unconscious experience of them. In other words, the immediate therapeutic interaction is not the primary focus of treatment, but its polestar.

DEFINING THE APPROACH

The communicative approach is a particular version of psychoanalytic psychotherapy in which special stress is placed on the patient's unconscious—encoded and disguised—communications as they illuminate both the vicissitudes of the therapeutic interaction and those of the patient's madness. It is an approach that decodes the patient's derivative, or encoded, material specifically in light of the implications of the therapist's interventions.

Communicative therapists accept the proposition that there is a significant unconscious dimension to *expressed madness* (*i.e.*, to all types of emotionally founded symptoms). Such therapists believe in principle that an important measure of symptom relief can arise from a correct interpretation of the derivative communications that illuminate the patient's unconscious experience. The approach recognizes other curative factors as well. The most important of these is the therapist's capacity for holding and containment, as reflected in his or her ability to make validated interpretations and to secure the ideal frame for the psychotherapeutic experience. A therapist capable of such efforts inevitably generates in the patient unconscious identifications and introjections of his or her well-functioning and positive capacities. Communicative cure, then, is founded on the therapist's genuine insight into the derivative communications that emanate from the deep unconscious system of the mind, as well as on the therapist's capacity for offering the patient secure-frame conditions to treatment (or, when deviations are inevitable, secure-frame moments at opportune interludes in the course of the psychotherapy).

The communicative approach adheres in principle to psychoanalytic conceptions of the role played by genetic and dynamic factors in madness, but it has also defined and delineated important issues in each of the other dimensions of the therapeutic experience (mentioned earlier; also see Chapter 7) and sees those issues as relevant to human interaction in general. The emphasis in the communicative approach is on the unconscious aspect of madness, but this aspect is very specifically defined in terms of derivative or encoded expressions. Communicative therapists are convinced that true unconscious meaning is expressed solely by way of *encoded derivatives*—communications in which the perceptions being expressed have undergone displacement from their actual stimulus and been symbolized in other terms. Therefore, unconscious meaning as it is relevant to the patient's madness cannot be identified either from a patient's *manifest expressions* or from the *implications* inherent in a particular behavior or communication.

It is the consistent illumination of *derivative* meaning that inevitably leads to an impression of the mind as encompassing two distinctive modes of thought, communication, experience, and information processing. As mentioned, one is a conscious mode, which governs manifest meanings, and to which is appended an accessible or superficial unconscious subsystem. This latter is the realm to which implied meanings belong. Distinct from this unconscious subsystem is the deep or inaccessible unconscious system, whose premises, areas of sensitivity, ways of processing information, and output are peculiarly its own. The communicative approach departs from psychoanalytically oriented therapy in its recognition of encoded messages as the only source of information about the deep unconscious system. Psychoanalytically oriented therapy traditionally works with the manifest contents of the associations from patients and with the evident implications of those contents. Decoding is not a central feature of such work. In other words, when the patient's associations refer to outside events, the traditional psychoanalytically oriented therapist interprets mainly by hypothesizing the feelings and meanings implied by what the patient has said or done. In contrast, the communicative approach proposes that all narratives, images, and dream reports whose subject matter pertains to experiences outside of treatment, as a rule, function as vehicles for encoded communications about the therapeutic experience.

The communicative approach accepts Freud's basic proposition (1900) that the mechanisms used to encode unconscious material for conscious expression are essentially those of displacement and symbolization, or disguise. (Condensation, concerns for representability, and secondary revision are of lesser importance.) Thus, the communicative therapist uses a method of decoding that undoes or reverses the patient's use of these two fundamental vehicles of human transformation, or camouflage. When such efforts are carried out consistently in light of the implications of the therapist's interventions, it emerges that a patient's initial encoded response to an intervention always involves his or her unconscious *perceptions* of the intervention's meanings. Following this, both consciously and unconsciously, the patient expresses a full range of *reactions* to these perceptions (see Chapter 3).

In substance, then, the communicative approach to psychoanalytic psychotherapy stands or falls on the correct decoding of the patient's encoded, or derivative, communications and on an understanding of their unconscious meanings and ramifications. For validation of correct interpretations, the approach relies on subsequent unconscious derivative communications from the patient, which typically extend a correct therapeutic intervention in unique and unexpected ways.

It is to be stressed that *interactional decoding*—decoding in light of the implications of the therapist's interventions (also known as *trigger decoding*)—is the only means by which a therapist can gain access to the deep unconscious system, and thus to the unconscious basis of the patient's madness. In substance, then, the communicative approach has developed a methodology that is faithful to Freud's original goal, which was to offer a cure for madness based on insight into truly unconscious factors.

DEFINING MADNESS

The communicative approach uses the term *madness* to refer broadly to all forms of emotional dysfunction. Madness in this sense is to be distinguished from colloquial allusions to psychosis. The term is intended, rather, to indicate a common foundation for all emotional disturbances, ranging from affective disorders such as anxiety and depression to psychosomatic symptoms such as asthma, peptic ulcer, and more general physical disturbances that have been shown to have emotional components. Underlying all such disturbances is what the communicative approach terms *core madness*. Core madness is made up of several basic elements. Its nucleus is a mass of primitive, realistic and unrealistic, distorted thoughts and images, aspects of which stem from mental functioning in the early months and years of life, and from those parts of the mind that remain primitive even into later years. These thoughts and images appear to be concentrated in the deep unconscious information processing system, and in the more stable pathological unconscious system of memories and motivations with which it strongly interacts. Their influence is thus outside of direct awareness, and is expressed only by means of encoded communication. Every individual contains a core of madness, whose structure may be relatively primitive or advanced—utterly terrifying or simply a cause for anxiety.

Contributing to core madness throughout life are self-contradictory messages, from others and from oneself, and intrapsychic and interpersonal conflict, all of which is inevitable in the living of life. Core madness also stems from the realization of the existential crisis—that with the gift of life comes death, itself a disturbing and contradictory message.

In general, core madness is organized around significant *life traumas*—especially those traumas that occur in the early years, although later life traumas are not without significance. These traumas virtually always involve some form of *death anxiety*—issues of separation and loss, the actual death of others, major illness, and major injury. Assaults of this kind are partly experienced through primitive and unrealistic (psychotic) perceptions and are often the occasion for minipsychotic acts (unrealistic but brief lapses in behavior) and for psychotic communications in nonpsychotic individuals (see Chapter 9). Communicative and interactional analyses of expressions of core madness in the course of psychotherapy testify to the critical role of death anxiety and its derivatives in the foundation of mad symptoms.

Core madness may be well or poorly defended against. The extent to which core madness is reasonably well managed such that symptomatic expressions are kept to a minimum depends on the nature of an individual's intrapsychic tendencies and defenses, interpersonal transactions, and further traumas, Under conditions that weaken the intrapsychic and interpersonal defenses constructed against core madness—and these include traumatic interventions by a therapist—there will be an open expression of emotional dysfunction. Such episodes constitute incidents of *expressed madness*. The symptoms involved range, as noted, from psychosomatic disturbances, to affective disorders and phobias and obsessions, to disturbances in interpersonal functioning. In addition to these symptomatic elements, expressed madness may involve disturbances in characterological tendencies and so may be classified in terms of level and

type of functioning—neurotic, borderline, psychotic, narcissistic, and the like.

In essence, then, both patient and therapist house a core of
madness, and both—the patient and, at times, the therapist—
will reveal manifestations of expressed madness. As stated
earlier, all forms of failure in role requirements are perceived unconsciously as expressions of madness. Indeed, correct intervention and frame management have been determined on the basis of consistent unconscious reactions in patients. Whenever a
therapist intervenes incorrectly through behavior, comment, or
mismanagement of the ground rules, the patient will experience
and communicate an unconscious perception of expressed
therapist-madness. The patient will also react to such unconsciously perceived madness in a variety of ways, most often
through unconscious curative endeavors and efforts to help the
therapist rectify his or her errant techniques.

The crux of the matter is that patients tend to reveal little in
the way of dysfunction in the presence of therapist-madness. In
contrast, expressions of therapist-sanity (as conveyed through
validated interventions) brings patient-madness to the fore. In
general, the conscious system of the patient, which controls behavior, tends unconsciously and defensively to prefer clinical situations in which therapist-madness occupies the bipersonal
field. Under such conditions, the patient's resources are mobilized and his or her madness recedes into the background,
where it serves mainly as a factor in selecting for encoded
representation pertinent aspects of the implications of the therapist's errant interventions. The patient finds much comfort in
being spared the role of the actively mad individual in the therapeutic interaction. In fact, in such situations, the patient is
given the defensive opportunity to express his or her own madness almost entirely through the way in which he or she selectively perceives the disturbance of the therapist.

Therapists also unconsciously prefer to function in mad fashion in the therapeutic interaction, largely because they are unaware of their own mad behaviors and are permitted in this situation to deny their existence. At the same time, entirely on an
unconscious level, they have the unique opportunity of receiv-
ing the patient's unconscious ministrations and efforts at cure.

All the while this is happening, both patient and therapist consciously believe that the cure of the patient is uppermost.

It is unconscious needs of this kind, characteristic of the unconscious subsystem of the conscious system, that readily entice both patients and therapists into some type of psychotherapeutic collusion and conspiracy. The unconscious needs for errant forms of psychotherapy in both participants to treatment tend to create a field of great hazard, one that is strongly influenced by the aberrant and pathological needs of both participants to the experience. The very vehicle through which we hope to alleviate expressed madness tends all too often to be constituted itself as a mad situation. Paradoxically, the frightened patient who is convinced that he or she is exceptionally mad finds a notable measure of unconscious relief in discovering madness in the therapist and in realizing unconsciously that therapy itself is imbued with madness. This is another reason for using a term as broad as the word *madness*, which can incorporate all types of emotionally aberrant symptoms and situations.

Supporting clinical material for these propositions has been presented and dissected in far greater detail in previous writings than can be attempted here. A brief vignette must suffice to illustrate what has been confirmed consistently by clinical observation.

The patient is an 18-year-old young woman who had made a suicide attempt with sleeping pills and alcohol. She was seen in an emergency room by a male therapist, having first been screened by a social worker who reported her findings to the therapist. The therapist also had brief contact with the patient's parents. He had asked them to wait in the waiting room while he held a 45-minute evaluation session with the patient. The therapist began this session by identifying himself as the evaluating consultant and asking the patient how he could be of help.

The patient initially ruminated about the problems she had, saying that she had to get over them, they weren't very important, etc. Twenty minutes of silence followed, during which the therapist intervened three times. First, he advised the patient to say whatever was coming to mind; second, he told her he was relying on her for information; and third, he acknowledged her expectation to be hospitalized, and suggested that she might be waiting for the therapist to tell her what to do.

After a bit more silence, the patient described her relationship with her stepfather, with whom she and her mother were now living. She spoke in detail of the anger in the man and of his uncontrolled sexuality. She then described sexual experiences with the stepfather and episodes of being beaten by him. When the patient had told her mother about these incidents, the mother did not believe her. Moreover, the stepfather was always prying into the patient's business. If the patient told her mother a secret, she was sure to tell her stepfather, who would then react violently to the information.

Without further pursuing this session, we may identify the patient's expressed madness as the suicide attempt. In the formal analysis of sessions to be described in Chapter 3, all forms of expressed madness—whether pathological symptoms or pathological resistances—are called *indicators*. An indicator, then, is a sign of expressed madness.

As this session unfolded, there were also indications of the life traumas around which the patient's core madness had been organized. Although not mentioned in the above-quoted opening part of the session, the patient had suffered the death of her father when she was three years of age. She had also been molested by several of her mother's lovers, experiences that had begun during the patient's latency. These incidents had created a dimension or core of madness within the patient that centered around issues of death, separation, and loss, all of which were perceived as violent forms of abandonment. In addition, a related aspect of her core madness involved incestuously tinged sexual experiences with attendant sexual conflicts and guilt, and a view of sexuality as intermixed with violence and destruction. These elements in the patient's core madness found expression not only in her suicide attempt (which had been prompted by the sudden decision of the patient's boyfriend to break up their relationship), but also established a constellation of unconscious fantasies, memories, and perceptions that became a vital part of the schemata with which this patient experienced the world—both consciously and unconsciously.

The patient was thus faced with trauma and danger situations both in the therapeutic relationship and in her outside life. In terms of her outside situation, the patient spoke directly of having been deserted by her boyfriend, and she drew a direct analogy to the experience of having lost her father. In addition, she carefully and manifestly analyzed the implications of these experiences, showing little evidence of the unconscious displacement and symbolization that is characteristic of unconscious thinking and adaptation. By and large, then, the patient was adapting to the outside trauma with communications that were mainly manifest. Although a careful analysis would undoubtedly reveal some unconscious response, the patient's primary reaction was straightforward and conscious, not derivative and unconscious. Conscious—though under unconscious *influence*.

The situation is rather different when we look at the therapeutic interaction. The trigger in the patient's outside life is the abandonment by her boyfriend. The triggers within the therapeutic situation include the setting (a hospital emergency room rather than the ideal of a private office), the therapist's power to hospitalize the patient, and the therapist's acceptance of information from a third party (later material indicated that the patient suspected such leakage and was concerned about violations of her privacy and confidentiality by the therapist). All these circumstances must be considered interventions, because a patient unconsciously understands all stimuli constituted by the therapeutic situation in terms of the therapist's participation in them.

On the conscious level, the patient says virtually nothing about these stimuli. On the other hand, she does represent their presence in the therapeutic interaction indirectly, by way of encoded derivatives—in particular, through her allusion to the mother's betraying her confidence by revealing secrets to the stepfather. The remainder of the patient's material organizes as encoded perceptions of the therapist, given particular and selective meaning unconsciously, in light of the patient's own core madness. Thus, the therapist's participation in this leakage—and, through condensation, his participation in the other triggers as well—leads the patient to unconscious perceptions of being sexually abused and having violence done to her.

As we will see, these are valid readings of the unconscious

implications of the actual interventions of the therapist. The patient's material organizes as a powerful unconscious and derivative response to these interventions. Repeated observations of this kind have led to the proposition that the unconscious meanings of a patient's madness is revealed almost exclusively as derivative responses to the implications of the interventions of the psychotherapist.

RECOMMENDED READINGS

Grotstein, J. (1977): The psychoanalytic concept of schizophrenia I: The dilemma. *International Journal of Psycho-Analysis* 58:403–426.
Grotstein, J. (1977): The psychoanalytic concept of schizophrenia II: Reconciliation. *International Journal of Psycho-Analysis* 58:427–452.
Langs, R. (1982): *Psychotherapy: A Basic Text*. NY: Aronson.
Langs, R. (1985): *Workbooks for Psychotherapists*. Vol. III: *Intervening and Validating*. Emerson, NJ: Newconcept.
Langs, R. (1985); *Workbooks for Psychotherapists*. Vol II: *Listening and Formulating*. Emerson, NJ:: Newconcept.
Langs, R. (1985): *Workbooks for Psychotherapists*. Vol. I: *Understanding Unconscious Communication*. Emerson, NJ:: Newconcept.

CHAPTER *2*

Emotionally Charged Messages

The therapeutic interaction is, as noted, best conceptualized as a spiraling interchange of conscious and unconscious meaning and information. The carriers of such meaning are termed *messages*. Messages may be verbal or nonverbal, that is, expressed through words, affects, and/or actions.

The communicative understanding of the therapeutic interaction is based on a proper conceptualization of the messages from patients and therapists—the free associations (and affects and behaviors) of the former, and the interventions (as noted, a term broadly defined to include the setting, all behaviors including silences, and the words and affects) of the therapist. In so doing, it is critical to maintain the distinction between surface information and other levels of meaning beyond the surface. An additional distinction is made between consciously perceived or available meaning and those meanings that register outside of awareness—unconsciously.

In general, conscious meaning may evoke realistic fear, but that fear will not be a factor in unrealistic anxiety, depression, and their consequences. Surface and conscious dangers are disturbing and call for adaptive efforts, but these efforts generally do not create madness directly; most such responses are conscious and direct, although they may spill over into unconscious reactions as well. It is the latent or implied meanings of danger situations—those that are unconsciously perceived and processed—that are generally the main basis of mad symptoms.

It is important to keep this distinction in mind, because a great deal of psychotherapy is directed toward surface dangers and their meanings, that is, toward problems that have little relevance to expressed madness (where the central issues are unconscious). In fact, we should clearly distinguish between the type of psychotherapy that deals with direct danger situations and the type of psychotherapy that seeks to illuminate and to resolve unconscious factors in madness. Patient-therapist contacts that deal with direct and immediate emotional difficulties are *counseling situations*. The focus of such efforts is on the surface and implied aspects of the patient's problems. All too often an expert healer claims to be carrying out psychotherapy when he or she is actually engaged in counseling. Moreover, in most such instances, the counseling efforts, directed as they are toward immediate reality and conscious meaning, *serve functionally as a way to avoid the unconscious meanings of the patient's madness.* As pointed out, many such meanings are expressed by way of accurate perceptions of madness within the therapist and in the nature of his or her interventional efforts.

LEVELS OF MEANING AND TYPES OF MESSAGES

All messages, whether verbal, affective, or behavioral, have a *manifest or surface content* and a set of *implications*. But some messages are derivative, and some are nonderivative. The present discussion focuses on verbal messages, and assumes, first, that there may well be an affective component, and, second, that a similar analysis could be carried out for behaviors, but with far less certainty.

A nonderivative message is simply an adaptive response to incoming and received messages (stimuli or triggers). Its main characteristic is the *absence* of encoded or disguised meaning. Figure 2-1 diagrams a nonderivative message. When analyzed

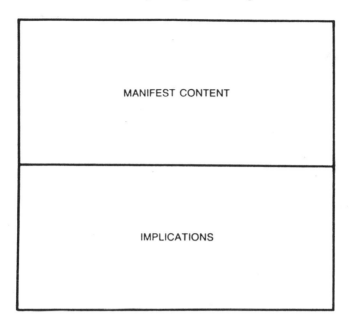

FIGURE 2.1
A Nonderivative Message

in light of the incoming messages, a nonderivative message reveals surface content and a set of implications, but no encoded or disguised meanings. The implications of a nonderivative message are, as a rule, processed both consciously and unconsciously by both sender and receiver. The implications that are conscious for the sender of a message may or may not be conscious for the receiver, and, conversely, the implications of which the receiver is aware may or may not fall within the awareness of the sender. Although there is often considerable overlap with respect to conscious and unconscious implications as experienced respectively by sender and receiver, there are often sharp differences.

In psychotherapy, nonderivative messages expressed by the patient tend to take the form of intellectualizations, generalizations, nonspecific comments, direct references to the therapist, efforts at analysis, and other types of speculation. Messages of this kind are expressions of the conscious system, even though some of the implications are outside of awareness. An *implica-tion* of a message may be defined as any nonmanifest meaning that is inherent in and can be extracted directly from the message itself. In ascertaining the particular implications of a message, one examines the overall surface context for nonmanifest meaning pertaining directly to the immediate area with which the surface message is concerned.

For example, a male therapist was seeing a female patient in psychotherapy for episodes of depression. The patient had been referred by the therapist's wife, who uses her maiden name in her work. In a session early in the treatment, the patient mentioned the referral source, and the therapist pressed the patient as to what she knew about the woman who had referred her to him. The patient responded as follows: "You're really pressing me, aren't you? All I know is that she works in the same school as me. I'm wondering why you're so concerned. Something seems to be bothering you. I really don't think you should press me so hard."

In this instance, the patient's free associations or messages appear to be basically nonderivative in nature. Their manifest meaning involves the patient's conscious perceptions of the therapist—the ways in which he is pressing her and concerned about what she knows about the referral source. She reacts by advising him to ease up. This is the manifest level of meaning and is identified by a summary of the direct communications.

To arrive at implications, we would attempt to identify the possible nonmanifest meanings in this message. What can we infer? What is the patient expressing indirectly? We answer these questions by examining the manifest messages themselves and extracting additional meaning. Some of these meanings may be conscious for the patient, others unconscious. Similarly, we may miss implications of which the patient is aware, and we may share with the patient conscious awareness of still other inferences.

For example, this message sequence seems to imply criticism of the therapist, discontent with his efforts, and an underlying sense of anger. The message may also imply thoughts of terminating the therapy and a perception of inappropriate aggression in the therapist.

The formulation of implications thus involves an examination of manifest messages as they create a sequence of communications in a particular immediate context. We accept the manifest context of the messages and search for evidence of hidden meaning. In this instance, the message scene or context involves the therapist and the therapeutic interaction. The patient has made a number of manifest comments about the therapist, and we have searched for possible additional implications inherent in those comments.

If we were engaged in *decoding* (see below), we would have suggested a set of nonmanifest meanings that actually belong to a *different* scene or context. Instead, since we are concerned with implications, we have tried to extract as many meanings as possible as they pertain to the area of the patient's immediate concern.

The distinction between inference making and decoding is critical. A nonderivative message does not have encoded meaning, though it does, as noted, have both manifest and implied meaning. Encoded meaning is created by displacement and symbolization, and decoding therefore requires an undoing of these two mechanisms—in particular, a shift from the manifest scene to a second, and different, scene or arena.

This is not to suggest that implications are merely straightforward and concrete. Implications can be highly theoretical. In the case just described, the therapist could speculate that the patient was expressing a measure of criticism, which suggests a harsh superego. One might infer the presence of oral or anal aggression. But none of this has anything to do with derivative meaning. All of these formulations take the basic message at face value, seek out nonmanifest meaning in terms of the direct area covered by the messages, and arrive at meanings of which a patient may indeed be unaware.

Once pointed out by the therapist, however, the implications of a message are often readily acknowledged. In fact, as some analysts have noted, many patients are more adept at identifying the implications of their own messages than their therapists. This is because the unconscious implications of messages belong to the conscious system and its superficial unconscious subsystem. As such, they arouse far less anxiety than encoded meaning. Implications are often clichéd and almost always involve personal impressions and speculations. Thus, they are open to a wide margin of error. And because they do not in any way deal with derivative meaning and the core madness housed in the deep unconscious system, interventions that point out the implications of a patient's associations or behaviors do *not* obtain derivative or unconscious validation. Instead, they evoke either conscious agreement or disagreement, and some measure of conscious elaboration. In fact, the only deep unconscious processing evoked by such interventions is the patient's unconscious perception of the therapist as defensively working in the area of implications rather than dealing with encoded meaning.

Let us turn now to encoded or derivative messages (see Figure 2-2). Whereas a *nonderivative message* has *two* levels of meanings, a *derivative message* has *three*. In this type of message, there is manifest content, conscious and unconscious implications, and encoded, or disguised (transformed), meanings. Each of these levels of meaning must be separately formulated; and each is processed distinctively by the human mind (see Chapter 9).

Derivative messages are virtually always constituted as narratives or images. They take the form of stories, myths, descriptions of recent or past events, plays, movies, and dreams, and other types of narrative content in which imagery is prominent. Derivative meaning is processed by the schemata of the deep unconscious system, and it seems likely that this processing is largely visual in nature—a highly effective means of dealing with incoming information and meaning.

Encoded messages, then, have manifest meaning, immediate implications, and transformed meaning. The most distinctive feature of the transformed level of meaning is that it is created by the unconscious use of the mechanism of *displacement*.

An encoded message is an adaptive response to a stimulus or trigger. It is the product of an interactional experience and can be understood only in light of a specific stimulus and the interactional context that has provoked it. It is a message that is

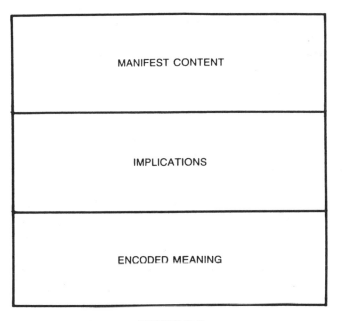

FIGURE 2.2
A Derivative Message

shaped by the trigger to which it is a specific response, an intermixture produced by the nature or properties of the stimulus and the nature or properties of the recipient and his or her inner mental tendencies. By and large, the human mind is so constituted as to selectively perceive stimuli accurately; otherwise, suitable adaptation would be impossible. *Reactions* to these perceived stimuli, however, are strongly shaped by the intrapsychic factor.

In psychotherapy, a therapist must understand that a free association constituted as a derivative is a transformed image produced in response to an earlier trigger. The image is a product of displacement and symbolization having operated on those raw or traumatic qualities of the trigger that are not permitted entry into consciousness.

The narrative level of an encoded message always concerns a manifest situation. However, the encoded level of meaning *pertains to a different situation, a latent or unconscious context.*

Encoded messages are therefore a way of unconsciously adapting to a traumatic trigger by working over the issues in another arena. The encoded image usually represents the trigger itself, its critical unconscious implications for the message receiver, and a variety of responses to this initial constellation. Many of these issues are represented in *symbolic form*, a term used in its broadest sense to allude to *disguise*—the representation of a particular person, incident, or meaning by a different but related image, chosen because the two elements bear some resemblance in form or meaning.

If a person is to cope successfully in adapting to emotionally charged messages, the human mind must respond on two levels: first, consciously and directly, and, second, unconsciously and indirectly. In general, the conscious response is limited to immediate issues and involves emergency responses and some extended direct coping. The unconscious response, on the other hand, is broad and intensive and takes into account significant emotional factors. It is on this level that the encoded and otherwise unconscious aspects of a traumatic trigger are received and worked over (indeed, this is one of the main functions of the deep unconscious system). And it is in the deep unconscious realm that adaptive failures may well lead to symptom formation. Conscious meanings are generally worked over directly, whereas implications are worked over both directly and indirectly or unconsciously. Encoded meanings are generally worked over only indirectly, with subsequent representation through derivative, or encoded, messages.

To state these propositions more clearly in terms of the model of the mind offered in Chapter 9, the unconscious components of a trigger message are received by the deep unconscious system and do not register directly in the conscious system of the mind. Information received by the deep unconscious system is processed outside of awareness, and the results of this processing are always reported out or revealed in the form of transformed messages. That is, all messages emanating from the deep unconscious system are subjected to displacement and symbolization. Thus, whatever processing and adaptation takes place in the deep unconscious system can be reflected only in encoded messages. Indeed, one of the central functions of this system appears to be the transformation of all outgoing information into derivative expressions. Thus, we may say that derivatives are entirely the product of the adaptational efforts of the deep unconscious system.

Manifest contents and conscious implications touch on meanings that are processed by the conscious system and then enter the conscious realm of experience. The conscious system has its own unconscious subsystem, in that its contents are not exclusively confined to immediate awareness. The main distinguishing feature of the conscious system, however, is that it processes meaning on its own terms, directly and without transformation (Chapter 9).

Each system deals with danger situations and sources of fear and anxiety; but whereas the conscious system has been designed to handle direct dangers related to immediate survival, the deep unconscious system has evidently been created to deal with nonmanifest or symbolic dangers—those that prevail in the emotional realm.

THE PATIENT'S MESSAGES

We turn now to the clinical relevance of these concepts. We may begin with the messages from the patient, with full recognition that they have been stimulated, or triggered, by the interventions of the therapist—and their implications. Experiences outside of psychotherapy are of secondary importance; they seldom evoke transformed or derivative communications. Furthermore, whatever their power, they are rarely the most significant factor in the vicissitudes of the patient's madness. As already noted, this power falls to the interventions of the therapist.

In communicative therapy, the fundamental rule of free association is invoked in the first session (see Chapter 5). Face to face in the first hour, and usually on the couch in subsequent sessions, the patient says whatever comes to mind. The therapist listens to these communications while observing the patient's bodily expressions, demeanor, actions, and affects.

The therapist recognizes from the outset that the patient's messages are adaptive reactions to his or her interventions. The therapist, therefore, attends to the patient's material for representations or direct allusions to these *triggers or adaptive contexts* (contexts or interventions to which the patient is adapting). In the course of free associating, the patient will often mention directly an intervention that the therapist has made—a remark or, more often, the way a ground rule has been handled. Sometimes this trigger itself will be given an encoded or derivative representation. For example, an overcharge by a therapist may be represented by a story about a merchant who had inadvertently charged too much.

Because adaptive contexts are always constituted as the interventions of the therapist, the more a therapist knows about the *implications* of his or her own interventions, the more readily a derivative message may be recognized—and a derivative meaning identified. In other words, the therapist's awareness of the adaptive contexts constituted by his or her interventions serves as a *guide* to deciding whether a particular expression is nonderivative or derivative in nature.

A derivative message from the patient is constituted as a narrative or image that conveys in displaced, and usually disguised, form a selected perception of an implication of an intervention from a therapist. In most instances, the narration of a story or of a dream that does *not* directly involve the therapeutic situation will carry encoded meaning. Such a narrative would reveal a displaced and disguised perception of the therapist. In those instances when an otherwise appropriate extended narrative does not reveal an encoded perception of a therapist in light of his or her interventions, the material must be considered to be nonderivative.

Patients tend to fall along a continuum: At one extreme are those who frequently communicate derivative perceptions; at the other are those who do so only rarely. Nonetheless, communication of derivative, or transformed, images appears to be a *basic psychobiological function* and a fundamental unconscious means of adapting to emotionally charged triggers. As a result, derivative communication is quite common in situations that evoke anxiety. This response is highly characteristic of reactions to alterations in the fundamental ground rules of psychotherapy and departures from the ideal frame (see Chapter 6). It has been clearly documented clinically that patients are exquisitely sensitive to the therapist's management of these tenets. Because ground rules constitute the basic core of the therapeutic relationship, and afford the therapeutic interaction its fundamental functions and meanings, departures from the ideal frame are powerfully evocative of derivative responses, even in patients who tend to rarely communicate derivative material.

Certain types of nonderivative associations are relatively easy to identify. Thus, the absence of a narrative—of a displaced story—is the hallmark of nonderivative communication. Nonderivative expressions are characteristically intellectualized, ruminative, and speculative. They often involve efforts at self-analysis or the analysis of others. Manifest allusions to the therapist and to the psychotherapeutic situation are seldom a vehicle for derivative communication, because *displacement* is the most salient feature of such expressions. On rare occasions, the patient may allude to one aspect of the therapeutic experience as a displaced representation of perceptions related to another aspect of that experience. This type of disguise is quite unusual, however, and most direct allusions to the treatment situation are nonderivative in nature.

Patients who speak of their problems with aggression, who speculate about the meanings of their own material, who scrutinize the therapist and attempt to directly analyze the implications of the therapist's interventions, and who talk in generalities are, in most instances, communicating through nonderivative material. The communications contain manifest contents, and they contain implications, some conscious and others unconscious, but there is no displaced and disguised imagery—no encoded representation.

Strictly speaking, in using the word *nonderivative*, we refer to associations whose possible displaced and encoded meaning is minimal. There is strong evidence that *every* association from the patient, whether ruminative or narrative, is created on the basis of inputs from both the conscious and deep unconscious systems of the mind. However, nonderivative material is in great measure a product of the conscious system (including its own unconscious component), whereas derivative material tends to reflect the greater influence of the deep unconscious system.

Material can be defined as primarily nonderivative in nature when there are no evident displaced and disguised meanings that can be understood as unconscious responses to an adaptive context of an intervention by a therapist. Quite often, as in the following excerpt, the emergence of nonderivative, or unencoded, associations is the result of inputs from both the therapist and the patient. As a rule, the therapist contributes by either failing to interpret the patient's derivative material or by intervening on a manifest-content and evident-inference level. The patient's contribution is usually one of basic communicative style. Certain patients are known as *nontransformers*—individuals who only rarely report out from the deep unconscious system by conveying transformed or encoded associations.

A young bisexual man became seriously depressed when his wife suddenly left him. He was being seen in once-weekly psychotherapy by a female therapist. In the first session of the sequence we are considering, the patient described in some detail a dinner with a homosexual, but platonic, friend whose present lover had contracted AIDS. The patient's present girlfriend was with him at this dinner, and much of the session was spent in describing the celebrative mood of the evening.

The patient then reported a dream about the therapist: He was in her office, which was furnished exactly as it is in reality. The therapist was saying that the patient would be all right whether he continued in therapy or not. After ruminating about the manifest dream and his uncertainties as to what he was getting from therapy, the patient asked the therapist if he was making progress. The therapist said yes, he was making steady but slow progress. With that, the session ended.

In the next hour the patient said that he had been thinking about what the therapist had said at the last session—"slow and steady." Actually, that had not corresponded to how he was feeling, he said, so her statement had seemed odd. Anyhow, he'd been thinking a lot about it and wondering if he really was moving slowly. In some ways, he actually felt he was moving fast. He had begun to wonder what the therapist wanted from him. He felt put down. He was trying hard; he really didn't understand what the therapist meant. After all, he might not be a trained psychologist, but he wasn't dumb. The therapist seemed to be intelligent, but not smart. She never pursued his sexual associations and seemed disinterested in the topic. In some ways he felt that he'd been fooling the therapist and maybe he was, after all, brighter than she.

Without pursuing the material further, we can begin our discussion by identifying the prevailing adaptive contexts. The triggers include the fact that the therapist practices in her home in the suburbs, completes a monthly insurance form for the patient, and tends to intervene on the manifest-content level and in terms of conscious implications.

An examination of the patient's material in each of these sessions, however, fails to reveal any displaced and disguised images that might readily be formulated as selected unconscious perceptions of the therapist in light of these adaptive contexts. In the first hour, there is a direct allusion to the way the therapist's office is furnished; this may well be an indirect reference to the home-office arrangement. However, the additional material is neither displaced nor disguised with respect to this adaptive context. Instead, the patient speaks mainly of his manifest feelings toward the therapist. As noted, manifest references to the treatment situation are almost always nonderivative in nature.

In the second session, the patient not only speaks manifestly about the therapist; he also intellectualizes and speculates—typical nonderivative expressions. In response to material of this kind, the therapist is well advised to maintain a holding, silent attitude—and to attempt to ascertain the ways in which he or she is contributing to the patient's nonderivative propensities. In the present instance, the therapist's manifest content-oriented, noninterpretive interventions to the effect that the patient is making steady but slow progress appear to have contributed significantly to this patient's massive use of nonderivative material.

The therapist's capacity to properly formulate the patient's material is sorely tested by patients who communicate extended narratives, and dream reports that simply fail to organize as meaningful derivative perceptions in light of the prevailing adaptive contexts. Such patients may be called *nonderivative narrators*, or *narrative-producing nontransformers*. As always, the key to determining whether material is derivative or nonderivative is to identify all activated adaptive contexts, and attempt to use them as potential organizers of the patient's associations.

A case in point involves a married man who is in psychotherapy because of a depressive reaction to his wife's having left him. The male therapist had at one point recommended a marriage counselor, and the patient and his wife were seeing this counselor at the time of the session excerpted as follows:

The therapist began the hour by informing the patient that a vacation day was pending in two weeks. The patient made a verbal note of the date and said that missing a session would be a relief, because he was extremely busy at work in his job as a real estate salesman. He could stop answering the telephone and still be occupied for at least three weeks. His co-workers were pressing him to help them with a variety of tasks—to evaluate a piece of property, to make a sale, to help someone on a deal, and so forth.

He then said that he had had two strange dreams the other night. In one, he is walking along a walkway toward a house. There are trees to either side of it and they are pretty. As he moves along, the trees get closer and closer together. Soon the branches are interlaced, and by the time he gets close to the house, he can't pass on the sidewalk. He has to go around the trees in order to reach the house. He feels it was stupid to plant young trees so close together; it is clear the trees are quite young and had been planted by someone.

The patient then spots two women appraisers who are at the house, Doris and Susan. Doris is sitting on a grassy knoll to the right of the house, and Susan is looking out of a window on the second story. The land slopes down along the side of the house to a garage. The patient slides down on his back and it's a lot of fun. But then the ground begins to move up on a wave, up to Susan't level. Whoo, he says, and she says it as well. The patient keeps going up and he feels scared, afraid it will go too far. Susan is looking out at him with a lewd expression. He wonders what will happen. The situation seems very unpredictable, but then the wave levels off and the patient feels all right.

The patient's second dream was also quite long and involved clubbing mice shaped like balls, which were hard to kill. And there was a third dream, about mice nibbling at cherries. The patient then spoke in some detail about a visit home, which was characterized by a striking degree of noncommunication among himself, his mother, his father, and his two brothers.

This session was initiated by the therapist's announcement of a pending vacation, a technical error that abrogated the patient's right to begin the hour with his own associations and concerns. The patient responded with some conscious thoughts about remembering the date, and some images about his coworkers pressuring him to help them with their work. This particular association has a derivative quality. It appears to encode an unconscious perception of extreme neediness within the therapist. The patient has unconsciously perceived him to have made the announcement about his vacation day in order to get the patient to work over the therapist's anxieties and pressures with regard to the pending separation.

The dream, on the other hand, seems to contain little material that might be organized as encoded perceptions in light of the hastiness of the therapist's intervention or his anticipation of being away from the treatment situation. Nor does the dream appear to organize around the two existing background adaptive contexts—an increase in the patient's fee, and the referral of the patient by the therapist to a marriage counselor.

To some extent the two women in the first dream may represent the patient and his two therapists, but the actual situation involves four individuals, because the wife is also seeing the marriage counselor. Even if one could make a case for this representation, it would be difficult to identify the patient's unconscious perceptions in light of this particular adaptive context, except to say that in some way he views it as highly disturbing (perhaps earth-shaking) and seductive (the lewd look from Susan). The rising earth is a psychotic image in a nonpsychotic patient and, as such, indicates extreme or psychotic anxieties (see Chapter 8).

Despite these small threads of possible displaced and disguised (encoded) perceptive meaning, there is no sense of clear encoded meaning and no quality of a coalescing derivative network—one that clearly and strongly touches on different meanings of an activated trigger. The patient himself appears to unconsciously recognize this absence of meaning, as reflected in his displaced allusion to not communicating with those in his family. However, we may accept this last image as an unconscious self-perception only if we are prepared to include the therapist as well—that is, to view the image as a condensed unconscious perception of some communicative failure on the part of both members of this therapeutic dyad. Nonetheless, overall, this is a rather typical lengthy dream that offers extremely little in the way of derivative expression.

To cite a brief example of what is clearly derivative communication, we may consider a female patient in once-weekly psychotherapy with a male therapist for immobilizing episodes of anxiety and depression. During an hour early in the therapy, the patient requested that the therapist see her husband with her. The therapist agreed. The patient then spoke about her boss at work. She said that he took advantage of his female employees by having affairs with them, even though he had virtually destroyed his own marriage by doing so. His wife was no longer talking to him. The patient suspected that this boss was actually a latent homosexual who became involved with so many women as a cover.

Here, the trigger is the therapist's having agreed to see the patient's husband. The patient responds with a displaced story that involves her boss in a situation at work. The narrative has a sequence of manifest contents that pertain to the boss's affairs. It would be possible to identify in this narrative a wide range of implications—not only about the boss, but about possible ways in which the patient is projecting her own unconscious needs and fantasies into his activities.

For our purposes, however, we are concentrating on the story as an encoded response to the adaptive context of the therapist's intervention and its implications. To decode the patient's transformed images is essentially to formulate the initial raw perceptions that the patient has unconsciously displaced and disguised.

The patient is indicating through derivative expressions her perceptions of the implications of the therapist's decision to see her husband. Despite the patient's conscious wish for such a meeting (an expression of her conscious system), her unconscious perceptions are that the therapist has decided to be unfaithful, to betray the patient by having an affair with the husband, to exploit the patient, to create a situation where the patient will no longer wish to communicate with the therapist, and to become involved with the husband in a latently homosexual fashion. All in all, this is a rich derivative network, one that conveys powerful unconscious perceptions selected in terms of the patient's own unconscious conflicts with respect to heterosexual and homosexual issues, infidelity, frame violations, and the like.

WAYS IN WHICH THE MATERIAL FROM PATIENTS MAY BE FORMULATED

Undeniably, the communicative therapeutic technique requires an understanding of the nature of messages and communications from patients if the therapist is to correctly formulate the meanings and implications of a patient's associations and behaviors. It should be noted again, from the outset of this discussion, that the only real guarantee of a formulation's validity is its obtaining encoded, or derivative, validation from the patient (Chapter 4). No matter how clever or appealing a hypothesis or formulation of the hidden or unconscious aspects of a patient's material, there is always a significant risk of error. Many formulations are defensive and self-serving for the therapist, and function as a way to avoid unconscious meanings that might disturb the therapist and his or her self-image. This can easily happen, because much of the patient's material contains, without his or her awareness, disturbing and yet incisive encoded perceptions of the vulnerabilities of, and errors by, the psychotherapist. The situation is also difficult because psychoanalysts and psychotherapists have not consistently depended on derivative validation to certify their formulations. As a result, many styles of formulating have gained wide acceptance, even though interventions based on such hypotheses receive no derivative validation when offered to patients.

The communicative approach has established the clinical finding that the patient communicates in psychotherapy as part of his or her adaptation to the therapeutic situation and to the ongoing interventions of the therapist. Such adaptational efforts are fundamental to the therapeutic interaction and experience. If a therapist wishes to generate a formulation and intervention that will obtain unconscious, or derivative, validation from the patient, obviously he or she must do so by correctly capturing the unconscious adaptive meanings of the patient's associations. Any other formulation—even of nonmanifest meaning—is in error, because it misrepresents the patient's unconscious experience and intended meaning. Manifest agreement with an intervention and direct elaboration by the patient are popularly regarded as confirmation, but it must be recognized that responses of this kind are entirely manifest and actually indicate *the absence of unconscious responsiveness*, an absence of insight into actual unconscious factors.

By far the most common types of formulations and interventions made by psychotherapists involve the manifest content of the patient's associations and the implications of that surface content.

Formulations of manifest contents and interventions that essentially repeat what the patient has communicated on the surface.   Interventions of this type are extremely common in the psychoanalytic literature, and they shade into interventions that include a small or large measure of direct implications. Clearly, a playback of the patient's manifest messages involves only the patient's conscious system. Interventions of this kind do not touch on the patient's unconscious conflicts, perceptions, fantasies, memories, and other types of inaccessible unconscious experience whose communicative expressions are always encoded and transformed. Manifest-content interventions, then, do not in any fashion illuminate the unconscious factors in a patient's madness.

Interventions that identify the implications of the patient's manifest associations. In this type of intervention, the therapist repeats the manifest content of the patient's associations, but also calls to the patient's attention an implication that may not have been noted. At times, the therapist may do this by summarizing the ramifications of a set of associations or by using some technical term to unify a variety of implied meanings inherent in the patient's material.

The therapist who intervenes by extracting meaning directly from the patient's associations almost invariably formulates the implications as aspects of an intrapsychic conflict within the patient. Emphasis is placed on the patient's fantasies and memories, and there is little or no place for genuine perceptions of any kind, especially perceptions pertaining to the therapist. Implications are almost never formulated in interactional terms.

The identification of implications, including those of which the patient is unaware, touches on issues involving the conscious system and its unconscious subsystem. Implications involve directly stated meanings rather than meanings that are displaced and disguised. Such meanings, as noted, belong to the conscious system and not to the deep unconscious system. Because the implications of a set of associations are often outside the awareness of the patient, the identification of such meanings has generally been considered a way of dealing with the unconscious factors in madness. It can be shown, however, that interpretations of what is implied by the patient's manifest associations never obtain derivative validation. Moreover, patients consistently perceive interventions of this kind unconsciously as erroneous, as expressions of therapist madness, and as a defensive means by which a therapist avoids the painful, valid unconscious perceptions of the patient concerning the therapist's own disturbance and madness.

Even when patients agree manifestly with a formulation of the implications of his or her material, on the unconscious or derivative level, confirmation is consistently absent. It is in this regard that we obtain our first glimpse of the way in which the conscious and unconscious systems operate—of how they process information, express needs, and generate communications related to madness that tend to be diametrically opposed. In general, much of what is desired and of emotional value to the unconscious system is opposed and degraded by the conscious system. And as we will see, it is the unconscious system that expresses and pursues emotional truths, whereas the conscious system is motivated in large measure by defensiveness and efforts directed toward the avoidance of unconscious meaning. It is this expressed need to avoid derivative or unconscious meaning that often leads patients to remain in psychotherapy with therapists who intervene exclusively on the level of implications.

The formulation of an unconscious fantasy. In this type of effort, which is relatively rare, even among psychoanalysts, the therapist attempts to undo displacement and disguise by postulating the existence of an isolated, encoded intrapsychic fantasy within the patient. The flaw in this approach is its assumption of a closed intrapsychic system in which the patient generates disguised fantasies on the basis of intrapsychic conflicts. Again: We are adaptive creatures. We interact with the environment. Our conflicts are precipitated by incoming stimuli as we attempt to respond and maintain psychic equilibrium. In all instances the patient initially responds to incoming messages with encoded perceptions. In other words, the patient registers and expresses his or her unconscious perceptions of the meanings of the adaptive context before reacting to it. And on occasion, the patient does react with responsive encoded fantasies.

Thus, the basic problem with formulating an isolated intrapsychic fantasy within the patient is that such an approach ignores the immediate adaptive aspects of the patient's encoded responses. The therapist must always consider the particulars of the ongoing therapeutic interaction, and recognize that the patient's encoded communications are constituted above all as unconscious responses to that interaction.

The deep unconscious system does, of course, contain and interact with residuals of unconscious fantasies and memories. However, clinical experience indicates that such fantasy-memory systems are mobilized in therapy only as part of a chain reaction designed to adapt to the implications of the therapist's interventions. For this reason, a therapist who wishes to formulate unconscious fantasy formations must first establish the presence of selected encoded perceptions in response to the therapist's intervations, and then define reactive fantasy responses. These are characterized by encoded communications that cannot be decoded as valid perceptions of the implications of the therapist's interventions, and which therefore must entail the patient's responsive fantasies and memories. The technical aspects of this conceptualization will be made clear in Chapter 3.

Interactional decoding. To summarize briefly, restatements of manifest content have no relevance to unconscious processes and meanings. The identification of implications extracted directly from the patient's material involves aspects of the unconscious subsystem of the conscious system. These aspects may be presently unconscious, but are directly and immediately accessible to consciousness. They pertain to the basic conscious system with which we process information. Formulations of unconscious fantasies isolated from the stimulus of the therapeutic interaction are merely hypothetical and of no *functional relevance* to the patient's immediate adaptive responses and to the unconscious meanings that he or she wishes to convey. Although they may be justified on theoretical grounds, they do not define the activated information being imparted from the deep unconscious system.

Interactional decoding is the only means by which the processing of messages and information that takes place in the deep unconscious system can be correctly identified and defined. Such decoding is based on the assumption that the therapist's interventions constitute the stimuli to which the patient is adapting by means of his or her free associations and derivative responses (when present). As stated, the patient first registers unconscious perceptions of the actual implications of the therapist's interventions, so that the patient's derivative responses are initially constituted as encoded images of these unconscious perceptions, selected in accordance with the patient's own madness. The perceptions themselves tend to be nondistorted and veridical.

Such unconscious perceptions of implications that are related to the patient's intrapsychic conflicts involve introjects that significantly influence the vicissitudes of the patient's madness—doing so in a variety of direct and paradoxical ways. Erroneous interventions tend to create introjects that reinforce the patient's madness. Nonetheless, the ability to view the therapist unconsciously as mad can sometimes bring relief to the patient—by permitting a nefarious unconscious comparison between the two participants to therapy. Valid interventions, on the other hand, tend to disrupt pathological maladaptations and to generate symptom relief based on insight into unconscious meaning and other related factors. (It is important to note, however, that valid, insight-offering interventions are unconsciously perceived as dangerous by the patient and may evoke temporary periods of regression.)

Decoding efforts carried out in light of the implications of the therapist's interventions will lead to further interventions that obtain derivative validation—both interpersonally (through the gradual emergence of positively functioning individuals) and cognitively (through unique encoded extensions of the therapist's interventions, which shed entirely new light on the nature of the patient's madness).

It is interactional decoding alone that correctly identifies the patient's experience of the psychotherapy as a process in the inaccessible unconscious system. Only the proper use of interactional, or trigger, decoding will thus obtain derivative validation.

This is a simple statement of fact, comparable to stating that respiration consistently involves the extraction of oxygen from incorporated air. Just as the extraction and metabolism of oxygen are a basic biological function, adaptation to the dangerous unconscious implications of incoming stimuli through derivative communication is a basic psychobiological function. The therapeutic relationship is unique in its paradoxical combination of danger and security; intimacy and separateness. Unconscious emotional adaptation is constantly occurring. The communicative approach attends to patients' unconscious adaptational responses to the therapeutic situation, because these responses reveal the fault lines of a patient's emotional functioning. It can be convincingly demonstrated that the activated unconscious meanings of the patient's madness can be defined only in light of his or her ongoing interaction with the therapist.

The need for a consistent way of formulating and intervening arises from the consistency with which a patient adapts to the therapist and the therapeutic experience. The interventions of the therapist must correctly state the realities of the therapeutic interaction as reflected in the patient's derivative communications. Otherwise, the intervention will not obtain derivative validation—largely because it is, perforce, fundamentally in error.

The following vignette, an extract from a highly deviant psychotherapeutic situation, will enable us to illustrate the four types of interventions just identified. The patient is a married woman in her mid-thirties. She sought psychotherapy for immobilizing episodes of anxiety that interfered with her job as an executive secretary. The male therapist had seen both the patient and her husband in the initial sessions. After two months, however, the patient had elected to come to sessions alone. The hour under consideration took place three weeks after this decision. Meanwhile, the therapist had discovered that his family was known to the patient's husband. Also, at the patient's request, he had reduced his relatively low fee. At times—including the previous hour—he had extended the patient's sessions by ten or fifteen minutes because she seemed to be in distress. Since being seen individually, it was the patient's habit to enter the sessions with two cups of coffee and to offer one to the therapist. The therapist accepted each time and drank the coffee during the hour.

In keeping with this practice, the patient began her session by offering the therapist a cup of coffee. The therapist accepted, and the patient began to speak. She mentioned that the color of the therapist's walls did not match the color of his carpet and drapes. She then said that her husband seldom satisfied her sexually. He would get an erection easily if she were menstruating, but not at other times. He was a needy man who took more than he could give.

The patient then thought of her boss, who was having an affair with another woman at work. He and this other woman would sit around drinking coffee and wasting time, waiting un-

til the end of the day so they could go to a motel. A man came
to the patient's house to paint the kitchen. The patient tried to
be nice and offered him a cup of coffee. He accepted, but then
made seductive moves toward her. Men are all alike, she said.
All they want to do is seduce women. It was a mistake to offer
the painter a cup of coffee; if all he wanted was sex, he shouldn't
have accepted.

Without pursuing this hour further, let us now develop
several possible formulations:

In terms of *manifest content*, it could be proposed that the
patient appears to be preoccupied with sexual concerns. She also
has a negative view of men as overly seductive and exploitive.
She is having sexual difficulties with her husband; she turns
away when another man becomes seductive after she offers him
coffee.

Although more could be developed along these lines, it is
clear that manifest formulations simply repeat manifest contents. Often, they do so in summary fashion or with a slight degree of inference. They either describe the surface of the patient's communications in intellectualized terms or, through the
selection of charged elements, become suggestive of evident conflict and issues. They do not, however, identify truly unconscious meaning.

In terms of *implications*, the material suggests that the patient is dissatisfied with her sexual relationship with her husband. It seems likely, too (*i.e.*, the associations also imply) that
the patient is struggling with impulses to be unfaithful to her
husband, which she projects onto her boss and onto the man
who came to paint her apartment. These associations also suggest that the patient may be jealous of her boss, and that, furthermore, she may be seductive at one moment and frightened
of her impulses at another. Witness her offer of coffee to the
painter, which is followed by a repudiation of his advances.
There is evidence, too, of a harsh or condemning superego in the
patient's attitude toward her boss and in her condemnation of
the painter—and of men in general.

The reader may well make many additional inferences based on this small extract. Each meaning is taken directly from the patient's associations and involves the immediate situation that the patient is describing—there is no change of scene. Some of the formulations draw on psychoanalytic theory, others rely on the therapist's intelligence and cleverness.

Many of these implications would undoubtedly fall outside the awareness of this patient, which is why formulations of this kind offer the illusion of interpretation—they make something conscious that has been unconscious for the patient. By this criterion, such formulations are axiomatically "interpretations." However, by the criterion of derivative validation, no insight into unconscious meaning is achieved. The formulation of unconscious implications is never followed by encoded validation from the patient. Once we consider the interactional derivative formulation of this material, it will be possible to understand why interventions based on this type of thinking are consistently perceived by patients unconsciously as a way of avoiding the therapeutic interaction and the patient's disturbing unconscious perceptions of the psychotherapist.

Turning next to the formulation of *unconscious fantasies and memories*, it could be proposed that the images of the husband involve a projection of the patient's own sexual conflicts. The situation with the patient's boss may be a "derivative of" primal scene experiences during which the patient had observed parental intercourse. These images may also defend against the patient's wish (or fantasy) to engage in sexual relations with the boss herself. The experience with the painter also suggests that the patient has fantasies of having an affair.

A relatively sophisticated psychoanalyst might also propose that the material reveals unconscious fantasies related to the therapist—so-called transference fantasies (see Chapter 8). Through displacement and symbolization, the patient seems to be imagining (fantasizing) a sexual liaison with the therapist and wondering whether or not he will be potent. These fantasies have an oedipal cast, as reflected in the story about the patient's boss. The painter is a stand-in for the therapist, and this incident also reflects the patient's conflict over her sexual wishes. There are signs of superego condemnation and guilt in the patient's critical attitude toward her boss and the painter.

At first glance, it must strike the reader that these formulations are, in fact, the product of decoding. Such efforts, however, are divorced from the therapeutic interaction. They assume fantasies within the patient that are simply played out like a tape loop, apropos of nothing. Despite their great conscious allure, interventions of this kind obtain no derivative validation.

Finally, in terms of *interactional decoding*, we must first identify the trigger or adaptive context that has set off this sequence of associations from the patient. Undoubtedly, the trigger here is the therapist's acceptance of a cup of coffee from the patient—a behavioral response on his part that has developed under pressure from the patient (an illustration of the circularity of the interplay between patient and therapist). The patient represents this particular trigger in her allusions to drinking coffee in both the story about her boss and her description of the incident with the painter. The material can therefore be formulated as reflecting the patient's encoded or transformed (displaced and disguised) perceptions of the implications of the therapist's intervention—his acceptance of the coffee—as well as her reactions to these perceptions. In substance, based on her own sexual fantasies and conflicts (which do not serve as the primary source of meaning, but, rather, have played a selective role in the patient's perception), the patient perceives the therapist's intervention as a modification in the usual boundaries and ground rules of relatedness (*i.e.*, as an affair) and as a form of seduction. Her main reaction to these perceptions is to condemn the therapist for being seductive and to advise him to behave otherwise.

In addition, through condensation, the patient's material also expresses a self-perception of her own seductiveness, and she condemns these impulses as well. Nonetheless, it is critical to identify the perceptive component of the unconscious meanings of the patient's associations *before* formulating the meanings that accrue to the patient's own needs, memories, and fantasies. In this way, the manner in which the therapist's interventions have triggered and shaped the patient's communicative and derivative material can be fully appreciated.

In the vignette at hand, the patient has set the stage for the therapist's intervention by her offer of coffee. But this offer itself was evoked in part by earlier triggers from the therapist, such as his seeing the patient's husband, his involvement with the husband's family, his reduction of the patient's fee, and his extensions of the patient's hour. Interactions of this kind are continuously circular in fashion, and such transactions contribute significantly to the vicissitudes of the patient's madness. The therapist's interventions must reflect a proper understanding and formulation of this unconscious dimension of the therapeutic experience and of the patient's free associations.

THE MESSAGES FROM THE THERAPIST

For the therapist, the ground rules of treatment state that silent listening should be maintained until the material from the patient calls for active intervention. Determining these moments is not a matter of guesswork. In following the *fundamental rule* of free association, the patient is developing a communicative network through which the unconscious meanings and sources of his or her madness are revealed. Ideally, the patient will unconsciously represent—directly, but in passing—the trigger or adaptive context to which he or she is meaningfully reacting at the moment. And this allusion will generally precede the development of a group of coalescing, highly meaningful, selected unconscious perceptions of the implications of that context.

In essence, then, the therapist maintains silent listening until the recipe for *intervening* has been fulfilled by the patient's manifest or clear derivative representation of an adaptive context and a set of derivative perceptions. Technically, the therapist's silence is in fact an intervention, a nonderivative message with a variety of implications (see Chapter 4). But our concern here is with active interventions, which are undertaken in response to derivative communication from the patient.

Of course, some patients in therapy communicate relatively few derivatives. It has been shown clinically that such patients may do just as well in the course of a psychotherapy as patients who communicate many derivatives. This suggests that the communication of derivative messages is not essential for sound cure. Nonderivative communicators unconsciously wish to avoid encoded meaning and to resolve their emotional difficulties mainly through the holding and containing capacity of the relatively silent, nonetheless attentive psychotherapist. Although derivative communicators also rely on the therapist's holding and containing capacity, they require as well specific interpretations of their encoded messages to resolve their particular measure of expressed madness. In general, the therapeutic situation is constructed and constituted by a set of ground rules that favors derivative communication from the patient to the greatest extent possible.

What active interventions are appropriate? A proper active intervention may be constituted either as a validated interpretation (an explanation of a segment of actively expressed madness in light of the prevailing adaptive context and the patient's encoded perceptions) or as constructive management of the ground rules. These are the only types of active intervention that are perceived unconsciously by the patient as expressions of the sanity and capabilities of the psychotherapist.

Of course, an active intervention may be erroneous, but an incorrectly fashioned effort at interpretation characteristically fails to obtain derivative confirmation, as do the great variety of noninterpretive interventions (*e.g.*, questions, clarifications, confrontations, so-called supportive interventions, and so forth). Furthermore, framework interventions are undertaken only to secure the frame at the behest of the patient's encoded derivatives. No others will obtain encoded validation.

Because derivative validation from the patient serves as a highly reliable guide to the appropriateness of interventions by the therapist, it is possible to clearly identify those kinds of messages from therapists that obtain confirmation from the patient and have insightful, curative effects. Such messages may be distinguished from those that are substantially harmful to the patient, though they may, paradoxically, bring the patient a measure of symptom relief—or initiate a significant measure of symptomatic regression.

The essence of the situation lies in the finding that the therapist is unconsciously "asked" by the patient to communicate through *nonderivative messages.* Ideally, the therapist intervenes with silence, interactional interpretations, or efforts to secure the frame. In interpreting, the therapist explains to the patient the unconscious meanings of his or her material. This is done by creating a synthesis of the patient's representations and attempting to show the patient how his or her communications and behaviors have been triggered by a specific event in the ongoing therapeutic situation—an event whose meanings the patient has unconsciously perceived and reacted to. The therapist also fully explains in this context the unconscious basis of any active symptom or resistance—that is, of any active form of expressed madness. In so doing, the therapist's intervention, though stated with suitable *affect,* is *explanatory* in nature and *cognitive-intellectual* in form. Similarly, handling a ground-rule issue through the directives contained in encoded form in the patient's derivative material is a cognitive effort at frame management and explanation.

Valid interventions, then, are constituted as messages that have manifest contents and a variety of implications. Quite often, both therapist and patient are unaware of these implications. It can be shown clinically, however, that the patient unconsciously perceives the more compelling implications of these interventions and processes these perceptions—this information—in the deep unconscious system. The patient then reports on the results of this processing through transformed or derivative messages. In other words, as with all therapeutic interventions, the implications of a therapist's correct interpretive or frame management efforts are selectively encoded by the patient and revealed in his or her associative material.

It is to be stressed that correct interventions are *nonderivative* messages. It is not uncommon, however, for a misguided psychotherapist to make use of derivative messages in intervening to patients—employing metaphors or feeling free to tell a patient a myth, narrative, dream, or bit of personal history in intervening. This type of effort is made or advocated by therapists who attend mainly to manifest contents and evident implications and have little or no appreciation of encoded communication.

It can be shown clinically that when a therapist communicates a narrative or image that the patient himself or herself has not expressed in a particular hour (this includes the therapist's reference to narrative material communicated by the patient in *prior* sessions), patients respond with nonconfirmation. Moreover, the patient unconsciously perceives the implications of interventions of this kind as major expressions of madness from the therapist, and as highly threatening and disruptive efforts by the therapist at projective identification into the patient. Rather primitive communicative and symptomatic responses tend to follow.

To summarize, the role requirements in psychotherapy favor both nonderivative and derivative communications from the patient, but restrict the therapist to nonderivative communications. Those therapists who communicate their own derivative expressions alter the therapeutic situation through expressions of their own madness. Under such conditions, the therapist is unconsciously seen as the *functional patient*, and the *designated patient* typically reacts by adopting the role of *functional therapist*. In addition, the patient experiences strong pathological and regressive pressures from the therapist, and will respond with powerful derivative images of a highly negative nature.

The distinction between the implications of a message and derivative meaning is often difficult to grasp. Implications, no matter how esoteric, are extracted directly from messages, whereas derivative meaning can be identified only through the specific reversal of displacement and symbolization.

The ramifications of these distinctions for psychotherapeutic technique are crucial, in that a validated interpretation relies on the therapist's capacity to distinguish manifest contents from implications, and both of these levels of meaning from the patient's encoded messages.

RECOMMENDED READINGS

Arlow, J. (1969): Unconscious fantasy and disturbances of conscious experience. *Psychoanalytic Quarterly* 38:1–27.

Arlow, J. (1969): Fantasy, memory and reality testing. *Psychoanalytic Quarterly* 38:28–51.

Bion, W. (1962): Learning from experience. In W.R. Bion: *Seven Servants*. NY: Aronson, 1977.

Freud, S. (1900): The interpretation of dreams. *SE* 4/5:1–622.

Freud, S. (1908): Hysterical phantasies and their relation to bisexuality. *SE* 9:155–166.

Freud, S. (1915): Repression. *SE* 14:141–158.

Freud, S. (1915): The unconscious. *SE* 14:159–204.

Langs, R. (1982): Some communicative properties of the bipersonal field. *International Journal of Psychoanalytic Psychotherapy* 7:89–135.

Langs, R. (1982): *The Psychotherapeutic Conspiracy.* NY: Aronson.

Langs, R. (1983): *Unconscious Communication in Everyday Life.* NY: Aronson.

Langs, R. (1985): *Workbooks for Psychotherapists. Vol. I: Understanding Unconscious Communication.* Emerson, NJ: Newconcept.

CHAPTER 3

Listening and Formulating

For the patient in psychotherapy, expressed madness is activated, sustained, intensified, or distinctly diminished in concert with the therapist's interventions. The vicissitudes of the patient's madness are adaptive and maladaptive responses to the triggers of the therapist's interventions. Similarly, the patient's free associations, and the meanings so contained, are efforts to cope with the implications of the therapist's efforts. In substance, then, the activated unconscious meanings of an expression of madness are both interactional and intrapsychic in nature, and they are part of the patient's ongoing efforts to adapt to the messages from the therapist.

It follows, then, that a validated intervention must take a specific and definitive form, one that captures the true meanings of the patient's material—the realities both of the patient's madness and of the therapeutic interaction. As discussed in the previous chapter, only two kinds of active intervention are appropriate: interactional interpretation and frame management at the behest of the patient's derivative communications. The present chapter focuses on efforts to establish unconscious meaning and to generate validated interpretations. Interventions that involve management of the ground rules are considered in Chapter 6.

Because all correct or validated interpretations must be interactional and take into account the unconscious aspects of the therapeutic interaction, it is possible to provide a model of the ideal intervention:

(1) I (the therapist) did such and such.

(2) You (the patient) unconsciously perceived the selective implications of what I did as this, that, and the other.

(3) All of this explains your (the patient's) current bit of expressed madness—symptom or resistance.

Only an intervention constituted in this fashion will obtain encoded or derivative validation from the patient. Thus, listening to and formulating the material from the patient must be designed to identify each of the three elements required for a potentially valid interpretive effort: (1) representations of adaptive contexts (the therapist's interventions—the triggers for the patient's responses); (2) displaced and encoded perceptions of the implications of the therapist's interventions; and (3) reactions to these perceptions—especially unconscious curative efforts by the patient on behalf of the therapist, and the vicissitudes of the patient's expressed madness. Whenever the patient provides material that touches on each of these three categories of adaptive response, the recipe for intervening has been fulfilled, and the therapist is likely to intervene.

THE TRIGGER OR ADAPTIVE CONTEXT

The therapist enters each session with a divided mind. With half the mind, the therapist is aware of his or her most recent interventions, the flow of the patient's current material, and the central issues in the treatment situation. He or she is familiar with recently activated adaptive contexts, the validity of recent interventions, the state of the ongoing communicative interaction, and, especially, with the state of the ground rules and whether frame issues have arisen. The therapist requires such knowledge to recognize the meanings of the patient's material and to generate potential formulations that can obtain silent validation and eventually be offered to the patient before the session is at an end.

Meanwhile, the other half of the therapist's mind is quite empty of desire, memory, or understanding, remaining open to the direction of the patient's material in a given hour, without foreknowledge or prejudice. This type of attitude is essential to sound listening as a safeguard against the all-too-human tendency to repeatedly rediscover that which is already known and to avoid that which is unknown.

Sound listening therefore requires both knowledge and ignorance, an ability to anticipate correctly and yet remain open to unanticipated discovery.

Freud (1900) taught us that the dream and all intrapsychic responses are stimulated by day residues, or triggers. In psychotherapy, triggers are constituted by the adaptive contexts of the therapist's interventions. Such messages ideally contain only manifest contents, or surface meanings, and implications (though they may also embody encoded messages when certain types of errant interventions are offered).

Adaptive contexts tend to have a wide range of implied meanings. Most of these meanings are universal properties of the trigger and can be identified through a careful analysis of the intervention itself. However, among the many meanings implied by a therapist's interventions, those to which the patient unconsciously reacts are determined by such additional factors as the status of the ongoing interaction with the therapist, the nature of recent transactions within the treatment, knowledge of the therapist as the message sender, the nature of the patient's own madness, the patient's assets and capabilities, and a variety of genetic factors related to the pateint's history and memory systems.

In substance, then, the trigger or adaptive context has a set of meanings to which the patient responds selectively based on intrapsychic and interpersonal factors. Identification of the adaptive context is therefore essential to the comprehension of the unconscious meanings of the patient's material. Without knowledge of the trigger, the therapist can only identify prominent themes in the patient's association, while remaining unable to assign these themes specific shape and meaning.

Technically, the therapist scans the patient's associations for representations, or portrayals, of the adaptive context. In simple terms, the therapist is searching for allusions to his or her interventions. These allusions may take two forms: direct or manifest, and indirect or derivative.

The ideal representation of an adaptive context is a manifest reference to a particular intervention of the therapist made by the patient in passing and without realization of its importance or ramifications. The patient may happen to mention a comment made by the therapist in the previous hour, or will directly allude to a particular ground rule that the therapist has altered or perhaps maintained. A direct statement of this kind facilitates interpreting, because an interpretive intervention is fashioned entirely from the material from the patient in a given hour. A direct allusion to a trigger is strong evidence that the patient on some level—often unconsciously—realizes that a particular intervention by the therapist has evoked an important measure of unconscious response.

A manifest reference to an adaptive context permits the therapist to clearly show the patient that a particular intervention is on the patient's mind, and from there, to demonstrate that the patient's unconscious or derivative reactions are clearly related to the trigger.

In addition to manifest references to interventions or adaptive contexts, patients will at times develop clear *derivative allusions* to a particular trigger. When a therapist has invoked a self-serving (vested interest) alteration in the ground rules, such as adopting a home-office, generally the patient will not allude to the intervention directly, but will provide, in selected sessions, a strong and clear *encoded representation* of the context. This type of *description, or portrayal,* although it is displaced or encoded and therefore indirect, is nonetheless a suitable vehicle for a particular type of interpretive intervention: *the playback of selected derivatives organized around an unmentioned but encoded adaptive context.* It is therefore critical that the therapist consistently scan the patient's material for encoded allusions to his or her interventions. During many difficult therapeutic interludes, recognition of this type of representation proves crucial.

On the other hand, the therapist should not reach for such

allusions. Although derivative representations are displaced and disguised, an encoded portrayal should be sufficiently clear that an unknowing but informed observer could, in most instances, make a highly educated guess as to the intervention involved.

For example, a therapist who had inadvertently overcharged a patient on her monthly bill recognized a derivative representation of the adaptive context when the patient alluded to an overcharge by her butcher. A therapist who changed an hour so the patient could keep an appointment with a dentist recognized the derivative representation of the adaptive context when the patient described her boss as being unreliable because he kept changing the hours during which the employees should be present at work. Another patient reported a dream: Strangers had invaded her bedroom and wanted to murder her. They seemed to know a lot about her, even though she had never seen them before. In this instance, the therapist recognized the displaced and disguised representation, or portrayal, of the trigger of his having signed an insurance form, released information about the patient, and so brought third parties into the treatment situation.

Technically, then, recognizing a manifest allusion to, or a clear derivative portrayal of, an adaptive context is one of the most crucial aspects of listening to and formulating the patient's material. Once a trigger has been recognized, the therapist can then silently formulate the main implications of the intervention. Those meanings that touch on issues of *communication* (*i.e.*, the extent to which a particular intervention promotes or discourages derivative communication from the patient) and on the *frame* (whether an intervention moves toward securing the frame or deviating) are among the most compelling for the patient. The therapist attempts to formulate as many implications of a represented adaptive context as possible before attending to the patient's derivative responses, which, as a rule, will contain extremely sensitive, selective readings of the meanings involved.

Clinical Illustrations

If the therapist is to intervene, the trigger or adaptive context must be represented in the material from the patient. It should *not* be introduced by the therapist. As noted, the representation may be manifest or derivative in form. Often, in the first instance, the allusion is so casual the therapist may overlook the representation. Or the patient will mention the trigger in some general rather than specific fashion.

For example, a patient may begin an hour by thanking the therapist for changing the time of his session, thus directly representing a deviant-frame adaptive context. If a therapist had instead refused to give a patient a later appointment, thereby maintaining the frame, the patient might begin the following session by saying that he'd had a hard time making the hour. This would be an indirect and general allusion to a secure-frame adaptive context.

Any mention of the therapist's silence, frame-management efforts, and other active interventions, as well as any allusion to the setting or other aspects of the conditions of treatment should be recognized as a manifest representation of an adaptive context. Once identified, the therapist then attempts to organize the patient's displaced and disguised material as encoded perceptions of himself or herself in light of the intervention at hand.

The following session involves a male patient who sought therapy with a male therapist because of marital difficulties and depression. Having found the patient difficult to work with, the therapist had suggested that the patient supplement his individual once-weekly sessions by going with his estranged wife to a marriage counselor who was also a man. Eventually, the patient did initiate such treatment, and at the time of the hour to be excerpted, he and his wife had been seeing the marriage counselor for several months. Quite recently, the therapist had increased the patient's fee by ten dollars per session. He had informed the patient that this increase was part of a general increase in his fees, based on higher costs.

The patient began the hour we will study by reporting a dream in which he has lost all his savings. He looks everywhere, knocks on doors, but doesn't know where they are. In a second and longer dream, the patient is trying to check out the value of a house he is interested in buying. His father assists him, though one of his hands freezes while he is holding the metal tape for measurements. The two men are in the interior of a house, and there is a woman who is sitting in a living room that resembles the therapist's office. The woman seems prepared to blackmail the patient for some reason.

The patient went on to speak about a family function he had missed, mainly because his wife wanted to pretend that the two of them were still together, whereas the patient wanted his own space and independence. If he had gone with her, he'd have felt mugged and exploited. The patient then said that in the sessions with the marriage counselor he felt hopeless about any possibility of repairing the marriage, whereas he did feel some hope in his individual sessions.

In this session, there is a manifest representation of the therapist's referral of the patient to a marriage counselor; this representation takes the form of a general reference to that particular situation, though it falls short of a specific reference to the actual referral. Nonetheless, the representation would permit the therapist to readily allude not only to the existence of two psychotherapies, but also to his own responsibility for initiating this particular situation.

The second deviant-frame adaptive context that the patient appears to be working over unconsciously and alludes to in this hour is the increase in his fee. The allusion is not manifest, however. What we have is a *derivative portrayal*, which appears in the first dream where the patient loses all of his savings. Were the patient to offer subsequent derivative perceptions of the therapist in light of this intervention—and perhaps clarify why he represented the therapist as a woman—the therapist could then offer the patient a playback of this encoded representation and the accompanying disguised perceptions (see Chapter 4). Such an intervention was feasible in this hour.

In general, when there are two active adaptive contexts, one represented manifestly and the other in derivative form, the adaptive context that has obtained encoded representation will tend to be more critical for the patient. The disguise reflects the patient's greater need for communicative defense because of a greater measure of anxiety. In most instances, this principle is far more self-evident than it is here. In the session extracted above, the greater measure of anxiety might exist simply because the increase in the fee was the more recent deviation.

Adaptive contexts are the stimuli for, and organizers of, the patient's selected encoded perceptions. When a manifest or derivative representation is identified, the remaining material should be treated as encoded perceptions to the extent that the images are displaced and disguised. The undoing of these two communicative defenses constitutes the decoding process. In sessions where displaced derivative images are evident, the therapist's task is to discover the adaptive context that organizes and gives the derivatives coherent meaning.

IDENTIFYING DERIVATIVE PERCEPTIONS

Identifying the patient's selected unconscious perceptions of the implications of the therapist's interventions is among the most difficult and yet rewarding tasks of the psychotherapist. The guiding principle for this effort is defined in the following question, which the therapist should ask continually of the patient's material: *What intervention, having what implications, did I make, such that this particular narrative or image is a valid encoded perception of myself?*

In principle, then, every image in the patient's associations should be tentatively accepted as some type of perception of the therapist until proven otherwise. In other words, the therapist should make repeated efforts to correlate or to fit a particular displaced image with an unconscious implication of one of his or her prevailing interventions. It is only after such efforts have failed to establish such a correspondence that one might tentatively consider a displaced image to involve a *reaction* to an encoded perception (see below).

Technically, the search for derivative perceptions preoccupies the therapist throughout each hour. In the presence of rumination, intellectualizations, and nonnarrative material, there is little likelihood that the patient is representing encoded perceptions. Nonetheless, even with this material, the major themes should be identified, because these may involve general perceptions of the therapist's endeavors.

The situation is different when the patient describes an image, dream, memory, or communicates some other type of narrative. We may recall that the patient is responding to the anxiety-provoking implications of the therapist's interventions (and these will exist with both validated and nonvalidated interventions) by processing these threatening meanings outside of awareness, in the deep unconscious system. The results of this processing are then transformed through displacement and symbolization into a narrative that, as a rule, involves a situation outside of treatment. Thus, whenever a patient begins to tell a story, recall a memory, or report a dream that does *not* deal directly with the therapist and therapeutic situation, there is a strong likelihood that the material is encoded, and that the encoding involves selected but accurate perceptions of the meanings of the therapist's efforts. It is therefore quite important for the therapist, first, to identify these encoded perceptions, and, second, to determine the specific intervention or adaptive context that has served as a trigger for these communications. The ultimate goal is to offer an interpretation that is quite *specific* about both the trigger and the perceived encoded meanings, selected in terms of the patient's own madness.

Decoding encoded material, as noted, involves undoing displacement and symbolization. A symbol is an image that stands for, or represents, another, latent repressed image. Though different in some respects, the two images always share some common meaning.

The decoding procedure involves, first, identifying in the manifest story a *theme* that has been displaced from the *initial context*, the actual trigger of the situation—in psychotherapy, the interventions of the therapist (Context I). The patient's manifest story is a second context (Context II) that represents Context I. Some confusion may arise from the fact that what we are calling the second context, the particulars of the patient's manifest narrative, is the context that we encounter first in the psychotherapy session. This manifest story contains the encoded images. It is the therapist's responsibility to trace the themes in the surface story back to their original context, and thereby to decode the transformed or disguised images into the initial, raw (anxiety-provoking) perceptions that required the use of a transformation process.

To summarize, the patient's manifest associations constitute a second context, one that contains in disguised form a series of themes that actually belong to the initial context which triggered the transformation process. To decode this material, the therapist lifts the main themes from the manifest narrative, and identifies and isolates each separate element. He or she then attempts to discover an activated intervention with implications related to these themes. The themes are then read in terms of that intervention, and their raw meanings are identified in light of the implied meanings of the therapist's efforts. It is important to identify both abstract themes and concrete themes in formulating the patient's material. The key is to discover a level of meaning that is shared by both the manifest and latent images.

To offer a brief example, a female patient in psychotherapy reported a dream in which a robber enters her bedroom. He tells the patient that he is there to give her a gift. But the patient knows that he is there to steal something from her, and that he might even kill her.

Rich narratives contain many themes. Here, there are themes involving robbery and theft, intrusion into the patient's space, entering a bedroom, offering a gift, and the possibilities of lying and of being murdered. Some of these meanings may be classically symbolic, in that we might wonder if the robber entering the patient's bedroom is a symbol for a penis entering a vagina. Similarly, a gift could represent a baby, and stealing could represent female castration.

In listening to associations, the therapist is well advised to attend to the material in loose fashion, identifying all possible levels of thematic content. As he or she does so, these efforts must alternate with a search for representations of adaptive contexts. In addition, even when a context is not represented in the patient's material for the moment, the therapist should attempt to identify a particular adaptive context whose implications bear a relationship to the themes that have emerged in the patient's associations. What possible intervention, the therapist might wonder, could account for images of breaking and entering, of a bedroom with its sexual overtones, of gifts and stealing, and of potential murder? Once the trigger has been identified, these themes can be lifted from the manifest story (Context II) and given dynamics, interactional life, and meaning in light of the implications of the precipitating intervention from the therapist (Context I).

Let us consider several hypothetical triggers for this material. Suppose, for example, that the therapist is a psychologist who referred the patient to a psychiatrist for medication. We would have little trouble identifying the theme of the gift as an allusion to the medication. We would also connect the image of stealing to the medication, as well as the image of breaking and entering—here, implying that the medication is in some way being forced on the patient and is experienced as a penetration. The theme of being killed would also be connected to the medication as having been selectively unconsciously perceived by this patient as toxic.

By identifying these themes and organizing them around the adaptive context of the referral to a medicating physician, we are able to lift them from the manifest message and to arrive at latent contents—a set of raw images that the patient found necessary to repress and disguise. In terms of these raw images, one could state that the patient unconsciously views the referral to a medicating physician as a violation of her therapeutic space (entering the bedroom). It is also seen as a gift that in actuality is depriving the patient of something and has become a way of stealing from her. Worse still, the patient sees the medication as destroying her and possibly the psychotherapy as well. The therapist and psychiatrist who are collecting fees for these efforts are seen as robbers.

It is well to remember that the referral to the medicating physician initially precipitated these anxiety-provoking perceptions, selected in terms of the patient's own madness; but the images did not register consciously and were therefore triggered outside of awareness. Nonetheless, the patient responded to these perceived implications of the therapist's intervention by processing the issues they raised for her in the deep unconscious system. The results of this processing were then transformed through displacement and symbolization into the dream images, which the therapist heard as the manifest dream among the patient's free associations. The listening-formulating process described in this chapter is designed to reverse these communicatively defensive processes and to arrive at the raw images with which the patient is coping. It is these raw images, rendered unconscious and processed in the deep unconscious system, that would account for the patient's expressed madness in a particular hour.

Let us now relate these themes to a different trigger. Let's suppose that the patient had asked the therapist to complete an insurance form, and that the therapist had done so. The manifest themes of this same dream report (Context II) would then be organized by this particular trigger (Context I), suggesting the following disguised raw images: The therapist has permitted the insurance company to intrude into the therapeutic space in criminal fashion. The insurance money appears to be a gift, but actually deprives the patient of something by stealing it from her. In some way, it is destructive both to the patient and to the therapy, and it has lead to the demise of treatment.

We can see now how a trigger shapes unconscious processing by creating a variety of emotionally charged issues. Some of these problems are processed consciously and in terms of direct meaning; other aspects—mostly in the form of implications, and sometimes in the form of incoming, encoded messages—are processed unconsciously. The latter efforts are then revealed through transformed images. Proper decoding involves knowledge of the stimulus that has shaped the disguise. In practical terms, decoding is accomplished by lifting the themes from the manifest story and understanding them in terms of the latent context—the evocative intervention of the therapist and its implications.

Let us now consider a final hypothetical trigger. In this instance, let us suppose that just after her previous session the patient had gone to use the bathroom. Not realizing that the lavatory was occupied, and finding the door unlocked, the therapist had inadvertently entered the bathroom while in use by the patient. In light of this particular adaptive context, the patient's dream might be decoded as follows: The therapist, by intruding on the patient in the bathroom, had done something criminal and sexual (the robber entering the bedroom). Unwittingly, the therapist may believe he is gratifying the patient (giving her a gift), but mainly he is taking something from her and doing something destructive to both herself and to the treatment.

In each instance, we have allowed the adaptive context to shape our decoding and to define quite specifically the nature of the raw images and perceptions that the patient had to repress and process in the deep unconscious system. In this way, we are undoing the effects of the transformations to which this type of processing is subjected. In simple clinical terms, the essence of decoding is identifying a theme in the patient's manifest associations that has powerful meaning in light of a latent context—one that pertains virtually always to the interventions of the therapist.

Alterations in the ground rules and erroneous interventions by the therapist are traumatic for the patient and experienced as mental assaults (as long as they are confined to words and feelings). In present-day psychotherapy, they are a major cause of derivative communication and bear a powerful relationship to the vicissitudes of the patient's madness. Frame-securing interventions also constitute danger situations for the patient (and for the therapist as well; see Chapter 6). In organizing the patient's material, frame-related interventions and their implications are the single most critical area of intervening around which derivative meanings should be formulated. In essence, the therapist's management of the ground rules and frame is the most significant class of intervention to which the patient responds.

Consider briefly a female patient who was offered the ideal conditions of treatment—a secure frame—in her first session. She begins the next hour by describing herself as a good driver on the whole. She then recalls that she's been anxious recently when driving the car, especially when her son is present. She remembers an incident where she lost control and went off the highway. She was convinced that both she and her son would die.

The themes here are those of cars, anxiety, losing control, going past the usual and safe boundaries, and concerns about death. We may also think of the car as a closed space, or claustrum, and recognize that thematically it is being described as dangerous and related to issues of death.

The patient's manifest thoughts and recollections are, as we have seen, the end of a long sequence that began with the trigger—intervention—through which the therapist secured the conditions of psychotherapy for this individual—a critical category of communicative expression from the therapist. The themes suggest that the patient's raw image of the secure frame is a mixed one: She alludes to herself as a good driver, thereby suggesting a positive unconscious perception of the therapist in light of his ability to propose a strong framework for the treatment. On the other hand, the patient sees the secure-frame space as dangerous, as a place where control may well be lost and issues of death experienced and confronted.

Here, too, we have lifted a set of manifest themes from the second or manifest context and related them to a latent or initial context constituted by a secure-frame intervention. The themes have helped us to define ways in which the patient unconsciously perceives the secure-frame therapist and the secure-frame treatment space.

In working with themes, it can be seen that it is quite important to attempt to formulate all possible levels of abstraction and meaning. As themes accumulate, they often help to point the therapist toward a particular adaptive context, especially if he or she is aware of the implications of his or her most recent and active interventions.

Work of this kind is not a simple cognitive effort. A therapist must be prepared consciously and unconsciously to modify his or her usual defenses against realizations related to his or her own errors and madness. A therapist must also be capable of accepting valid perceptions that run counter to his or her own self-image. Indeed, there are no natural-born psychotherapists, given that we defend ourselves against such experiences from the beginnings of life. All of us, on the other hand, appear to be natural-born patients, capable of communicating meaning and of conveying nonmeaning as required. In this respect, the work of the psychotherapist is far more difficult than the work of being a patient, albeit the patient experiences greater pain, because he or she is so vulnerable to the influences of the therapist's sanity and madness.

It is well to remember that the patient's free associations are the *end* of a journey. In order to arrive at a correct formulation of unconscious elements, and especially of unconscious perceptions, the therapist must retrace the patient's steps, identifying both the processes that have led to his specific endpoint and the trigger that set the journey in motion in the first place.

In time, the psychotherapist who treats every narrative and image from a patient initially as a valid reading of the implications of his or her interventions will discover that the therapeutic context and efforts have vast complexes of meaning previously unrecognized. Attention to derivative communication provides access to the deep unconscious system, the world of unconscious experience. Consistent listening and formulating of this kind provides the groundwork for distinguishing between the two basic systems of the mind. It also affords the therapist a singular opportunity of generating interpretations based on the deep unconscious processes that give meaning to madness.

A study of the patient's encoded images in light of the adaptive contexts of the therapist's interventions reveals that the traditional concept of transference seldom obtains and only under specific circumstances; the major *intrapsychic* influence in the patient's experience of the therapeutic interaction is one of *selection*, not distortion. Patients select for representation those implications of a therapist's intervention that are pertinent to their madness. When an intervention involves an alteration in the ground rules or an erroneous verbal effort by the therapist, the patient unconsciously perceives the implications with virtually no secondary distortion—but with major genetic repercussions, because an errant therapist is repeating on some level a past pathogenic trauma for the patient. In other words, a patient does not unilaterally introduce erroneous and distorted perceptions of the therapist.

On the other hand, when a therapist's intervention is validated and his or her efforts are directed toward securing the frame, the patient's initial perceptions and reactions to these perceptions tend to *exaggerate* and overstate the paranoid-like anxieties and dangers surrounding the secure frame as entrapping and claustrophobic. On occasion patients will manifestly present a distorted view of the therapist and treatment experience, but such distortions are a product of the conscious system. Those perceptions that register in the deep unconscious system tend to be essentially nondistorted and veridical in nature, because they are inaccessible to manipulation by conscious processing.

These realizations are critical for technique, because they shape the nature, tone, and attitude reflected in the therapist's interventions. Mistaken impressions that patients are introducing distorted views of the therapist are based on manifest-content/evident-implication types of listening, and on a failure to understand the patient's derivative messages. Such interventions tend to accuse the patient, whereas interventions that recognize encoded and valid perceptions tend to be balanced: They acknowledge the therapist's responsibility for the trigger that set off the patient's associations, while holding the patient accountable for the selectivity of his or her perceptions and the ways in which he or she reacts to these perceptions. The failure to appreciate the perceptive aspects of the patient's narratives and images is one of the most crucial problems in psychotherapy and psychoanalysis, one that has existed since their beginnings.

REACTIONS TO UNCONSCIOUS PERCEPTIONS

As noted, the therapist is obligated to consider every image from the patient as a conveyor of a valid encoded perception of the actual implications of his or her efforts before concluding that such material contains some other form of expression. Only when an image appears on repeated examination to possess no measure of perceptive value may the therapist consider it as a *reaction to perceptions*. In all instances, however, the sequence is the same: the trigger (an intervention by the therapist) is followed first by the patient's conscious and unconscious perceptions, and only then by his or her reactions to those perceptions, especially responses to those perceptions that are outside of awareness.

Among the most common reactions to unconscious perceptions are efforts to *correct, cure, and assist the psychotherapist* in re-establishing sound interventions when he or she has been in error; and *vicissitudes of the patient's madness*, constituted mainly as symptoms (intrapsychic and interpersonal) and resistances. Other reactions include *efforts to harm the therapist;* the *evocation of memories;* and, at times, *responsive distortions.*

These reactions may involve further encoded responses, primarily in the form of *derivative efforts to direct the therapist to the correct intervention that has been missed.* This occurs in particular with respect to securing and rectifying deviant ground rules. Patients will also engage unconsciously in efforts at explanation that constitute *unconscious interpretations* to the therapist. The meanings of these endeavors are available to the therapist only if he or she identifies the trigger or intervention that has set them off, and then recognizes the patient's imagery as displaced and disguised reactions to these triggers.

At times the patient's responses to unconscious perceptions become symptomatic and behavioral. *Pathological resistances or symptoms*—using the term in its broadest possible sense— may increase, or the patient may verbally attack the therapist, threaten to terminate, or perhaps actually leave the treatment. These manifestations of psychopathology or forms of expressed madness—in substance, symptoms and resistances—are technically termed *indicators.* They are indications of emotional disturbance as well as indications for intervention.

Indicators are the immediate expressions of patient-madness that are available for interpretation in a given hour. Indicators usually appear early in the session and in the patient's manifest associations. The patient may mention an anxiety attack or a depressive episode, or will describe some other sign of emotional dysfunction. He or she is late for a session or has missed the previous hour. It is the the therapist's goal in each session to interpret the unconscious meanings of activated indicators in light of pertinent triggers and the patient's unconscious perceptions of the therapist. Insight into this unconscious structure of the patient's expressed madness is a critical avenue of symptom relief.

When an indicator stems from a frame deviation or, at times, from a critical secure-frame moment, the therapist also endeavors to interpret the patient's response in light of his or her relevant, selected encoded perceptions of the frame-management adaptive context. Such work is the basic substance of ongoing therapeutic endeavors and the means by which activated symptoms and resistances are interactionally interpreted so that their unconscious basis may be revealed and adaptively resolved.

It is to be stressed again that the therapist should attend to each segment of material from the patient in order to assign it to one or more of these categories: representations of adaptive contexts, encoded perceptions, reactions to these perceptions, and, in particular, pertinent indicators of madness. The therapist's goal is to synthesize an interpretation that explains the vicissitudes of the patient's madness in light of the pertinent trigger and the patient's selected encoded understanding of the therapist's efforts.

This is the only type of listening and formulating that leads to derivative validation of interventions, because the deep unconscious system is inaccessible to intervention except *by invitation*. The patient *invites* the therapist to enter the system by alluding to an activated trigger and communicating transformed images that express the processing that has taken place in this otherwise inaccessible realm of the mind. It is only at such moments, when the patient has made the processing of the deep unconscious system accessible to the therapist's interventions, that it becomes possible for the therapist to generate insight into the workings and meanings of this part of the mind. (This is so even though the patient does not consciously recognize that such communications have been made; the images involved are transformed, and the actual perceptions lie outside of his or her awareness.) It is at these moments alone that processes otherwise confined to the deep unconscious system are made available to the realm of conscious experience (see Chapter 9). As we will see, clinical experience indicates that the conscious system abhors such information and knowledge, and that insights of this kind remain available in most instances for only short periods of time. Nonetheless, important therapeutic processes are set into motion in this way, processes that can then become the basis of insightful and adaptive cure.

A Clinical Illustration

Turning to a clinical illustration, we may consider the psychotherapy of a severely depressed woman whom the therapist had first seen as a service case in an inpatient hospital setting. He had agreed to continue with the patient on her discharge from the hospital, and had proposed a low fee. The patient paid for the therapy herself and was seen on the couch.

Six weeks after her discharge from the hospital, the patient began a session by describing a job offer from her father that would give her financial security, but bind her unreasonably to her family. Her father's need to keep her close by had been a factor in her divorce; in a way, all of the members of the family had drawn her back into the fold and she had succumbed.

She said that she had dreamt about working for her father in his appliance store. In the dream, she has been awarded a free trip by an appliance manufacturer, but doubts that she should accept. She has a broken tape recorder and she goes to the hospital to have it fixed. The people there aren't able to fix it, but they become overbearing in trying to do too much for her. They should have backed off and given her some room.

The dream led to the patient's recollection of a situation in which she was riding the subway with her sister when they were both quite young. The sister became frightened and wanted to get off the train, and the patient helped her to get out. During much of her life, the patient had set the world right for everyone else and failed to take care of her own needs.

This session is a good illustration of those hours in which there are relatively strong and coalescing derivatives, but no manifest mention of an adaptive context (see below). Under these circumstances, the therapist should wait for the emergence of a direct allusion to the context, but also be prepared to offer a playback of these derivatives, in the absence of a manifest representation of the trigger, if a good encoded representation of the adaptive context and a general bridge to therapy is available (see Chapter 4).

The central adaptive context for this hour is the low fee that the therapist is charging his patient. There is also a background adaptive context, in that the patient was seen in a hospital and the therapist had no choice but to maintain hospital records.

In formulating derivatives, the therapist should first attempt to identify the best encoded portrayal, or description, of the adaptive context and to separate this particular derivative expression from those encoded images that reveal the unconscious meanings of a particular adaptive context. In this instance, it would appear that the dream image of obtaining a free trip from an appliance manufacturer is the clearest encoded representation of the reduced fee. This portrayal also carries with it a measure of meaning—in this instance, it reflects the patient's unconscious perception that the reduced fee constitutes no fee at all—free psychotherapy.

In listening to and formulating the additional material, we would seek to identify encoded meanings in light of the low-fee adaptive context. There are many displaced and symbolized images here, each revealing a particular and selected meaning of the trigger. The allusion to being offered a job by her father, one that would bind her to her family, indicates that the patient unconsciously perceives the low fee as a special arrangement, one that implies obligation, nepotism, or, possibly, incest.

Though on the conscious level, the patient is grateful for the low fee, the unconscious perception is rather different (this situation is typical of the conflict between the two systems of the mind—conscious and unconscious; see Chapter 9). In the deep unconscious system, the deviant ground rule is perceived as inappropriately binding the patient to the therapist in a manner comparable to the situation with her father. Implied here is a valid encoded perception of a similarity between the therapist's low-fee offer and the ways in which the father pathologically bound his daughter to himself—an aspect of their relationship that had contributed to the patient's sense of hopelessness and depression.

The deep unconscious system stresses these similarities, while the conscious system ignores or denies them. To put it another way, the deep unconscious system tends to process and to identify similarities between situations and people, whereas the conscious system defensively stresses differences—here, for example, the conscious mind would point out that the therapist certainly is not the patient's father. Nonetheless, the low fee, despite its well-meaning aspects, is unconsciously perceived as a seductive offer that does not permit sufficient distance between patient and therapist, and interferes with the patient's efforts at independence and autonomy. The therapist, then, on the unconscious level, is repeating the past and present pathogenic traumas and triggers that, in the patient's outside life, have significantly contributed to her depressive symptoms.

The image of the broken tape recorder is a condensed derivative. It is both a derivative representation of the records the therapist kept during the patient's hospitalization, and an encoded perception of the therapist in light of the reduced fee. Here, the raw or unconscious meaning is that the trigger has damaged the treatment.

We may note, then, that the theme of the broken tape recorder can be decoded in two distinctive ways, depending on the guiding adaptive context. In terms of recordkeeping, the theme shared by the manifest and latent contents is that of records and recordings—the tape recorder on the manifest level and the hospital record on the latent level. On the other hand, in light of the low fee, the stress is on the damage that is being done. Because both records and low fees are deviations that damage the therapeutic hold and therapeutic experience, the theme of a tape recorder can touch on both through condensation—the main theme being the means by which the ideal ground rules have been altered (see Chapter 6).

This exercise demonstrates the importance of isolating every single image in the patient's material and attempting to decode its meanings in light of the adaptive contexts at hand. It would have been easy to relate the tape recording only to the record-keeping, failing to recognize that it conveyed an unconscious meaning pertaining to the low fee as well. There is no substitute for checking and rechecking one's formulations—especially if the ongoing material from the patient does not appear to be adding fresh derivative meaning.

The allusion to the hospital touches on the adaptive context constituted by the therapist's treating the patient in a hospital setting. Fixing the tape recorder could involve the patient's conception of the therapist as trying to help the patient with her depressive illness and also to repair the damage to the treatment situation (the therapist had already begun interpretive and rectifying efforts related to some of the deviations in the psychotherapy).

The allusion to the confused people at the hospital may well reflect a split image of the therapist: understanding some aspects of the patient's material and engaging in rectifying efforts, and, on the other hand, failing to understand some aspects and not engaging in the rectification of other deviations.

Finally, the image of the people at the hospital trying to over-indulge the patient is an encoded perception of the therapist in light of the low fee, which is perceived in selective and valid fashion as a form of overindulgence.

This completes the present exercise in decoding perceptions. (The reader may wish to attempt to decode this material in light of the recordkeeping adaptive context.) We turn now to those associations that appear to reflect the patient's *reactions* to her selected unconscious perceptions of the therapist in light of the low-fee trigger.

As noted, the single most important patient-response in this regard involves efforts to help the therapist to correct and rectify his or her errors. The patient communicates corrective encoded images and often engages in unconscious interpretations as well. The sensitive therapist can benefit if he or she is able to identify the disturbing adaptive context and understand the patient's encoded communications as a response to perceived difficulties in the therapist.

The present vignette contains several models of rectification, or correctives. All are conveyed on a derivative level, given the patient's conscious appreciation of the therapist's wish to treat her and the fact that she has raised no conscious objections or criticisms. Nonetheless, based on the patient's unconscious sensitivities and perceptions, she is advising the therapist against offering an intervention that binds the patient inappropriately to him. This advice is conveyed in derivative form in the patient's comment that her family should allow her a greater degree of independence.

Another rectifying image appears in the patient's thought that she should not accept the free trip from the appliance manufacturer. This is a strong and clear derivative that speaks against her having accepted the low fee.

Next, the patient alludes to the need to fix the tape recorder—a directive to repair the damaged container and frame. Then, finally, she alludes to the people at the hospital who are trying to do too much for her and who should give her more breathing space. Several times over, then, the patient is appealing to the therapist to stop his overindulgence and to secure the frame by charging her his usual fee.

To some extent the patient's material also contains reactive unconscious interpretations. Through her derivatives, the patient is suggesting that the therapist has a pathological symbiotic need to merge with the patient or bind her to him. In her final associations, the patient unconsciously proposes that the therapist is experiencing secure-frame anxiety (claustrophobic anxieties as portrayed by being in the subway; see Chapter 6). Furthermore, she indicates that the therapist has unconsciously asked the patient to be his caretaker—in substance, his psychotherapist. The patient bemoans the fact that this leaves little room for her own satisfactions.

When an interpretation or ground-rule management intervention fails to obtain derivative validation (see Chapter 4), the therapist is well advised to attend to encoded patient perceptions and reactions constituted as efforts to assist the therapist in setting the situation straight. In this way, the therapist is not only able to properly help the patient, but to help himself or herself as well.

TYPES OF SESSIONS, TYPES OF COMMUNICATORS

There are three basic types of sessions that can be identified when the listening process involves careful attention to triggers and derivative communications:

Sessions in which meaning is absent.   In this type of hour, the trigger may be represented manifestly or in clear derivative fashion, but there are no coalescing, encoded perceptions. This type of session may also unfold in the presence of encoded perceptions without a clear representation of a pertinent adaptive context. Finally, there are many sessions in which there is neither representation of a trigger nor evident encoded perceptions. It follows, of course, that the therapist is essentially silent during such hours, which tend to be spent in efforts at generating meaningful formulations and in recognizing that such endeavors are not possible.

Sessions in which the adaptive context is alluded to early in the hour, and the therapist awaits the communication of encoded perceptions.   Usually in sessions of this kind, which are not uncommon, one adaptive context is represented manifestly, and another alluded to derivatively. Clinical experience has shown that, as a rule, the adaptive context represented in derivative form is far more important to the patient than the one alluded to directly. The therapist must therefore listen to the patient's derivative material with respect to both contexts, generating potential formulations. An intervention is usually made once the meaning of the early material has been developed, confirmed by silent validation in the coalescence of ongoing diversely meaningful derivative perceptions, and an opportune moment for comment presents itself (see Chapter 4).

Sessions in which allusions to derivative perceptions are made in the initial part of an hour—images that organize well around an adaptive context known to the therapist.   The therapist then basically waits for the patient to allude directly or in clear derivative fashion to the trigger before intervening. In those hours where there are abundant narratives and images, but the pertinent trigger is unknown, it becomes the responsibility of the therapist to discover from the patient's themes and images the likely adaptive context that can account for the material. Silent validation of a hypothesis of this kind is constituted by the patient's subsequent allusion to the trigger, at which point the therapist is likely to intervene.

Patients tend to manifest one of two basic communicative styles. In one group, the trigger is usually represented manifestly and derivative perceptions tend to be abundant. These patients may be called meaningful communicators, in that they engage openly in the process of transforming the processes of the deep unconscious system into available encoded images. We may also call them *transformers* in recognition of the central role played by this function in their free associations.

The other group of patients are *nontransformers*, in that they tend to produce many hours without unconscious meaning. In those sessions where an adaptive context is alluded to manifestly, derivative perceptions are unlikely to emerge. Similarly, if there are one or more derivative perceptions of an effort by the therapist, the trigger is not likely to appear. Nonetheless, on rare occasion, such patients will put together a meaningful hour—a representation of an adaptive context and one or two pertinent encoded perceptions, doing so mainly when there is a ground-rule issue at hand.

It has been discovered clinically that transformers tend to have stormy therapeutic experiences. They tend to be quite anxious and to struggle continually with highly disturbing imagery that stems from the psychotic core. Nontransformers, on the other hand, tend to have more quiet therapeutic experiences, and they often spend much time engaged in efforts at self-analysis that pertain to the conscious rather than to the deep unconscious system.

Either type of patient may do well or poorly in psychotherapy. Transformers tend to be terrified of the secure frame, of secure-frame meaning (see Chapter 6), and of the very derivative images that facilitate their treatment experience and their development of insight into the processes of the deep unconscious system. These patients benefit not only from such insight, but from the therapist's capacity to hold and contain their communications and projective identifications, which are often violent and potentially disruptive.

Nontransformers tend to have rather active and threatening psychotic cores, but have been able to seal off derivative expressions of these disturbing inner contents. Rather than permit the emergence of transformed images from the deep unconscious system, they unconsciously safeguard against such expresisons. Therapeutic work with nontransformers requires patient holding and containing, and the therapeutic use of appropriate silence. Such patients gain some superficial or conscious insight and only a minimal understanding of the processes within their deep unconscious system. Nonetheless, they tend to do well in psychotherapy in ways that suggest some strengthening of their defenses in the deep unconscious system, and some modification of the pathological aspects of these defenses.

The symptom alleviation experienced by nontransformers through the therapist's holding capacities, with few interpretive interventions, appears to reflect the natural healing processes and tendencies that seem to exist in all patients. The therapist's holding capacities facilitate these healing processes and appear to provide the optimal conditions under which this self-healing can take place. In fact, otherwise well-meaning therapeutic interventions can disrupt such processes within the patient—particularly if such interventions stem from pathological needs within the therapist to be active—and convey detrimental implications.

It is essential that the therapist accept and respect a patient's communicative style, because psychotherapy takes a distinctive course depending on that style. But perhaps the most fundamental factor determining the course of treatment is the therapist's ability to properly listen to and formulate the patient's material.

A Clinical Example

The following vignette illustrates a session in which the adaptive context was represented at the beginning of the hour, and the therapist then listened for derivative perceptions so he could intervene interpretively. The patient is a man in his thirties. The therapist had seen him for a year in psychotherapy before a second period of therapy was initiated two years later. The first period of treatment had begun because the patient had become depressed when his wife had an affair with another man, for whom she eventually left the patient. The patient was also having difficulty in establishing a new relationship with a woman.

This first therapy had ended under unusual circumstances. The therapist, who practiced in Chicago, was forced to close his city office when his office building was sold and the new landlord insisted on immediate occupation of the therapist's office space. The therapist thereupon offered to see the patient in his suburban office, and the patient went for two sessions but then terminated.

The following is an excerpt from the first hour when the patient returned to therapy two years later:

The patient began the session by alluding to his previous therapy and to the time that had elapsed since he had last seen the therapist. He indicated that he had gotten his accounting business together and that it was going well. He owed his ex-wife a lot of money and still felt attracted to her, and that was bothering him a great deal. After all, she had left him for another man, whom she had ultimately married, keeping the marriage a secret from the patient for almost a year.

Two years ago, when the patient was in the therapist's office, everything had seemed too chaotic. He had felt too flooded with emotion. He had given his ex-wife a huge sum of money, and she had spent it all on drugs. Both the ex-wife and the man she married are social workers; they met at the hospital at which they both worked. But now the ex-wife had been abandoned herself, and she was afraid she'd lose any chance of getting back with the patient if he returned to therapy. But why in the world would he want to go back with her anyway? Everyone was telling him he should stay away from her.

His upset over the loss of his former wife had continued after the first therapy ended. The patient began to be distracted and did crazy things. He would schedule one client and then someone else would ask for the same time, and he'd agree, thus ending up with two appointments for the same hour. He would realize it, but would tell neither of them, and sometimes they would both show up. On other occasions, he would tell one of the clients at the last minute that he couldn't make it as planned. He even did this several times to women he was dating, arranging to see two of them on the same night. With all the chaos she had caused, why would he ever want to see his former wife again?

The patient spoke further of details related to his ex-wife's having been abandoned, and to the way in which her new lover–husband abused her. He recalled an occasion where he had to come to a restaurant to take care of the ex-wife when this other man had attacked and suddenly left her. He had even allowed her to sleep in his apartment, though there was no sexual contact.

It was late in the session when the patient began to describe how upset the ex-wife was at the present time. Her mother was ill, and the mother's doctor, who had been giving her vitamins, missed a tumor that was developing. The tumor proved to be malignant and required radiation, but it took another doctor to give her proper care. Because of the divorce agreement, the patient was paying his ex-wife's taxes. But a lien had been placed against her wages because the government had failed to record the payments. It was an aggravating oversight. The patient then said that he tends to over-protect his ex-wife as if she were a child.

At this point, some ten minutes before the session was to end, the therapist intervened. Before briefly considering the intervention, we may review some of the features of this particular hour.

The patient begins the hour by alluding to the previous chaotic therapy. Therefore, by implication he directly touches on the prevailing prior adaptive context—the therapist's sudden inability to see the patient in his city office and the shift to his suburban office. There then follows a series of selected encoded perceptions of the therapist in light of this unusual adaptive context.

In substance, the therapist is unconsciously perceived as having abandoned the patient in a manner comparable to the way in which the patient's wife left him—suddenly, unfaithfully, and because of something he had kept secret. The therapist's departure from the city was seen as destructive and self-serving (the allusion to the wife spending money on drugs). In addition, through the material related to the patient's own scheduling problems, the therapist's interventions are seen as crazy, out of control, and conflicted. Toward the end of the sequence, they are also seen as a malignancy and as a mistake.

These are all powerful encoded perceptions. They emerge in an unusual type of first session, yet they typify patients' encoded reactions to all adaptive contexts that precede an initial consultation hour—the nature of the referral, the first telephone call, and whatever (see Chapter 5). As is the case here, the derivatives evoked by these triggers tend to illuminate the patient's early resistances (which in this instance involve an unconscious reaction to the therapist's deviant prior intervention—his sudden change of office). In this regard, there are many derivative allusions to questions in the patient as to why he had returned to the therapist (expressed through the references to questioning why he would return to his ex-wife). The patient had also shown some hesitation on the telephone about returning to treatment. This is an important *indicator*, one that would require interpretation in light of the prevailing triggers and the patient's unconscious perception of the therapist.

As for reactions to the patient's unconscious perceptions of the therapist's difficulties with his office, there is the initial allusion to the patient's having gotten his business together—a derivative model of rectification. There is also the derivatively expressed concern that it is a mistake to return to the therapist, especially in light of his unfaithful behavior. The patient is reacting strongly to his unconscious perceptions of the therapist by questioning whether there is any sensible reason to return to treatment with a therapist who has made such a major error. There is also the suggestion that a proper cure could take place only in the hands of a different therapist—a new physician, like the one who took care of the patient's former mother-in-law.

This session reveals a special and important type of unconscious perception. It involves situations in which the patient has fulfilled the recipe for intervening by clearly representing an ac-

tivated adaptive context and by conveying a variety of coalescing and meaningful encoded perceptions. In the deep unconscious system, the patient knows that he has communicated
sufficient material for interpretation by the therapist. There is
no conscious awareness that this is so, nor can the patient consciously synthesize the material on his own to produce insight
into his unconscious meanings. Still, on the unconscious level,
patients consistently know when the time has come for the therapist to intervene—interpretively or otherwise.

This appears to be the case in the present hour. The patient
represented the critical adaptive context at the beginning of the
session. He then offered clear derivative perceptions of the
therapist's abandonment, destructiveness, and crazy behavior
with his schedule. When he alluded again to the theme of
abandonment this time the victim was the patient's ex wife
and the perpetrator was her current lover—the therapist should
have intervened. Support for the hypothesis that the patient unconsciously knew that the intervention should have been made
is to be found in the derivative allusion to the doctor who missed
the former mother-in-law's serious pathology. This perception
is restated in a second derivative related to the error and oversight made by the income tax bureau. Indeed, it was these allusions to error that alerted the therapist to his failure to intervene and prompted him to finally interpret the patient's
material.

In listening to material from patients, it is important to monitor themes of not hearing, missing something, making mistakes, failing to appreciate pathology, and the like. When these
themes appear toward the middle or latter part of a session, it
is extremely likely that the therapist has missed an
intervention—an interpretation or frame-securing effort. It be-
hooves the therapist to carefully re-evaluate the patient's material in order to find the missing intervention. Such a quest
should begin with a reconsideration of all prevailing adaptive
contexts and should be followed by a reconsideration of the patient's derivative material. This type of derivative directive is an
excellent supplementary guide to intervening.

The indicators in this hour include the patient's uncertainty
about returning to treatment, his upsetting attraction to his

former wife, and his destructive behavior at work as manifested by scheduling problems. In virtually every instance in which a patient develops new symptoms after a psychotherapy, it will be found that the expressed madness is based unconsciously on unresolved deviations (and less so, other types of error) that prevailed in the psychotherapy. The patient unconsciously enacts these deviations and incorporates the unresolved madness of the psychotherapist into his errant daily behaviors. Whenever a patient returns for a second period of therapy, the therapist should be alert to this likelihood. It has been possible to document influences of this kind in patients who have returned to a therapist even twenty-five years after an initial period of therapy.

In brief, the therapist did interpret the patient's reluctance to reinitiate therapy, his strange attraction to the former wife who had abandoned him, and his scheduling problems as related to his own abrupt abandonment of and scheduling problems with the patient during the first psychotherapy. The patient responded with a small measure of derivative validation. He indicated his awareness that the therapist often commented on his material as involving disturbing aspects of the interpersonal interaction between them. He remembered that in the first therapy he would deny the therapist's intervention during the session, only to think about it later and realize that the therapist was right. He also recalled that while sitting in the therapist's waiting room he had seriously questioned whether he really wanted to get back into this mess. The patient then indicated that he nonetheless wanted to resume therapy, and the therapist structured a once-weekly treatment situation.

Validation may have been restricted in this instance because the therapist did not offer clear assurances that the earlier difficulties in treatment would not be repeated. Still, there is a small measure of cognitive validation in the patient's realization of his distinct uncertainty about beginning therapy again, and, more particularly, in his comment that the therapist was quite right in the past—a weak cognitive, but clear, positive interpersonal type of confirmation. Whenever possible, the therapist should rectify an alteration in the ground rules when directed to do so by the patient's encoded material. In situations of this kind, rectification takes the form of a pledge to the patient that to the greatest extent possible the deviation will not be repeated (see Chapter 6).

RECOMMENDED READINGS

Bion, W. (1967): Notes on memory and desire. *The Psychoanalytic Forum* 2:271–273.

Freud, S. (1926): Inhibitions, Symptoms and Anxiety. *SE* 20:75–172.

Freud, S. (1900): The interpretation of dreams. *SE* 4/5:1–622.

Langs, R. (1982): *Psychotherapy: A Basic Text.* NY: Aronson.

Langs, R. (1985): *Workbooks for Psychotherapists. Vol II: Listening and Formulating.* Emerson NJ: Newconcept.

CHAPTER 4

Intervening and Validating

The foregoing chapters have delineated the three basic spheres of intervening: *appropriate silence* in the absence of meaningful material, *interpretive efforts* in the presence of such meaning, and *managing the ground rules* of psychotherapy. Although the specifics of handling the ground rules are discussed separately in Chapter 6, it should be noted here that ground-rule issues almost always constitute the primary source of anxiety and danger for the patient in psychotherapy. As a result, this arena not only involves frame-management responses, but is the main sphere for interpretive intervention as well. Secondary adaptive contexts—that is, adaptive contexts unrelated to the frame—are generated only by a therapist's error in technique, usually by a missed or errant intervention. Thus, in principle, a well-run psychotherapy is a ground-rule issue psychotherapy, except when the therapist has introduced a measure of error into the treatment experience.

In general, interpreting the encoded perceptions and reactions to perceptions that involve framework issues proves to be more felicitous than efforts to interpret the patient's unconscious reactions to erroneous interventions. In fact, the latter adaptive contexts are not generally represented in the patient's material; the therapist becomes aware that he or she has committed an error by hearing the patient's corrective derivatives—and can benefit from these correctives by silently rectifying the errant situation, even though intervention to the patient may not be possible.

The process of intervening may be described as follows:

(1) The therapist listens and formulates interactionally in terms of therapeutic triggers and encoded perceptions (as well as reactions to these perceptions). In so doing, he or she develops an initial *silent formulation or hypothesis,* which is *not* imparted to the patient. The therapist then seeks ongoing validation of this hypothesis, mainly through the emergence of fresh derivative images that lend it unexpected support, or through a direct allusion to a postulated, but previously unmentioned trigger.

(2) In those sessions in which a trigger is clearly represented, and derivative perceptions conveyed, the therapist will intervene at a propitious moment. When the patient represents the trigger early in the session, intervention will take place after silent validation and with the emergence of a dramatic derivative. At other times, an intervention will be offered when the patient alludes in some fashion to the psychotherapeutic situation, creating a bridge that invites interpretative comments.

In those hours where encoded perceptions appear in the patient's material before the trigger has been represented, in principle, intervention will take place when a direct or a clear derivative representation of the adaptive context has emerged. Practically speaking, however, it is generally advisable for the therapist in this situation to wait for one additional derivative image before intervening. Clinical experience has shown that the derivative material following this type of delayed manifest representation of the adaptive context is often especially meaningful.

(3) After intervening, the therapist is obligated to listen to the patient's responsive material as a *commentary* on the intervention. This commentary will either contain or lack encoded *validation* and may itself include *encoded perceptions* of the implications of the intervention.

True psychotherapeutic or psychoanalytic validation must involve responses from the patient's deep unconscious system, and therefore can be conveyed *only through transformed or en-*

coded images. Such validation is termed *derivative validation,* and is to be distinguished from direct or conscious agreement with an intervention. Support from the conscious system involves a different, limited, and more superficial type of insight. In addition to this basic type of validation, in most situations, the confirmed intervention will lead to some degree of conscious working over and conscious working through.

Derivative validation takes two forms: *cognitive* and *interpersonal.* Cognitive validation is the emergence in a patient's material of a displaced and disguised (encoded) narrative or image that reveals an entirely new dimension of the patient's madness, a dimension that clearly extends the therapist's interpretation. Material of this kind typically serves as a *selected fact* (Bion 1962) that provides *new* synthesis and meaning to the patient's material and emotional dysfunction.

Cognitive derivative validation is always a surprising and powerful experience for the therapist, and once interpreted, has great impact on the patient as well.

In this regard, it is to be stressed that the emergence of new derivative material is *not* a form of validation per se. Patients typically respond to erroneous and personally revealing interventions with rich derivative material. However, a proper formulation of this material shows it to be not derivative confirmation, but a response to a nonvalid and traumatic intervention. Indeed, especially rich narratives and images (often with negative undertones) should prompt a therapist to search for errors in his or her efforts.

Interpersonal validation is the emergence in a patient's material of well-functioning figures, quite often involving an allusion to something done well and effectively by the patient himself or herself. These displaced and disguised images represent the unconscious perception and introjection of a therapist capable of a sound interpretation. They convey the ego-strengthening aspects of such interventions. However, they do not embody the specific insights that have been offered to the patient, and they usually do not involve an extension of these insights—as happens with cognitive validation. For this reason, interpersonal validation is somewhat less cogent than cognitive validation, though ideally both are present in response to a sound interpretive effort by the therapist—or to an effective and correct period of silence and/or a proper framework-management endeavor.

In the presence of powerful derivative validation, the therapist should offer an additional interpretation. If both cognitive and interpersonal validation are absent, however, the therapist should consider the intervention to have been in error, because the initial nonconfirmation of ultimately validated interpretations is quite rare. Thus, in the absence of derivative validation, every effort should be made to reformulate the patient's material and to discover the correct formulation and interpretation available at the moment. Negative interpersonal images and nonvalidating derivative material should be taken seriously and should lead the therapist to search for an overlooked adaptive context and to reformulate the patient's material accordingly.

SILENCE

Appropriate silence is one of the most difficult interventions for a therapist to make. The communicative criteria for silence are quite clear: The therapist should maintain silent listening until the patient has fulfilled the recipe for intervening by representing a trigger and providing a coalescing set of two or more derivative perceptions.

Therapists appear to have a strong need to be active. They feel devalued and of little use to the patient when they remain silent. Nonetheless, it is critical for the therapist to have *faith* in patients, because they will indeed communicate a network of meaning in sessions where they experience an unconscious need for interpretation or a frame-management response. Sometimes a dread of meaning or the need to lie fallow will precipitate a period of time during which no activated emotional triggers and issues are represented in the patient's material. At such times, the only valid intervention available to the therapist is that of nonintervention—silence. Essentially, it is the patient who creates the session, *including* the therapist's interventions, and the patient should be allowed to create therapeutic silence as well, when the need is for quiet holding.

In most instances, appropriate silence obtains interpersonal derivative validation toward the end of the hour—largely through the emergence of references to well-functioning individuals other than the therapist. The therapist should be alert, however, in sessions where he or she has maintained silence, for images in the patient's material of people who have failed to see or hear or respond to someone in need—and to other themes that could suggest the possibility of a missed intervention. Quite often, images of this kind are accurate unconscious perceptions of a therapist's failure to properly formulate the patient's material and to intervene in the presence of a well-represented trigger and a series of derivative perceptions. Thus, themes of inaction, absence, and failure to help should alert the silent therapist to the strong possibility of the presence of interpretive material that should be more clearly formulated. With the patient's derivative perceptions as a guide, it is often possible to discover the missing adaptive context and to offer the correct interpretation to the patient before the hour is at an end.

We can see, then, that there are two basic forms of silence: valid and invalid. Valid silence tends to be confirmed interpersonally toward the end of the session, whereas invalid silence— *those silences that actually constitute missed interventions*— will tend to generate derivative images of missed opportunities and of people who have not heard or have been disappointing.

Valid silence is experienced as sound holding and containment, whereas invalid or erroneous silence is experienced as abandonment—and as hurtful and damaging. It is therefore critical for the therapist to maintain a validating listening attitude whenever he or she believes that the patient's material does not call for active interpretation.

INTERPRETATION

The communicative approach calls for refinements in the definition of an interpretation. Interpretations may deal either with manifest contents and implications (touching on issues in the conscious system and its superficial unconscious subsystem); or with transformed communications and the processess within the deep unconscious system.

In either case, the patient is made conscious of a communication and meaning contained in his or her messages of which he or she was unaware. However, there are distinct differences in the types of insights involved. Insights that involve the conscious system virtually always pertain exclusively to the patient and to his or her intrapsychic issues, taking into account neither the therapeutic interaction nor the patient's unconscious perceptions of the therapist. Such insights tend to be direct and self-evident—of a type that can be formulated by patients and therapists alike. Although some contents of the unconscious component of the conscious system are indeed outside of awareness and are often unrecognized by the patient until an interpretation brings them to his or her conscious attention, these contents are relatively nonthreatening and easily worked over. Usually the insight involves the identification of a pattern of behavior heretofore unrecognized by the patient, and the result may be a degree of conscious determination to change that pattern—with varying degrees of success. The point is, however, that insights of this kind are actually welcomed by the conscious system, while deep unconscious contributions to expressed madness remain entirely untouched.

Clinically, interpretations of superficial unconscious meanings and implications are experienced by the patient in two distinct ways. On the conscious level and within the conscious system, the new understanding, however self-evident, is accepted and worked over superficially. But within the deep unconscious system, the perceptions revealed through transformed messages indicate a view of *the therapist* as frightened by the deep unconscious system, defensive, and inclined to intervene without meaning.

We see again that the conscious and unconscious systems often hold opposing views, and this state of affairs obtains on most—if not almost all—basic issues. The therapist who is guided by the patient's conscious communications will have a far different view of the treatment experience than the therapist who also decodes derivatives and gains access to the deep unconscious system. In general, what the conscious system accepts, the unconscious system questions, and what the deep unconscious system expresses, the system of consciousness fears and avoids.

Interpretations confined to the conscious system should be termed *superficial interpretations* to indicate their lack of attention to derivative expressions. Interpretations that involve efforts at interactional decoding can be called *deep interpretations* to indicate that they are designed to gain access to information in the deep or inaccessible unconscious system.

Deep interpretations are always interactional in nature, because they are designed to identify the patient's immediate efforts to process emotionally charged information and to adapt. Most of the deep unconscious system is inactive at any given moment, because its components (schemata) are aroused only by immediate adaptive contexts (emotionally charged issues). As noted earlier, in the therapeutic setting, the deep unconscious system is especially focused on the interventions of the therapist and the frame, whereas the attention of the conscious system tends to wander and only rarely to be occupied with the therapeutic interaction. (There are, of course, situations in which the patient is consciously preoccupied with the therapist and the therapeutic experience, but such preoccupations are usually stimulated by errant and deviant interventions; and they are generally confined to conscious meanings with little derivative undertones.)

As stated, interpretation of the deep unconscious system can be made *by invitation only*. The indications, from the patient that deep unconscious meaning is available for intervention are constituted by a well-represented adaptive context and the communication of a coalescing, selected set of encoded perceptions. It is at such moments that the active processing of emotionally charged information and meaning, including genetic repercussions and other ramifications, is openly conveyed by the patient through transformed images. At such moments, the therapist can synthesize the patient's derivative perceptions with the prevaling adaptive context, and make use of that basic constellation as a means of explaining activated aspects of the patient's madness.

Deep interpretations always take into account the trigger of the therapist's interventions, the patient's selected encoded perceptions, and the patient's reactions to these perceptions. The patient may well communicate such elements in fragmented and disorganized fashion; it is the responsibility of the therapist to give organization to such scattered material and to make the patient aware of its decoded (raw) meaning. In so doing, the therapist places active meaningful information derived from the patient's deep unconscious system into the his or her conscious system. Clinical experience has shown that such information often has a very short half-life, in that the conscious system repudiates and defends itself agains the incorporation of meanings stemming from the deep unconscious system. The contents of the deep unconscious system are surrounded with intense anxiety, dread, and panic, and the conscious system continuously erects defenses against these affects (and the related danger situations and meanings).

Nonetheless, despite its rapid decay rate, conscious insight of this kind evidently sets in motion important processes— responsive working through on both the conscious and unconscious (derivative) levels, and positive unconscious introjective identifications with the well-functioning therapist. (In contrast, superficial interpretations tend to lead to negatively tinged incorporations.) A deep interpretation also possesses strong holding and containing qualities. All of this contributes to the alleviation of the patient's expressed madness.

In principle, a deep interpretation should begin with an allusion to the adaptive context—the intervention to which the patient is reacting. The patient's encoded perceptions of the therapist in light of this intervention should then be identified, after which the patient's reactions to these perceptions can be developed—especially those pertaining to the vicissitudes of the patient's madness and to any unconscious effort to cure or assist the errant therapist. As noted, once the interpretation has been offered, the patient's responsive material should be analyzed for the presence or absence of validation, and for the patient's unconscious perceptions of the therapist in light of this fresh intervention.

THE PLAYBACK OF SELECTED DERIVATIVES

An interpretation is essentially an explanation, a definitive portrayal of stimulus and response, cause and effect. In substance, the therapist explains to the patient that an intervention to which the patient has alluded has led to a variety of unconscious perceptions, and that these have had certain definitive effects on his or her symptoms and/or resistances. Interpretation is feasible only when the patient specifically alludes directly and manifestly to an adaptive context. Without a clearly identified trigger or stimulus, the therapist cannot specifically state the ramifications of his or her intervention for the patient. Interpretations must be specific, must involve clearly defined adaptive contexts, and should include well defined selected encoded perceptions. Efforts to identify a patient's general impressions of the therapist tend to be followed by nonvalidating material.

In principle, in the absence of a manifestly represented adaptive context, a definitive interpretation is not feasible, because the therapist should not directly introduce an adaptive context that the patient has not mentioned manifestly in his or her associations. In this way the therapist respects the level of the patient's communicative defenses, and works with activated material rather than with images introduced arbitrarily by the therapist himself or herself.

There is, however, a type of modified deep interpretation: *the selective playback of derivative perceptions organized around an unmentioned, but derivatevely represented adaptive context.* This type of intervention is called for when the following components are available in the patient's material: (1) *a clear and strong derivative representation* (encoded description or portrayal) *of an activated adaptive context,* which indicates that the patient is dealing with that context, though on an unconscious or derivative level; (2) *the equivalent of a direct allusion to the trigger*—namely, a general or nonspecific reference to therapy and an encoded portrayal of the specific intervention with which the patient is dealing; and (3) *a set of coalescing and selected derivative perceptions* of the therapist in light of the activated, encoded adaptive context. The general bridge to therapy is particularly important, because it enables the therapist to demonstrate to the patient that some issue in the treatment experience is indeed on his or her mind.

In intervening with a modified interpretation, the therapist is not in a position to show a definitive sequence of cause and effect. Instead, he or she must make an incomplete intervention, demonstrating to the patient that a particular set of themes (conveyed by images that contain a derivative portrayal of the adaptive context) is connected both to the psychotherapeutic situation (as indicated by the general bridge to therapy) and to another set of derivative images (the selected derivative perceptions).

In general, an intervention of this type begins either with the bridge to therapy or with the derivative portrayal of the adaptive context. Once these two elements have been played back to the patient, the encoded perceptions can be played back as well and a link proposed between these three basic elements.

In principle, validation of this type of playback is ideally constituted by a modification in the patient's communicative disguises, so that the prevailing adaptive context is mentioned manifestly in the patient's associations. Confirmation is also indicated by positive interpersonal images and fresh encoded perceptions that extend the therapist's intervention in a unique manner.

The playback of selected derivatives must be distinguished from the type of confrontation that directs the patient to unnoticed manifest associations. A playback of derivatives has a specific structure; it must include a derivative portrayal of an activated adaptive context and a playback of selected encoded perceptions. Furthermore, a playback is not designed to override the patient's communicative defenses. It must be confined to situations where an adaptive context is not alluded to manifestly, for example, in situations where a therapist has altered one or more ground rules in self-serving fashion—a circumstance under which the patient is unlikely to allude to the adaptive context directly.

SOME BASIC PRECEPTS

Valid silence, deep interpretations, selected playbacks of derivatives, and secure-frame management responses are the only interventions from psychotherapists that obtain *derivative* (unconscious) validation. All other interventions are unconsciously perceived by the patient as mad, destructive, defensive, and replete with a wide range of destructive and disruptive implications. Despite the patient's surface acceptance of many of these interventions consciously (*i.e.*, by the conscious system), they have a powerful and disruptive influence on the deep unconscious system—and on the patient as a whole. It is mainly because interventions of this sort can lead paradoxically to a measure of relief for the patient that they continue to be offered in the psychotherapeutic situation. Such relief is founded on the patient's unconscious realization that the therapist is as mad as, and perhaps madder than, the patient; or the result of a nefarious comparison between patient and therapist, which favors the patient; and such means of "cure" as the therapist's pathological sanction of mad patient behaviors, punishments that assuage the patient's guilt, or excessive and bountiful pathological forms of gratification. The effects of such interventions are unconsciously perceived by the patient, who may respond with a measure of symptomatic relief. Nonetheless, it can be shown that in almost all such instances, the patient is also harmed by these mechanisms, and these consequences are usually overlooked on the conscious level by all concerned.

Both interpretive and ground-rule interventions must be consistently checked against the presence or absence of derivative validation. Ideally, both interpersonal and cognitive validation will follow any correct and timely intervention, including an attempt to secure the frame, which is usually accompanied by an interactional interpretive effort.

To illustrate: The patient is a man in his thirties who sought psychotherapy for impotence, which occurred particularly when his wife took the initiative in sexual relations. This was his second marriage, and the patient was depressed about his symptoms.

The patient was seen on the couch, twice weekly. Three months into therapy, as he was leaving the hour, he turned to the therapist and mentioned that, by the way, the therapist had seen his first wife in therapy many years ago. The next two sessions seemed to be barren of derivative meaning; also, the patient said nothing more in any fashion about either his revelation or his first wife. There were many silences, and the patient asked many direct (but unanswered) questions of the therapist.

In the hour prior to the one under consideration, the patient spoke at length and in great detail about a man from whom he and his present wife had bought a piano. The salesman was pressuring them to buy many supplementary items. From time to time, the patient would complain about how difficult the therapy was. He was also frequently silent, and occasionally turned to look around at the therapist. The therapist did not intervene in the session. (Evaluation of the patient's material suggests that the silence was appropriate.)

The patient began the following hour by saying that he was trying to remember where they had left off the previous week. He'd been feeling pretty awful, even though he'd had some good sex with his wife the night before. Afterward, he was unable to sleep. He had run out of tranquilizers [evidently prescribed by someone other than the therapist] and lay there feeling sorry for himself. He felt himself to be in poor shape. "I don't really want to be in therapy," he said. "I can hurt as much at home as here."

After a long silence, the patient said that the sex with his wife last night reminded him of sex with his first wife. Suddenly he just had the thought that he'd like to kill his present wife, and that made him feel bad. These sessions were tough on him. He'd be wiped out after the hour, and here he had a business appointment with a difficult customer today [the patient sells insurance]. "Why don't you say something?" he asked the therapist.

The therapist intervened and suggested that the sessions were on the patient's mind and that he was feeling drained. Also, he had now revealed that there was another therapist involved in treatment, someone who was currently giving him medication. He had mentioned having sex with his present wife and said that it reminded him of sex with his first wife—the wife the therapist had seen some years ago. An image of a killer had followed, and this seemed to indicate that the therapist's participation in the therapy under these conditions was really hurtful to both the patient and the treatment situation.

The patient responded by saying he felt that he and the therapist were getting close to doing something that was very disturbing. He had the thought of grabbing the therapist by the shirt and telling him just that. And yet, in another way, the patient felt a great sense of relief and suddenly felt less tense. He was thinking of a picture he had had framed and kept for a long time in the basement, though recently he had placed it in his bedroom. In the picture there is a young boy with an older man, who reminded the patient of his grandfather. This grandfather had taken the patient to church and taught him many things. The picture had a sense of the old man's teaching the young boy many wonderful things. In the picture, it's just the two of them. "Why don't you teach me?" he asked the therapist. Now he suddenly had another odd thought—an image of someone pumping gas. With that the hour was at an end.

The prevailing adaptive context is the therapist's prior contact with the patient's first wife. There can be no doubt that this touches on one of the unique premises of the deep unconscious system, which understands certain situations to be inherently in contradiction with others. The contradictions perceived by the conscious system are quite different. Thus, in the conscious system, the therapist can certainly treat the patient's ex-wife and then, years later, treat the patient. But in the deep unconscious system, the therapist who has treated a man's ex-wife can never be a therapist to that man. The deviation destroys treatment— the most likely meaning of the sequence in which the patient mentions his ex-wife and then thinks of murdering his present wife. This contains an unconscious view of the therapist as destroying the patient and treatment because of the deviation.

As is true of many patients who suffer from impotence, this patient was a *nontransformer*—someone who tends to report few derivative images. In the present hour, the initial material involves two *indicators*—the sleep problem and the use of tranquilizers (a major resistance). It includes little, however, in the way of selected encoded perceptions—at most, that the therapist and therapy are not in good shape.

In the patient's idea that the gratifying sex with his present wife was like sex with his first wife, we have an *indirect allusion* to the deviant adaptive context. We also have a clue as to the unconscious sexual implications of the deviation. Destructive or murderous implications follow, and then there is a shift away from further derivative meaning.

With nontransformers, often a therapist must intervene with only a marginal representation of an adaptive context and a single encoded derivative perception. A patient's complaint about the therapist's silence or a request that the therapist speak is frequently a sign that the therapist has missed a valid interactional interpretation. Though the patient's request usually involves a noninterpretive response, the meaning generally reflects the patient's unconscious realization that he or she has fulfilled the recipe for intervening—a representation of an adaptive context and the presentation of important selected unconscious perceptions. The patient needs the therapist to give cause and effect and integrated meaning to the fragments of his or her associations.

Thus, the therapist was well advised to intervene at this point in the hour. In principle, however, the intervention should have been a playback of derivatives rather than an interpretation, which required the therapist himself to introduce the adaptive context. It would have been better, too, if the therapist had begun the intervention with the adaptive context and traced the patient's images and indicators from there.

Nonetheless, the therapist did capture the essential unconscious meaning of these associations: that the deviation was harmful to the patient and the therapy. Had he engaged in a playback, the intervention might have been stated in this way: "You're talking about the pressures you're feeling here and the disturbance that you're feeling in connection with therapy [this is the general bridge to the treatment situation]. You mention that you have been taking tranquilizers, suggesting that you have brought a third party into your treatment [this is both an indicator and a derivative representation of the adaptive context: The therapist had seen the patient's wife and was now seeing the patient—this, too, is a threesome]. You speak of having had gratifying sex and then mention your first wife [another tie to the adaptive context and to one of its unconscious meanings]. Immediately following there is an image of murder [an encoded perception]. It would seem that last night you had a threesome on your mind—you, your wife, and your former wife [another derivative allusion to the adaptive context]. You're making many connections to therapy today, so it seems that you are concerned with the sense of a threesome here in therapy that in some way involves me, yourself, and your former wife [*shaping* the representation of the adaptive context and the derivative material]. Whatever it's about, someone or something is being harmed and destroyed [again, shaping the derivatives to point toward their unconscious meaning].

In the actual session, the therapist, as noted, offered an interpretation by manifestly specifying the derivatively represented adaptive context. The interpretive effort included allusions to the patient's unconscious perceptions of the destructive aspects of the trigger. However, the therapist failed to use the adaptive context and unconscious perceptions to explain the acting-out indicator, which was the patient's major reaction to these perceptions—his contact with a third party to treatment and his use of medication. In all, then, although some elements were lacking, the intervention did capture the main thrust of the patient's material.

We may turn now to the patient's responsive commentary on the intervention. The image of grabbing the therapist by the shirt appears to have at least two meanings: First, it is an unconscious perception of the assaultive and homosexual qualities of the therapist's need to introduce in this session the fact that he had seen the patient's wife when the patient himself had not alluded to it. And second, it suggests an unconscious perception of the therapist in light of his "decision" to see this patient after having seen his wife. Simultaneously, through condensation, the image hints at the patient's own unconscious reason for seeking out this particular therapist. On both sides, the issue is one of assaultive contact and unconscious homosexuality. In seeing the patient under these circumstances the therapist has enacted a perverse deviation which has strong seductive aspects (see Chapter 6). At the same time, the patient is acting out a comparable need. These themes are extended in a more sublimated fashion through the image of the grandfather who teaches the grandson, which is followed by one final, strong, symbolic, though instinctualized representation in the image of pumping gas—sticking a nozzle into the opening of a gas tank, a strong encoded image of homosexual penetration.

In this instance, then, the cognitive response includes encoded unconscious perceptions of the therapist's need to thrust the adaptive context manifestly at the patient. Nonetheless, the cognitive imagery is derivatively validating, because it also extends the therapist's interpretation in an important way. In the deep unconscious system, once a third party has been introduced into the therapeutic space, he or she is always there. The patient's cognitive response reveals that the patient has unconsciously selected the therapist because in the deep unconscious system, the ex-wife will be present in every session, protecting him from his own unconscious homosexual fantasies and needs. It may well be that the ex-wife would also protect the patient from unconscious perceptions of the homosexual needs of the therapist. In this regard, it should be stressed that the cognitive material now adds a selected unconscious perception of the therapist as homosexual in light of the dynamics involved in his acceptance of a male patient after having seen the patient's wife. (In the deep unconscious system this is viewed as a direct decision by the therapist regardless of whether the therapist did this by deliberate choice or not.) The therapist's latent homosexual issues are selectively perceived through the lens of similar issues in the patient.

We may consider this material to be validating on the cognitive level, because the patient's previous material had not revealed the unconscious homosexual issues in the referral. In addition, the patient's responsive images have now led to the development of an important hypothesis regarding the patient's impotency—his presenting problem. It can now be proposed that the patient's difficulty is based on unconscious, passive-feminine homosexual conflicts and perceptions/fantasies in his interaction with his second wife (recall the fact that this symptom intensifies when the wife is the sexual aggressor). Cognitive validation will often illuminate in new ways the unconscious dimensions of both the therapeutic interaction and the patient's symptoms.

Interpersonal validation is, of course, reflected in the image of the kindly grandfather who is teaching the young boy. The therapist's intervention is unconsciously perceived as having taught the patient something important in the context of a constructive and warm relationship.

Finally, we may consider the patient's question as to why the therapist doesn't teach him anything. At first this image seems to contradict the positive images that have apparently validated the therapist's intervention interpersonally.

The most likely formulation of this query, however, is an allusion to the fact that this particular deviation cannot be rectified and that the patient is faced with a deviant-frame therapy with this particular therapist (see Chapter 7). In substance, such a therapy will limit what the patient can learn, though the present hour indicates that the learning can reach a considerable degree of importance.

In summary, then, this particular interpretation produced cognitive validation in revealing the patient's unconscious homosexual perceptions and fantasies which both reflected the patient's view of the therapist in light of the existing frame deviation and gave new meaning to his chief complaint. Interpersonal validation emerged by way of an allusion to a warm teaching relationship. These are good illustrations of the types of validation and insight that evolve from sound interactional interpretations.

We turn now to an additional vignette involving a ground-rule issue and an intervention through which the secure, or ideal, frame was maintained. As such, the vignette anticipates Chapter 7's discussion of the management of the ground rules of treatment.

The patient is a man in his thirties, a plumber who was seen in once-weekly psychotherapy by a male therapist for episodes of anxiety, depression, and guilt because his teen-age son had become profoundly depressed and needed therapy. There were no known deviations in the treatment situation.

Two months into therapy, the patient began a session by attempting to hand an insurance form to the therapist and requesting that the form be completed. The therapist suggested that the patient hold on to the form so that they might see what came to mind.

The patient spoke first of the local baseball team, which was on a winning streak. One of the workers at work had loosened a valve and there was a major gas leak. There had nearly been an explosion. The man was a goof-off; he should have followed the safety rules.

The patient's girlfriend was working as a waitress. Two extra waitresses had shown up at work the other night, and the girlfriend was upset because one of them was put into her area, resulting in her making less money.

When the patient asked the therapist to clarify his position on the insurance, the therapist intervened. He pointed out that the patient had come back to the insurance form because he had in effect just told the therapist what it would mean if he were to go along with filling out the paper. His indirect images indicated that it would be a way of blowing up treatment, and the therapist would be seen as a "goof-off" who was not following the rules. Completing the form would also be a way of invading the patient's private space, thus taking something away from the patient. The patient seemed to be indicating that the therapist should follow the rules and not complete the form.

The patient responded by saying how impressed he was with the way the therapist puts things together. He then said that his car had not been running well, but that he had fixed it. He had owned two other cars, which he had just sold. For once he had decided to put his investment in one car and to forego unnecessary back-up vehicles. He then wondered how he should relate to the daughter of the woman with whom he was now living—what should his role actually be?

In the next hour, briefly, the patient began by telling the therapist that something good must be happening in therapy, because he had been suffering from both depression and disturbing physical symptoms, but now they were gone. At work, he had had to get into a very tight place. In the past, he would have been terrified of not being able to get out, and his body would have ached. This time, however, he felt comfortable and the job went extremely well. In fact, he actually fixed a waterline that hadn't worked for twenty-five years. He had spent time with his son, who seemed less depressed. With tears in his eyes, the patient spoke of how much better everything seemed to be of late. He seemed to be getting in touch with some really powerful feelings in the therapy.

The indicator/gross behavioral resistance in this session is the patient's request that the therapist fill out an insurance form, thus altering the patient's total responsibility for payment of the sessions and compromising the total privacy and one-to-one relationship of the treatment. The *anticipated adaptive context* is that the therapist will sign the form. The patient's derivative perceptions in light of this trigger/possibility are well stated by the therapist in his interpretation. He begins with the patient's manifest representation of the anticipated adaptive context, and then indicates to the patient his indirectly represented, derivative perceptions of the therapist in light of his anticipated completion of the form. The therapist has also used the patient's own *model of rectification*, his derivative directive that the therapist should follow the rules—that is, should not complete the insurance form and should maintain the frame.

The patient's response constitutes both cognitive and interpersonal validation. The former is reflected in the patient's derivative indication that the insurance company would be viewed as a superfluous form of back-up. The allusion to the patient's girlfriend's daughter also suggests an unconscious incestuous issue—namely, that introducing the third party would create a situation in which role-requirement issues would be a problem. Interpersonal validation is reflected in the patient's description of his own ability to repair his car and to get along without unnecessary back-up vehicles.

The second session begins with an allusion to symptom alleviation. Recent clinical investigation has shown that the vicissitudes of symptoms in patients are closely correlated with framework interventions. Exacerbation of symptoms tends to appear with major alterations in the ground rules. In patients especially terrified of the secure, or ideal, frame, regression may be observed after sudden and unexpected frame-securing efforts, but typically this is followed by symptom relief. In this particular instance, the patient finds immediate ego strength and symptom alleviation in the therapist's maintenance of the ideal ground rules. In most instances, there will indeed be a significant measure of symptom relief in response to interventions of this kind.

The patient also represents the secure-frame's claustrum qualities in his allusion to the tight space at work. He derivatively reveals his comfort within the secure frame of therapy and the constructive accomplishments that can take place within its confines. This is followed by other positive images as well as the experience of strong affects.

By combining an excellent interpretation with a frame-securing effort, the therapist offered this patient an ideal communicative intervention. The result was a significant measure of symptom relief. This type of therapeutic work occurs only from time to time in the course of a sound psychotherapy, but it builds toward a lasting cure.

RECOMMENDED READINGS

Brenner, C. (1955): The validation of psychoanalytic interpretation. Reported by J. Marmor. *Journal of the American Psychoanalytic Association* 3:496–497.

Dorpat, T. (1984): The technique of questioning. In J. Raney (ed): *Listening and Interpreting.* NY: Aronson.

Freud, S. (1912): Recommendations to physicians practicing psychoanalysis. *SE* 12:109-120.

Freud, S. (1913): On beginning the treatment (further recommendations on the technique of psycho-analysis I). *SE* 12:121–144.

Freud, S. (1914): Remembering, repeating and working-through (further recommendations on the technique of psycho-analysis II). *SE* 12:145–156.

Freud, S. (1915): Observations on transference-love (further recommendations on the technique of psycho-analysis III). *SE*
   12:157–171.
Freud, S. (1915): The unconscious. *SE* 14:159–204.
Gill, M. & Hoffman, I. (1982): *Analysis of Transference*. Vols. 1 &
   2. NY: International Universities Press.
Greenson, R. (1967): *The Technique and Practice of Psychoanalysis*. NY: International Universities Press.
Langs, R. (1985): *Workbooks for Psychotherapists. Vol III: Intervening and Validating*. Emerson, NJ: Newconcept.

CHAPTER 5

The First Session and the Phases of Psychotherapy

The goals of the first session, as they are commonly understood, are relatively self-evident and well known. To these the communicative approach has added several distinctive features, along with defining specific technical precepts to guide the therapist in handling the session.

In principle, the initial session should not be treated as an exception with respect to technique. On the other hand, although ground-rule management is normally carried out only at the behest of the patient's encoded communications, the therapist is obliged in this first session to define the ground rules and conditions of treatment without recourse to the patient's derivative directives. This effort is the only departure from ideal and usual technique that is acceptable. All other deviations are consciously accepted by the patient, but perceived unconsciously in negative terms.

In the first hour the therapist must, of course, make an assessment of the nature, degree, and classification of the patient's psychopathology and interpersonal disturbances. The therapist should also determine the extent to which the patient shows not only *gross behavioral resistances* (manifest obstacles to therapy, such as silences, inattention to the therapist's interventions, lateness, and proposed modifications of the ideal frame; see Chapter 7), but also *communicative resistances* (in the presence of activated adaptive contexts and frame issues, failure to communicate meaningful material—well-represented triggers and coalescing, selected encoded perceptions).

It is not uncommon for patients to propose modifications in the ideal conditions to treatment in a first session, and often this is done with conscious innocence but strong unconscious investment (stemming from the superficial unconscious subsystem). Such proposals should be regarded as major indicators and signs of madness. They require interpretation and secure-frame response in the first hour, because they involve prevailing adaptive contexts and the patient's encoded perceptions and directives. At issue is the extent to which the patient will be offered secure-frame psychotherapy (in which all of the ideal ground rules—unconsciously requested by all patients—are established and maintained) or deviant-frame therapy (clinical situations established with a basic modification in one or more of the fundamental rules of treatment). Because each of these paradigms is a definitive form of psychotherapy with its own distinctive positive and negative features (see Chapter 7), the therapist's responses to resistances in the first hour—especially those involving alterations in the framework—are of utmost importance.

The therapist should also attempt to determine whether the patient appears likely to remain in treatment and to generate a workable therapeutic experience. This is not to imply that a patient's apparent resistance should determine his or her candidacy for therapy, but only to suggest that the psychotherapist be prepared for likely issues and eventualities.

Assessment should also be made of any suicidal or homicidal risk, or the presence of overt psychotic disturbance, as well as of the patient's assets and areas of conflict-free functioning. Genetic material, as made available in the patient's flow of free associations, should also be evaluated at this time, in order to illuminate the patient's history, current and past functioning, introjects, and the like.

It is to be stressed that it is not necessary to directly question the patient in any of these areas in order to carry out a sound and effective evaluation. At bottom, all a therapist truly needs to comprehend in the first hour is whether the patient shows a significant measure of suicidal or homicidal risk, and whether a treatment relationship can be established. Additional information is valuable, but not vital.

THE FIRST TELEPHONE CALL

Almost always, the initial contact between patient and therapist involves a referral and telephone call. On the telephone, the therapist should be concerned and empathic, yet proceed with dispatch. In all instances, the therapist should ask how the patient obtained his or her name, because certain answers to this question will preclude consultation contact. In addition, if there are indications of suicidal or homicidal tendencies, the therapist should briefly clarify these feelings and expressions, and establish a basic agreement with the patient that no action will be taken before the consultation. In the presence of such impulses, the first appointment should be made as quickly as possible. Under no circumstances, should there be a delay of more than six or seven days between the first phone call and the actual initial hour.

The first telephone call should not entail an extended interaction, except with regard to the referral source. There are certain contaminants that warrant another referral in lieu of consultation contact. First, the patient should not have been referred by relatives of the therapist, because the patient's contact with these relatives violates anonymity to an extent that is often not reparable.

Second, in the unconscious system, the therapist cannot be a social acquaintance in any sense and a psychotherapist at the same time. Any individual with whom the therapist has had prior personal, business, or social contact should be referred to someone else.

Third, the therapist should not see those individuals who have obtained the therapist's name from another patient of the therapist's—present or former. Patient-referrals create major disruptions in the therapeutic experience for both patients involved. Unconsciously, neither of the two patients feels that he or she is in therapy, and each patient considers the other as the therapeutic target of the therapist. There is always a sense in such patients that the privacy of the psychotherapy has been violated (the other patient is experienced unconsciously as ever-present). Furthermore, the relative anonymity of the therapist is modified in actuality, because each patient knows of another patient who is being treated by the therapist.

The therapist who accepts a patient-referral is seen unconsciously by the patient as depressed, greedy, and in need of pathological objects. It is not uncommon to discover that patients involved in this type of referral have suffered significantly from the syndrome of premature or overintense exposure to death anxiety (Chapter 9). They utilize this type of referral situation unconsciously as a means of defending against further separation and loss experiences. In the deep unconscious system, the presence of three individuals in the psychotherapy—two patients and the therapist—all but precludes the possibility of total loss: If one member of the trio dies, two survive and loss is denied. With this type of interactionally enacted defense in place, the meaningful exploration and analysis of the patient's death-anxiety issues is largely rendered impossible.

If a referral is warranted, for example, because the patient knows the therapist's family, the therapist should not become self-revealing and state his or her reasons during the telephone conversation. The therapist should simply inform the patient that it is not possible for the therapist to see him or her; this is done in a respectful manner, but in a way that does not violate the privacy of other patients and the anonymity of the therapist.

In principle, it is best not to discuss the fee with the patient until the consultation, so that the patient begins to experience the therapist's exploratory attitude, and recognizes that action-discharge efforts at relief will be precluded if possible.

The therapist should see a patient in consultation only if it is clear that there is an available hour and that the time is suitable for the patient. Wherever possible, the time used for the consultation hour should be used for the subsequent therapy as well. If necessary, the therapist should certainly offer the patient directions to his or her office, but should do so without becoming overindulgent.

THE COMMUNICATIVE ASSESSMENT

At the appointed time of the first session, the therapist should greet the patient in the waiting room by name and with a handshake. The therapist should then introduce himself or herself and motion to the patient to enter the consultation room. The therapist follows the patient and closes the door to the consultation room behind them, thus securing the privacy of the frame. The patient should be allowed to find the appropriate seat and should be seen face to face. When necessary, the therapist may have to motion the patient to the proper chair, after which the therapist should also be seated.

The first hour should begin with a therapeutically oriented question from the therapist such as: "With what may I be of help?" The patient is then allowed to say whatever comes to mind—to free associate. If silences are relatively rare or absent, all the therapist need do is to listen and formulate. However, if silences do occur, the therapist's initial response should be to invoke the fundamental rule—to advise the patient that it would be best for him or her to say anything that comes to mind, whatever it may be, and to allow the session to unfold in that manner. Persistent silence is to be interpreted in light of prevailing adaptive contexts and the patient's encoded perceptions of the implications of the therapist's interventions.

The therapist's listening stance relies on silent holding and silent formulating. Unconsciously, the patient perceives questions and other active interventions from the therapist as reflections of the therapist's anxieties and madness. There is no substitute for attentive listening, nor should the therapist implicitly promise a mode of therapy in which he or she will be excessively active, only to alter the technique in subsequent sessions.

As a rule, the patient communicates on two levels in the first session. Manifestly, he or she will attempt to inform the therapist to some extent about the nature and history of his or her madness. At the same time, these manifest associations often serve a derivative function in terms of which the patient recounts the history of the therapeutic interaction to that point. In this respect, the therapist's interventions during the first telephone call, the type of physical setting he or she has created, and his or her initial therapeutic stance are all significant adaptive contexts for the patient's selected and responsive encoded perceptions. When gross behavioral resistances appear, such as silence, their unconscious meaning will always involve these active triggers and the patient's responsive, encoded perceptions. Most first sessions show a measure of gross behavioral or communicative resistance that calls for interpretive response from the therapist.

Basic Areas of Assessment

Silent listening facilitates a number of assessments made by the communicative therapist. First, he or she evaluates the intensity and degree of primitivity in the patient's psychotic core. Patients who are overtly psychotic, such as those who are schizophrenic or manic-depressive, evidence both a gross psychosis and a highly primitive psychotic core. Associated with such a core is an extremely primitive and terrifying deep unconscious system. As a result, these patients are in terror of derivative expressions. Derivatives are themselves anxiety-provoking, but are even more dreadful when experienced as a means of access for both patient and therapist to the unconscious meanings of the patient's primitive madness.

Psychotic patients are especially terrified of sane and valid interventions from the therapist, because such efforts do not support their defensive need to cover over and deny their own madness and its derivatives. Psychotic patients also tend to be terrified of the ideal, or secure, frame because their quota of death anxiety tends to be quite severe and associated with disruptive perceptions and fantasies. At the same time, the secure frame offers these patients a significant sense of holding and containment, and helps to strengthen their ego functioning and healthy defenses (see Chapter 7). Communicative psychotherapeutic work with such patients is a very delicate balancing act, because there is considerable risk of premature termination due to their inordinate dread of unconscious meaning.

Nonpsychotic patients also contain a psychotic core, and many well-functioning patients reveal significant vulnerabilities to psychotic anxieties. Quite often, these problems emerge in the initial session, only to disappear from subsequent hours except under unusual circumstances. It is therefore crucial that the therapist be alert to manifestations of such vulnerability, because they serve to forewarn the therapist not only of the excessiveness of the patient's anxieties, but of the likelihood of unconscious primitive processing and thinking.

There are several common signs of an overly active psychotic core and a tendency toward experiencing psychotic anxieties. Such anxieties are usually intimately connected with a high level of death anxiety and death-related issues. In the session, psychotic vulnerability to such issues should be considered, first, in the presence of what have been termed *mini-psychotic acts*. Such behaviors are constituted by momentary breaks with reality that are quickly repaired. For example, the patient may sit in what is obviously the therapist's chair, or may attempt to leave through the wrong door at the end of the session. A slip of the tongue is a minor mini-psychotic act, as are all forms of momentary misperception. The appearance of phenomena of this kind in the first hour suggest special vulnerabilities in the patient.

A second indicator of this type of issue is the recounting of early memories or recent events in which there are bizarre occurrences, or a direct allusion to psychotic experiences and/or individuals. A history of attempted suicide, homicide, or other indications of overt psychosis in the patient's parents suggests the likelihood of psychotic introjects and notable psychotic anxieties. Early and unusual experiences involving loss, separation, physical illness, and death also point in this direction. Patients who are themselves faced with a fatal illness or with a recent accidental death to which they contributed are similarly vulnerable.

Another indication of psychotic anxiety is the emergence of an encapsulated psychotic symptom in the patient's own history. This applies to patients who are currently functioning quite well, but who nonetheless show in this fashion psychotic vulnerabilities.

Finally, the persistence of a strong need for deviation also suggests psychotic anxieties and a dread of the secure frame—and of secure-frame meaning. Certain patients find relief from their madness and its unconscious meanings by engaging the therapist in deviations that create mad images of the therapist—images that enable the patient to cover over his or her own psychotic expressions and anxieties. In addition, the creation of a deviant frame tends to diminish separation- and death-related anxieties by providing the patient with significant manic defenses. Implications of fusion and denial accrue to virtually all alterations in the ground rules. Thus, the persistent need for defense through deviation is typically a defense against psychotic anxiety (see Chapter 7).

The therapist who recognizes this type of vulnerability in a patient will be prepared to intervene with respect to the intense anxieties aroused in him or her by secure-frame efforts. Such patients are often disposed toward the premature termination of meaningful psychotherapy; so the recognition of this type of vulnerability facilitates both understanding and interpretation.

A difficult question arises as to whether a therapist should ever participate in a proposed deviation as a way of keeping such a patient in treatment. Clinical findings make clear the fact that this type of participation is unconsciously perceived by the patient as quite mad and destructive, even though it is welcomed by the conscious system. Also, patients unconsciously expect therapists who understand derivative communication to be capable of creating and maintaining a secure frame. When the therapist shows one of these capabilities and not the other, he or she is unconsciously perceived as psychotically split. Perceptions of this kind tend to drive the patient mad and often themselves lead to premature termination, or generate gross behavioral resistances and symptomatic regression in the patient. Moreover, because the invocation of deviations tends to offer pathological defenses against psychotic anxieties, the latter do not emerge with related imagery in a way that permits their analytic resolution through interactional interpretations.

Communicative Style

In the first session, the therapist should also evaluate the patient's communicative style. As noted, one type of patient—the transformer—tends to communicate well-represented adaptive contexts and derivative perceptions. Another type—the nontransformer—appears to be communicatively resistant and to generate little in the way of meaning. Although both types of patients can engage in effective and successful psychotherapy, it is important for the therapist to identify the patient's communicative tendencies.

Nontransformers, who also tend to question the therapy, attack the therapist's approach, and engage in violent efforts at pathological projective identification into the therapist, are a serious problem. Whereas nontransformers who are accepting of the therapist's silence and holding tend to do very well in treatment, those of this group who are agitated and discontent with treatment are generally terrified of their own derivatives and the related psychotic and death anxieties. They dread any measure of unconscious meaning in the course of their psychotherapeutic experience. Because these patients cannot tolerate and seldom express derivative meaning, interpretation is not possible.

At the same time, the therapist's holding capacity and ability to create a relatively secure frame constitutes a danger situation that is a source of extreme anxiety. In their daily lives, these patients are often without adaptive recourse. Similarly, within their psychotherapy, they can tolerate neither meaning nor nonmeaning. Interventions that lack interactional and derivative meaning are not only unconsciously perceived as destructive, but consciously attacked as well. Yet the therapist's silence provokes attacks on his or her lack of response. It requires a great deal of patience under pressures of this kind for a therapist to wait for the representation of an adaptive context and derivative expressions, but this is the only means through which these patients can experience a successful psychotherapy.

Response to the Ground Rules

The patient's attitude toward the ground rules, or frame, must also be evaluated, because this is one of the most vital areas of meaning and experience in communicative psychotherapy. As noted, certain patients insist on deviant conditions to treatment—alterations in the ground rules that provide them with major defenses and other pathological satisfactions that essentially preclude or limit meaningful communication and analysis. In the first session, these patients show major secure-frame anxieties, including critical claustrophobic and paranoid images and concerns. Validated interpretation of such images tends to reassure the patient and to support his or her adaptive resources, though simultaneously, such interpretations constitute danger situations, because they mobilize further terrifying secure-frame meanings and anxieties within the patient. Here, too, the therapist must strike a delicate balance; careful attention must be paid to the patient's derivative communications. Under pressure from these patients, therapists tend to shift to manifest-content listening and to deal with the conscious system. They fail to realize that the patient's unconscious reactions to such work often have a powerful negative effect on the subsequent interaction.

It should be noted again that both deviations in the ideal ground rules and the establishment of a secure frame constitute danger situations for the patient. In either context there will be meaning and opportunity for interpretation, although the deviant-frame situation defensively excludes some issues. In the first session, the therapist attempts to appreciate the specific issues and vulnerabilities of the patient, the genetic experiences that have contributed to these vulnerabilities, and the risks involved for the continuation of the psychotherapy. Signs of premature termination, including the possibility or likelihood that the patient will not return to treatment after the first hour, call for careful and specific interpretations in light of prevailing adaptive contexts (almost always ground-rule issues, secure or deviant), and the patient's derivative perceptions as they illuminate the mobilization of primitive issues and meanings, as well as extremes of anxiety.

STATING THE GROUND RULES OF THERAPY

Twenty or thirty minutes into a forty-five- or fifty-minute first session, the therapist should formally state the ground rules of treatment to the patient. This step should be taken sufficiently early to allow time for subsequent exploration and interpretation of any ground-rule issues raised by the patient in response. Prior to this effort, the therapist should intervene interpretively in the presence of significant indicators and clear communicative material.

The therapist should begin his or her definition of the ground rules by stating that he or she can be of help to the patient. In this context, the patient's evident emotional difficulties can be acknowledged, but no effort should be made to formulate the nature of these difficulties or their basis—except as permitted by interactional interpretation.

Next, the therapist should state his or her fee, because deciding on the frequency of sessions often depends on this factor. A single fee should be cited as current, and there should be no need for negotiation. A subsequent increase or decrease of the fee typically proves disruptive of the treatment and constitutes a disturbing alteration in the ideal frame.

The therapist should then propose a frequency of sessions. If it is evident that the patient cannot possibly afford more than one session per week, once-a-week sessions should be recommended. In most situations, the ideal recommendation is twice-weekly psychotherapy, but the patient should be given a choice between once-a-week and twice-a-week treatment. More frequent sessions are recommended only rarely, mainly in the presence of an extraordinary emergency or with a patient who has insisted on intensive treatment. Therapists should rightfully develop a strong faith in once- and twice-weekly psychotherapy as highly viable and effective treatment modalities.

With the frequency established, the therapist should propose specific hours. The consultation hour should, as a rule, be used for at least one of the weekly sessions. Once the hours have been established, the patient is informed that the time is set aside for him or her, and that he or she has full responsibility for all sessions for which the therapist is available. The therapist should then clarify his or her present vacation plans, doing so as clearly as is possible at the moment.

The therapist also states the length of the sessions, which will be identical to that of the first hour. The patient is informed that the therapist will not prepare a bill, and that it is the patient's responsibility to keep track of the number of sessions in each month and to pay the therapist at the beginning of each new month for the previous months' sessions.

Finally, the therapist should in all instances recommend that the patient be on the couch for subsequent hours. The patient is simply informed that lying on the couch and saying whatever comes to mind facilitates the treatment process. The couch has been found empirically to be an essential part of the ideal, or secure, frame unconsciously requested by patients.

The remaining ground rules—those of total privacy, total confidentiality, the relative anonymity of the therapist with no deliberate self-revelations, the use of neutral interventions, the absence of physical contact except for the handshake at the beginning and end of the psychotherapy, and such—are not usually specifically defined for the patient, but become evident through the therapist's behaviors and verbalizations.

In the course of the initial phone call and from the beginning of the first hour, the patient accumulates impressions of the nature of the ground rules or frame. He or she is soon aware of the extent to which treatment will be constituted as a secure- or deviant-frame treatment experience. The absence of third parties in the therapist's office, the sense of privacy and confidentiality, and the basic listening attitude of the therapist register both in the patient's unconscious and conscious thinking early on, as does the existence of deviations, whether in a clinic setting, a group practice, or unilaterally developed by a private therapist. Either experience evokes both conscious responses and a sensitive unconscious reading of the implications involved. Ground-rule adaptive contexts are the most critical interventions to which a patient responds unconsciously (and often consciously) in the first hour.

Technical Issues in the First Hour

How, then, should the therapist respond if the patient proposes a modificaiton in one or more of the ground rules offered by the therapist? On occasion, a patient will ask for irregular hours because of a job commitment or perhaps request to be excused from responsibility for all sessions because of travel requirements at work. Probably the most common request for deviation, however, is asking the therapist to prepare a bill with a diagnosis or to directly complete an insurance form.

In principle, the therapist should respond to such requests in one of two ways, depending on the available material from the patient. Usually this type of request appears toward the latter part of the first hour. Quite often, the patient has already communicated derivative material concerning the *unconscious implications* of this type of deviant intervention—encoded perceptions that forewarn the therapist. Indeed, this is one of the few instances in which the patient responds to an *anticipated adaptive context* based on a proposal that he or she has already made or plans to make. In addition to these encoded perceptions, the patient's material will often include derivative directives as to how the therapist should manage the request. In all instances, the encoded material points toward the need to maintain the secure frame.

In many instances, then, the therapist can respond to the patient's request to deviate with an interpretation. The main represented and activated adaptive context is the expectation that the therapist will carry out the proposed deviation. The therapist should allude to the direct representation of the anticipated trigger. From there, the goal is to demonstrate to the patient what his or her encoded perceptions of the therapist would be were the latter to deviate as requested. In addition, it is critical to show the patient how his or her own encoded-material points to the need to preclude any such deviant intervention.

The patient's response to an intervention of this kind is typically split or mixed, reflecting the rather opposite needs of the conscious/superficial unconscious and deep unconscious systems. Thus, the patient's encoded response to such interventions will, as a rule, reflect both interpersonal and cognitive validation—new derivative images that further amplify in unique fashion the therapist's interpretive and framework-management effort.

And yet, despite this indication of strong unconscious support for the therapist's position—material that can also be interpreted to the patient—conscious objections to maintaining the frame are not uncommon. In this regard, patients tend to be divided: One type, for various reasons, will accept the wisdom of maintaining and securing the frame, and engage in further cooperative therapeutic work with the therapist toward this goal. Another type, however, will either directly object to his or her own validated communications or agree with the therapist initially, only to then generate fresh conscious opposition. Some of these latter patients will not return after the first hour because their dread of the secure frame and of secure-frame unconscious meaning is extraordinary; they will not risk an experience of that kind. Others will remain in treatment, struggling consciously against the therapist's secure-frame interventions, while continuing to support his or her position on the derivative level. Careful and sound therapeutic work that concentrates on interactional interpretations and pays attention to the patient's derivative directives toward maintaining the secure frame is essential in these instances.

There are, however, sessions in which the patient's material prior to the introduction of a proposed deviation does not permit interpretation and frame-securing responses. Although this type of first hour is less common than those in which derivatives are available, the therapist has no choice but to intervene—when the patient raises a frame issue, a response must be made. In the absence of derivative meaning and directives, the therapist should indicate that he or she is offering to the patient the best possible conditions for the therapeutic work. Any proposal to modify these conditions, such as the one the patient has presented, should be explored over several sessions so that the answer as to how the situation should be handled can emerge from the patient's own associations.

In this way, the therapist adopts an interpretive attitude and implicitly invites the patient to engage in derivative communication. In contrast, a direct response would discourage derivative expression and lead to engagement on the manifest level. Such engagements are always destructive to the treatment; most often, the therapy becomes an open battlefield on which the therapist can only be defeated—that is, the pathological and defensive components of the patient's conscious system will hold sway over the healthy components of his or her own deep conscious system.

As noted, some patients will respond to this position by engaging unconsciously in the necessary exploration, providing the therapist with derivative directives to maintain the frame. Some of these patients will, in turn, forego the deviation and accept secure-frame conditions to the treatment. Others will acknowledge the meanings and directives interpreted to them, and still insist on the deviation. The therapist may then have to choose between terminating the case or participating in the deviant-frame therapy—though always with some hope of securing the altered ground rule or creating other secure-frame moments. In general, the latter course, though rarely successful (see above) seems most advisable, because the communicative therapist is in a unique position to help the patient understand the unconscious meanings of the deviation, whereas a noncommunicative therapist virtually ignores such issues. As mentioned, however, under deviant conditions created in this way the deep unconscious system constricts its communications, and the conscious system uses the deviation as a powerful means of denying interpretive meaning. The consequences of alterations in the ground rules stand among the least understood aspects of the psychotherapeutic encounter (see Chapter 7).

The following illustrates how an adaptive context that precedes the first hour affects the therapeutic exchange:

The therapist in this case is a male social worker married to another social worker. The wife had taken a job at a family service clinic, and the patient we are considering had at one time also worked at this clinic. She had left soon after the therapist's wife had begun to work there.

When the patient, a black woman in her twenties, went to the clinic for help, she spoke briefly to her former co-worker. When it became clear that clinic policy would preclude therapy for this woman because she had once worked there, the co-worker referred her to her husband, without revealing the relationship. (The wife uses her maiden name professionally.) Both husband and wife are Caucasian.

The patient's initial telephone call to the therapist was brief, though she did inquire as to whether he would accept her present insurance. The therapist said yes, but suggested that the matter be discussed further when he saw the patient.

The patient was five minutes late to her session. She nearly sat in the therapist's chair after entering his consultation room, and the therapist had to redirect her. When they were both seated, he asked the patient how he could be of help. She responded by apologizing, and said that she really hadn't thought she was supposed to sit in the really good chair.

The patient then asked if the therapist had talked to Helen Young [the therapist's wife]. The therapist responded that he had not talked to Ms. Young about her, and that all he knew was what the patient had told him on the telephone—namely, that Ms. Young had referred her to him.

The patient said that she was hoping the therapist had been in touch with her so she wouldn't have to talk so much. She ruminated about not knowing what to say and eventually suggested that they talk price. When she pressed him about the fee, the therapist suggested that she continue to say whatever came to mind.

After some hesitation, the patient said that she had been sick with the flu and had stayed home. According to her mother, she had had a nervous breakdown, but she herself felt it was only the flu. It had happened once before. But maybe her mother was right; the patient had felt suicidal at times.

The patient spoke again about how difficult it is to do therapy. She was able talk to people she knew, but not to a professional like the therapist. After expressing further concerns about doing therapy, the patient indicated that her problems began when she got a full-time job and could not take care of her young daughter. She was divorced and so involved in her work that she could not give the child the attention she needed. She had therefore given her daughter to her husband, who had insisted on legal custody, only to lose his job and go on relief. The patient felt furious that her daughter was on welfare and felt demeaned. Welfare people snoop about and there is no privacy, she said; they're always around somewhere. The patient was now paying for her daughter's support and resented not having legal custody. She should have kept the daughter with her.

The patient described her work as a secretary and her constant problems with money. These problems were especially bad during her marriage when her husband would lie to her and secretly spend all they had. He would even steal her credit card and use it behind her back. He hid the charge slips in her drawer, but the patient found them.

At this point, the therapist intervened without alluding to the patient's possible derivative perceptions of the connection between himself and his wife. Nonetheless, he structured a psychotherapy for the patient, and she has continued in treatment. Here, let us analyze the patient's material in order to better understand the structure of the first hour.

It can be seen that this patient showed strong, initial gross behavioral resistances—she was frequently silent, had difficulty in free associating, and spoke repeatedly of difficulties in doing therapy. These resistances should be accounted for in light of the prevailing adaptive context—here, in the main, the identity of the referring therapist and the expectation of the inclusion of a third-party payer through insurance. Both the referring therapist and the insurance company are third parties to therapy, so that the patient's derivative perceptions in response to these two triggers are likely to overlap. (We are, of course, assuming that the patient consciously or unconsciously knows of the relationship between the two therapists—a highly likely possibility.) It would therefore be important to determine whether there are distinctive derivatives that point more to the trigger of the wife as the referring source than to the insurance situation.

In either case, it can be seen that as the patient eventually gets around to describing her emotional problems and their recent sources—her suicidal depression, problems with her daughter, and divorce—she is also encoding derivative perceptions in light of the two activated adaptive contexts at hand. By and large, the patient's conscious system addresses her need to convey her problems to the therapist, while her deep unconscious system seeks to communicate the triggered selected unconscious perceptions that have registered within its confines. The patient's free associations reflect an unconsciously created combination of these two inputs—a remarkable achievement indeed.

The first derivative expression is the behavior of the patient—her almost knowing decision to sit in the therapist's chair. This action does not speak to the anticipation of the release of information to an insurance company, but appears to relate more strongly to the referral adaptive context. We may decode the message as indicating that the therapist is in serious need of help, and that the situation is steeped in confusion. In the unconscious system, the referral of a patient from wife to husband is seen not only as exploitive, but also as a contradiction—once the pateint has seen and worked with the therapist's wife, she cannot be the rightful and appropriate patient of the husband/therapist. In the deep unconscious system, a personal relationship of that kind precludes a therapeutic liaison.

The referral adaptive context is touched on manifestly at the very beginning of the hour, and the patient also mentions the price of therapy quite soon. The allusion to her own decompensation suggests an unconscious perception of the therapist as behaving in psychotic fashion—the referral source disturbs the patient's sense of reality (*cf.* her going to the wrong chair as well). There is then a reference to the patient and her mother as having different opinions about the nature of the patient's illness, a possible representaiton of the therapist and his wife.

The material that follows strongly supports a knowledge in the patient on some level of the therapist's marriage. In addition, it reveals an unconscious motive in the patient for having accepted a referral of this kind. The patient has sent her daughter off to live with her former husband; she is suffering from depression and guilt because she has done so. Unconsciously, she has selected a treatment situation in which a wife has also placed someone with her husband—this time the patient. Quite often, patients unconsciously seek out treatment situations in which the therapist enacts a situation that is comparable to the madness with which the patient is suffering or has suffered in the past. The unconscious realization that the therapist can participate in a destructive custody arrangement reassures the patient that her own behavior need not be condemned to the point of suicide.

The patient states that the custody situation is compounded by the fact that her daughter is on welfare. We may decode this as indicating that the referral from wife to husband is aggravated by the therapist's immediate acceptance of a third-party payer—

the insurance company is represented by the welfare agency. The third party produces a situation of snooping and destroys privacy; and the nature of the referral makes the patient something of an orphan.

The exploitive and greedy aspects of a wife-to-husband referral is further worked over unconsciously in the images of the husband's clandestine spending sprees and his stealing the patient's credit card. This alludes as well to some of the destructive implications of third-party payers, though the themes of dishonesty and secretiveness appear to touch mainly on the referral situation.

Had the therapist understood these derivatives, he would have carried out a playback version of an interpretation (see Chapter 4), because neither adaptive context is represented manifestly. The intervention might have been stated as follows: "You have mentioned Helen Young, and you have also said that we should talk price. You are concerned about the difficulty of doing therapy, and I think you are trying to tell us in some way that there are problems that exist well beyond those you have identified directly and consciously. As for price, you have been talking about welfare and people that snoop and destroy privacy. You have also mentioned dishonest ways of spending money and connect all of this to something that appears to be quite destructive. These images must in some way have something to do with the problem of price and the way in which the fee for your therapy will be handled.

"But then again," the therapist would have continued, "you have, as I said, also mentioned Helen Young. You said something about talking to her and then went on to speak of a sickness and something that is extremely disturbed, disturbing, and self-destructive. You spoke of a woman who turns someone over to a man in a manner that is also highly destructive and demeaning. You talk of people who will do anything to have money and you speak as well of dishonesty and secrets. Here, too, it would appear that there is some secret that you are trying to get at, because it pertains to your therapy and to your referral to me from Helen Young. Actually, there appear to be two hidden problems to your treatment, one related to price or fee and the other related to my contact with Helen Young."

It seems very likely that the patient would offer derivative support for this playback, and that she might now feel that she could safely allude to both of these contexts. The proposed intervention is in striking contrast to the therapist's actual comment that he had not talked to Ms. Young about the patient and that all he knew is what the patient had told him on the telephone. Although this statement was technically true, his reference to his own wife as "Ms. Young" and his implication that there was no other contact between them is disingenuous and will be unconsciously perceived by the patient as sick or even out of touch with reality—psychotic. The patient's first derivative images following this intervention did indeed reveal perceptions of this kind.

In principle, then, the session illustrates the need to interpret early resistances, such as reluctance to engage in the therapy in light of prevailing adaptive contexts and selected encoded perceptions. Many initial sessions take place in the context of some type of deviation, and often the alteration in the ideal ground rules is self-serving for the therapist. As such, there are powerful unconscious needs in the therapist to avoid the patient's manifest and especially derivative allusions to the deviation. Such an attitude, however, precludes sound interpretations and appropriate efforts at framework rectificaiton to the greatest extent feasible.

The therapist should also be mindful that deviations limit the patient's communicative material and have other actual, detrimental consequences for both patient and therapist and the therapeutic experience and outcome. A deviation such as a referral from a therapist's wife cannot be rectified and may produce lasting emotional damage in a patient. Nonetheless, there are many patients, such as the woman described above, who have powerful pathological unconscious reasons for unwittingly seeking out a deviant therapist. In such instances, the therapist may in fact obtain a paradoxical cure through madness, but the risks are great and the side effects often of major proportions.

Let us consider briefly another initial hour of a therapy. The patient is a woman who was being seen by a social worker in a small town for episodes of anxiety. The social worker, a young man, felt stalemated with the patient and referred her to a colleague by telephone. The second therapist agreed to see the patient. In his next session with her, the social worker suggested that the patient call the therapist and arrange a first session.

The patient began this initial session with the therapist by describing her therapy with the social worker, especially her sense that talking to him was going nowhere even though he seemed to be a nice young man. Responding to the patient's extended description of talking to the social worker, the therapist intervened and told the patient exactly what the social worker had said to him on the telephone (the information was minimal). He then assured the patient of the confidentiality of their sessions, emphasizing that he would not be in contact with the referring social worker again.

The patient then spoke about the death of her mother, which had taken place when the patient was fourteen. That loss was followed by the death of her closest girlfriend, her boyfriend, and soon after, her father. Every time something nice took place, she said, something awful happened. The patient had gotten married, they had bought a nice house, and suddenly she had felt depressed. Two years ago, she had had a baby and everything was fine, but then the anxiety attacks began. Recently, it had reached the point where the patient had to quit her job because she couldn't handle the pressure.

At this point, approximately midway in the hour, the therapist told the patient that he felt he could be of help to her. He said that his fee was forty dollars per session, that the patient would be responsible for the time they set for the sessions, that he expected to be paid at the beginning of each month for the prior month's session (he would not be handing her a bill; the patient should simply keep track of the sessions and pay the fee accordingly), that therapy would work best if she were on the couch, that the sessions would be fifty minutes in length, and that he expected to be in his office for all sessions except during three weeks in August—some three months hence. (It had already been established on the telephone that the particular time of the present session was acceptable in general for the patient.)

The patient agreed to therapy and asked how long the therapist thought treatment might last. Very quickly, she told the therapist she didn't want him to answer. She reviewed out loud the conditons of the treatment, and then asked about insurance—how would the therapist handle that? The therapist responded by suggesting that the patient continue to say whatever came to mind.

The patient paused a moment and then began to appear sad. She spoke of how unfair it was that she must get along in life without her parents. Her father-in-law and mother-in-law were very poor substitutes. Her father-in-law smoked and drank too much, and her mother-in-law was crazy. The patient was frightened of being overly dependent on her husband, and her older sister treated her as though she were a little child, which was repugnant to the patient.

While seeing the social worker, the patient had gone to a physician who had prescribed medication, but she felt like a zombie and stopped taking the pills. After her mother died, the patient's family had held on to the mother's house. When the patient got married, her sister had said that the patient could buy their parents' home, but then she set the price too high and the patient did not make the purchase. Besides, the house would have been someone else's house, not her own. She could never feel right living in someone else's space.

The therapist intervened again. He stated that the patient's images seemed to shed light on how the therapy would be influenced if he were to complete an insurance form. After bringing up insurance, her thoughts had gone to her father-in-law, who drank too much, and to her wish not to depend excessively on her husband. She had also mentioned that her older sister treated her like a child, much to her irritation, and that she had stopped the medication that had been offered to her. There was also the image of living in someone else's house and her objection to being in someone else's space. All of these images pertained to the meanings of bringing the insurance company into the treatment situation—there would be an addiction-like overgratification, an excessive type of dependency, an infantilization of the patient, and the loss of the patient's own space. The images indicated that the patient would not want this type of excessive dependency, nor did she wish to be treated like a child or given artificial support similar to medication. She was indicating quite clearly that she wanted her own space and that the therapy should be free of such contingencies.

It was now near the end of the hour. The patient said that she felt she could not afford treatment without insurance because money was very tight. She explained the details of her financial difficulties, but ended the hour by agreeing to return the following session.

This particular consultation begins as a relatively secure-frame situation. There had been a professional referral in which a minimum amount of information was imparted to the present therapist. The one-to-one relationship with privacy, confidentiality, and relative anonymity appear to be present. In approaching such an hour, the therapist can expect, first, to be in a position to learn something about the patient's symptoms, their etiology, and the relevant genetic history; and, second, to acquire considerable information regarding the patient's tolerance of the secure frame and her related anxieties.

The therapist noted the patient's repeated references to the social worker early in the hour. Suspecting an *implication* (note that this is *not* an encoded level of meaning) that the patient was concerned about the therapist's prior contact with the social worker and possible future contact, the therapist intervened to frankly and briefly describe the little information that had been imparted to him by the social worker and to assure the patient of the confidentiality of her sessions. This was an active, secure-frame intervention, with the potential to evoke secure-frame anxieties.

The patient responded to this intervention by revealing a traumatic sequence of death experiences and her sense that every good thing in her life is eventually spoiled. She also described both depression and anxiety attacks, and, finally, alluded to having quit her job.

This material suggests that the patient's depression and anxiety attacks are significantly connected to death anxiety and to the series of losses that the patient suffered in early adolescence. The material also suggests superego issues, survivor guilt, and a form of success neurosis in which the patient has an unconscious need to spoil or destroy moments of satisfaction. This, in brief, formulates the *dynamics* and *genetics* of the patient's madness. These initial speculations are *inferences* extracted from the patient's immediate material. It is this type of information that we derive from manifest contents and conscious implications.

We may shift now to the level of encoded meaning. As we know, a patient's encoded material tells two stories—one conscious and the other unconscious. The latter level of information is organized as derivative responses to triggers constituted as interventions from the therapist.

The first set of interventions involves the telephone conversation between the patient and the therapist, during which the first hour was arranged. In addition, the comments made by the referral source would also be experienced by the patient as adaptive contexts or triggers for which—as perceived by the deep unconscious system—the therapist would be responsible.

In this hour, there is no evidence of significant encoded response to these two initial triggers. The patient's comments in this regard are manifest and direct, mainly nonderivative in nature. The few seemingly minor comments the patient makes about her interaction with the social worker could involve encoded perceptions of the interaction with the therapist, but these are relatively insubstantial.

The therapist's first intervention in the session was based on inference rather than decoding. In principle, it is only in the first session that a therapist may intervene appropriately on this level and obtain a confirmatory response. The therapist should in all other sessions be confined to dealing with the patient's derivative expressions, but in the first hour he or she has the responsibility of establishing the ground rules of treatment, and this effort must be carried out, in almost all instances, without directive derivative material from the patient.

The therapist's first intervention in this hour, then, established a secure-frame gound rule related to confidentiality, an effort that was apparently necessary, given the implications of mistrust and uncertainty in the patient as to the possibiilty of leakage. (In principle, a therapist should establish a particular ground rule when called for by the patient's material in the session, reserving the remainder of these rules for a basic frame statement about half way into the session.)

The material that followed the therapist's intervention may be viewed, in part, as an unconscious response to that effort.

Two formulations are possible. The first would propose that the establishment of confidentiality was unconsciously perceived by the patient as destroying the therapist and/or the therapy—that is, as a form of death. There are also images of good things being spoiled and of quitting one's job. This formulation, however, is not in keeping with our knowledge of how patients in general respond to a secure-frame intervention nor is it supported by the patient's later material. Nonetheless, one must seriously consider such a formulation until additional material either supports or refutes the clinical hypothesis.

An alternate formulation would propose that the patient's responsive associations reflect a common form of secure-frame anxiety—one that centers on death-related issues based on the claustrum properties of the secure frame. Patients who have suffered major traumas related to death, as the patient has, are especially sensitive to such concerns.

In this light, the patient's images of satisfying experiences being ultimately spoiled would embody an unconscious perception of the *constructive* aspect of the therapist's intervention and the patient's expectation that something else will ultimately destroy the treatment—perhaps this reflects her anticipation of the insurance issue that soon followed. On this level, the patient's image of quitting her job because of excessive pressures would represent the patient's own thoughts of taking flight from secure-frame treatment.

The therapist's next intervention was to structure the treatment situation, whereupon the patient introduced a deviation. She tentatively asked the therapist to complete an insurance form and thereby release information to a third party. The therapist correctly responded by asking the patient to continue to free associate, expecting that her subsequent associations might well contain encoded images that would identify exactly how the patient would unconsciously perceive the therapist should he comply. This indeed appears to have been the case.

The insurance situation constitutes an *anticipated adaptive context*. The images that follow may be decoded in light of this expected trigger. The patient's derivatives indicate that if the therapist were to sign the insurance form, the patient would unconsciously perceive him as dead or absent—a death-related deviant-frame image. The therapist would fail in his appropriate function as a parental substitute, in part because his action would have self-serving and destructively addictive qualities. The deviation would create a situation of excessive dependency and would be a way of infantilizing the patient. It would be comparable to using medication—a situation to which the patient had objected and finally stopped. This latter was the patient's own *model of rectification*—a directive that the insurance should not be used.

Insurance would also create a situation in which the patient was no longer in her own private space—a situation to which the patient also objected (another model of rectification).

The therapist responded to this material with an interpretation that, in substance, corresponds to the formulations presented here. Granted, the patient responded with a few words that were entirely nonconfirmatory; however, in the following hour the patient did offer derivative validation and evidenced additional secure-frame anxieties—responses to the anticipated exclusion of the insurance carrier from the treatment situation.

Perhaps the main omission in the therapist's intervention is some reference to the manner in which the insurance deviation would have served to alleviate the patient's secure-frame anxieties, especially her death anxieties. In addition, as the patient reminded the therapist by alluding a second time to the death of her mother, the therapist who signs an insurance form is in some sense abandoning the patient and functionally dead. This genetic dimension should have been included in the therapist's interpretation, for example, by pointing out to the patient that her first thoughts following her questions about insurance coverage involved having to get along without her parents. This sequence suggests that in some way the therapist would be lost to the patient as the parents had been lost, were he to complete the insurance form.

We see then that in a first hour it is possible to establish adaptive contexts constituted by the therapist's interventions and to interpret the patient's derivative material accordingly. It is also possible to incorporate genetic information and other aspects of the patient's dynamic issues (as revealed in manifest contents and implications derived from these contents) into the interpretation of unconscious meanings. It is work of this kind that implictly indicates to the patient both the conditions of treatment and the means by which the therapist will intervene. In this way, the therapist establishes with the patient not only a conscious therapeutic alliance, but an unconscious one as well.

Finally, one could argue that in this session the patient had come to the therapist with an unconscious wish to find a replacement for her lost parents, especially her dead mother. Interestingly, although the insurance deviation would have provided some type of pathological satisfaction gratifying such wishes, it would also have *repeated her loss* on an unconscious level, rather than actually providing a substitute object (person). In general, deviations partially gratify unconscious wishes even as they recreate the traumatic situation that keep such wishes alive. Securing the frame frustrates unconscious wishes of this genre. When they arise in the first session, the therapist should regard them as *indicators* (signs of madness) in need of interpretation. These are some of the complexities of the transactions of the first hour.

THE OPENING PHASE

The first session sets the tone for the opening phase of therapy. This phase may last weeks to months, and usually blends into the long middle phase of treatment during which the major therapeutic work is carried out. Typical of the opening phase is the patient's initial response to the conditions of treatment— whether secure or deviant in nature. The patient also establishes his or her communicative style and, in general, makes clear the key issues in his or her madness—the key issues for the therapy.

Both core and expressed madness will tend to organize around life traumas that evoke a significant measure of death anxiety and its derivative anxieties. Traumatic situations—the early loss of a parent or sibling, illness, injury, abandonment by a parent—tend to create overwhelming interpersonal and intrapsychic conflicts. These traumas do damage to narcissistic balances, and they generate highly conflicted and primitive responses in the deep unconscious system. The deep unconscious system thus becomes the repository for the implications of these experiences which are so anxiety-provoking and terrifying that they are barred from consciousness.

These episodes also tend to foster a pathological development of the conscious system, in which a major pathological influence is exerted by the manic defenses of denial and merger and the need for deviations from the ground rules of society and life. Issues of this kind are mobilized by the initial ground rules of the psychotherapy, and their explication and working through characterize the opening phase of treatment. In addition, the initial gross behavioral resistances created as a defense against these core conflicts require interpretation in light of activated adaptive contexts and the patient's derivative perceptions.

During the opening phase, the risk of premature termination is relatively high. Because of this, the therapist should become sensitive to the particular ground rules that are at issue for the patient. In general, efforts to alter a ground rule are designed to seal off from communicative expression a deep unconscious response to the unconscious meanings of the patient's core and expressed madness. The patient defensively substitutes derivatives that are related to the alteration in the frame for the derivatives related to his or her core issue—and the latter seldom emerge in meaningful, interpretable form under such conditions. At the same time, the deviation provides the patient with a host of pathological defenses and gratifications that preclude meaningful derivative material in these areas.

In contrast, the secure frame, or the act of securing an aspect of the frame, unleashes the patient's derivative responses to the treatment situation in a way that connects these images to the unconscious meanings of the patient's core madness. Seen in this light, it is easy to understand why one or another of the ground rules of psychotherapy may become the central battlefield on which the struggle to develop a successful, truly insightful psychotherapy unfolds. The dread of secure-frame experience and unconscious meaning cannot be overestimated. Careful interactional interpretation of the relevant images and anxieties is indispensible for maintaining the therapy. The danger of secure-frame annihilation is experienced as quite real by secure-frame sensitive patients. This sense of reality must be interpreted along with the other elements that emerge in the patient's material (see Chapter 6).

A second type of initial treatment experience is one in which there are few transformed images and an almost total absence of derivative meaning. The patient is readily recognized as a nontransformer, and the therapist begins to listen silently, thereby expressing his or her sound holding and containing capacities. Most of these patients tend to settle into a quiet course of therapy that is highly defensive on the communicative level, but often quite effective. A few, however, become pathological projective identifiers into the therapist and attack him or her for the slow progress in therapy—and, mainly, for his or her failure to intervene (despite the absence of meaningful material). With this latter type, the therapist might wait patiently for an occasional expression of derivative meaning in light of a represented adaptive context, and intervene only at such moments or at times of serious crisis with threat of premature termination. Intervention made under the latter conditions will, in general, be successful in proportion to the degree to which the patient provides a meaningful communicative complex.

THE MIDDLE PHASE

The opening phase runs into the relatively long middle phase of psychotherapy. In this phase, the patient will from time to time create a ground-rule issue, doing so with a frequency that reflects the acuteness of the patient's anxieties and conflicts, and a measure of the patient's active therapeutic need. Some patients seldom create ground-rule issues and therefore seldom require interventions. Their therapeutic cure relies on silent holding and containment and their own inner ability to heal themselves—a process the therapist should not disturb with unneeded comment. These patients are able to render their inner defenses less pathological, especially those in the conscious system. They also modify their internal derivatives, as contained in the deep unconscious system, less primitive and disruptive.

Remarkably, such effects are seen in many of these patients over a course of months, despite the absence of active intervention by the therapist.

At moments of therapeutic need, patients will consciously attempt to alter a particular ground rule and then produce derivatives that advise the therapist to maintain the frame. If the therapist does so, the patient is then faced with a strong secure-frame moment and will communicate responsive derivatives. Typically, such derivatives lend themselves to interpretation and to conveying to the patient his or her own directives toward maintaining the ground rules.

It is to be stressed that this type of therapeutic work is always significantly related to the unconscious meanings of the patient's core and expressed madness, including genetic development. The unconscious meanings of a ground-rule issue consistently touch on the unconscious meanings and genetics of the patient's psychopathology. Because of this, an adaptive cure of the patient's symptoms will be fashioned by (1) maintaining the frame (which virtually always provides a holding experience and introject far different from that of the pathogenic parent, whose behaviors are typically deviant) and (2) interpreting the patient's derivative material as it expands into dynamics, genetics, and other areas (offering insights into deep unconscious meanings that were previously inaccessible to consciousness for the patient). Such insight and cure are possible also because following a ground-rule management intervention, the patient usually shows active signs of madness—indicators—that can be meaningfully interpreted in light of that adaptive context and the patient's responsive unconscious perceptions. In many of these situations, genetic material will emerge in a particular hour and enable both an interpretation of the issues in the immediate therapeutic interaction along with an interpretation of their relevance to earlier genetic experiences and issues.

THE TERMINATION PHASE—AND AFTER TERMINATION

The goal of psychotherapy is the insightful and truly constructive resolution of the patient's interpersonal or symptomatic disturbance—characterological or otherwise. The average communicative psychotherapy will take one to three years to carry out. At some point, it becomes clear, usually through *indirect* signs, that the patient's difficulties are beginning to be, or have been, resolved. In most instances, the patient will at this point begin to talk *in derivative fashion* about termination by alluding to experiences of endings, separations, and the like. The therapist is often in a position to offer a playback of these derivatives in light of a representation of the patient's expectation that the therapist will permit termination. Such playbacks typically lead the patient to think consciously about ending therapy and, in time, to set a termination date.

In communicative psychotherapy, the patient alone decides on when termination should take place—whether immediately or over so many sessions, weeks, or months. The therapist should accept the patient's decision in this regard and simply continue to interpret the patient's derivative material, when available, in light of prevailing adaptive contexts. As noted, in addition to all other existing contexts, the patient's realization that the therapist is prepared to end the therapy—to allow the patient to leave—is an important anticipated context during this period. Patients appear to have considerable unconscious wisdom in determining just how long working through termination should take in respect to their own needs to complete the therapy; and the therapist must respect this decision unless the patient's derivatives begin to contradict his or her conscious thoughts—an occurrence that is quite rare.

The termination phase is distinctive both in arousing major separation and death anxieties and in fostering their working through in light of the adaptive context of the therapist's preparedness to no longer see the patient. A planned termination should entail the completion of treatment, and there should be no compromise, such as pre-arranged or proposed follow-up visits.

During the termination phase, patients vary in the extent to which they communicate meaningful derivatives and engage in active working through. Some patients do so to a major extent, especially those who have suffered from significant death-anxiety issues. Other patients become communicatively defensive, and may spend just one or two sessions in this period expressing derivative meanings, even in the course of a a six-month termination experience. As always, the therapist must allow the patient to create the psychotherapy and interventions, accepting the patient's unconscious wisdom in this regard. Each patient requires his or her own distinctive way of completing therapy, and if this need is accepted by the therapist (unless contradicted by the patient's derivatives), virtually all such terminations are quite successful, and there is no need for a patient to return for additional treatment.

The last session is conducted in a manner similar to all other therapy sessions. At the end of the hour, the therapist should shake hands with the patient and wish him or her the very best of everything. There is no need to tell the patient that the door is always open or to suggest in any fashion that the patient could, if necessary, return to therapy—a comment that is often unconsciously experienced as an invitation to return and merely reflects the therapist's own separation anxieties.

All therapists experience a significant measure of anxiety and loss with the termination of a patient. This creates a strong unconscious need within the therapist to deviate through such means as altering technique toward the manifest-content level (a form of manic defense and merger), the proposal of follow-up visits, and, in extreme instances, a shift to a social relationship with the patient. Wishes of this kind should not be enacted, but should be subjected to self-analysis. The patient requires a clean and clear termination experience.

Implied here is the necessity that the patient and therapist have no further contact after termination. During the post-termination period, the patient is actively working over and solidifying the therapeutic experience and the introjects of the therapist. Any modification of a clear termination will detrimentally affect these efforts.

Separation and death anxieties are universal, and are not necessarily resolved within the therapist. As a result, the therapist's unconscious needs to pathologically and defensively deviate in the final sessions of a psychotherapy are a major risk. The therapist's capacity to maintain the frame and the basic interpretive attitude to the very last moment of treatment, and to accept the termination as complete and definitive, is very much appreciated in the patient's deep unconscious system. In the patient's conscious system, however, the therapist will find a willing ally for pathological alterations in the frame and in the basic therapeutic stance.

Ideally, as noted, there should be no contact between patient and therapist after termination. The therapist should not accept referrals from a terminated patient, because this can have pathological consequences even after termination. On the other hand, if the patient gets into further difficulty and seeks out an additional period of treatment—or perhaps a consultation session—the therapist should be available and carry out the necessary therapeutic work. In a vast majority of instances, an unexpected exacerbation of symptoms or the development of new symptoms after the completion of a therapy *is connected to a deviation in the original treatment situation that has gone unrectified and uninterpreted.*

To the end of the treatment and beyond, the communicative approach requires the psychotherapist to think interactionally with respect to any form of expressed madness shown by the patient, any symptom or resistance, and any regression after a successful termination. There is no underestimating the powerful influence of the psychotherapist on the patient's madness and its meaning, a responsibility that is often difficult to acknowledge, understand, and accept.

RECOMMENDED READINGS

Firestein, S. (1978). *Terminations in Psychoanalysis*. New York: International Universities Press.

Freud, S. (1913). On beginning the treatment (Further recommendations on the technique of psycho-analysis, I). *SE* 12:121–144.

Gill, M., Newman, R., Redlick, F., & Sommers, M. (1954). *The Initial Interview in Psychiatric Practice*. New York: International Universities Press.

Langs, R. (1973). *The Technique of Psychoanalytic Psychotherapy*: Vol. 1. New York: Aronson.

Langs, R. (1978). Some communicative properties of the bipersonal field. *International Journal of Psychoanalytic Psychotherapy* 7:87–135.

Langs, R. (1982). *Psychotherapy: A Basic Text*. New York: Aronson.

Langs, R. (1985). The first session. *Yearbook of Psychoanalysis and Psychotherapy* 1:125–150.

CHAPTER 6

The Ground Rules or Frame of Psychotherapy

We are accustomed to speaking of the ground rules, the framework, and the frame when referring to the basic tenets and conditions of the psychotherapeutic experience. However, the crucial component of this dimension of psychotherapy lies in *the therapist's management of the basic rules of psychotherapy.* The manner in which a therapist expresses himself or herself with respect to these rules is undoubtedly the most critical area of communication and expression within the therapeutic interaction. And although this chapter discusses the ground rules of treatment, it should be understood that in all instances what is meant is the manner in which the therapist establishes and maintains these ground rules, and his or her direct, behavioral, verbal, and interventional communications in this regard. The patient's deep unconscious system is virtually zeroed in on the implications of the therapist's management of the frame.

The ground rules of treatment define the therapeutic space and set the manner in which the treatment will be carried out. They define the mode of cure and mode of relatedness between patient and therapist, establishing the necessary distance and interpersonal boundaries between them, and expressing as well the therapist's capacity to hold and contain the patient's expressed madness. The specific nature of the satisfactions and frustrations within the treatment experience are defined by these rules, including the possibility of pathological components. The therapist's management of the ground rules also reveals a great deal about his or her own inner balances and capacities, and signals to the patient the type of communicative interaction and the level of communication the therapist expects from the client.

In substance, then, the ground rules define the basic or core relationship and mode of interaction between patient and therapist. They may be explicitly stated or implicit in the therapist's behavior and the physical setting, but in either case, they are fundamental to the curative process that will unfold in the treatment experience.

THE SPECIFIC GROUND RULES

The ground rules of psychotherapy presented here are confined to those tenets *that have obtained consistent derivative validation from psychotherapy and psychoanalytic patients.* Whenever a ground rule is invoked or modified, the therapist should examine the patient's subsequent material for both validation and derivative perceptions. The deep unconscious system expresses an extremely consistent and evidently universal need for an ideal set of ground rules. When these rules are invoked, the patient validates them in derivative fashion, whereas all modifications of these ground rules lead to nonvalidating images and highly destructive derivative perceptions of the therapist.

Thus, the patient's encoded or derivative communications have served as a guide for defining the ideal conditions of treatment and, accordingly, the specific nature of *secure-frame psychotherapy.* As noted earlier, any treatment situation that is constituted in terms of the specific modification of one or more of these ideal ground rules is to be considered a form of *deviant-frame psychotherapy.* Secure-and deviant-frame psychotherapy constitute the two basic forms of treatment experience.

There are two basic types of ground rules for psychotherapy, and both have obtained consistent derivative validation from patients. *The fixed frame* is constituted by a set of ground rules that can be maintained with great consistency and specificity. These include a single setting in which the therapist sees the patient, preferably an entirely private office suite in a professional building; a single and fixed fee; and a specified time and duration for each session.

In addition, there are other relatively stable, though more fluid, ground rules. These include advising the patient to use the couch in all but the initial hour; the adoption of the fundamental rule of free association by which the patient is advised to say whatever comes to mind; the evenly hovering attention of the therapist sitting out of sight behind the patient; the use of neutral interventions constituted by appropriate silences, interactional interpretations, and managements of the ground rules carried out at the behest of the patient's derivative communications; the relative anonymity of the therapist (i.e., no deliberate self-revelations, no offer of personal opinions and information); total privacy with a one-to-one relationship; and total confidentiality.

These ground rules alone have obtained consistent derivative validation from patients all over the world. This finding indicates that there is only one ideal framework for psychotherapy. A patient and therapist are not free to choose any frame that feels comfortable or to proceed on the basis of no ground rules at all. Every departure from the ideal ground rules is experienced unconsciously by the patient as aberrant and deviant, and all such departures, however unconsciously, provide both patient and therapist with a variety of pathological satisfactions and defenses. Furthermore, all modifications in the ground rules appear to preclude a significant measure of meaningful communication and accessible interpretive work, especially in so far as the patient's core madness is concerned. Thus, even though considerable insight may be developed in deviant-frame therapy, the limitations must be taken into account.

SECURE-FRAME PSYCHOTHERAPY

The communicative approach has shown that there are two meaningful classifications of psychotherapeutic and psychoanalytic experiences. The first involves listening, formulating, and intervening. The therapist is either attending to and interpreting interactional derivatives or is not. Of course, some therapists do shift about, one moment interpreting interactionally, then shifting to manifest content and evident implications. In these situations, however, the patient unconsciously perceives the therapist as split, and in most cases, the predominant mode is noninteractional.

The second classification involves the ground rules of treatment. Psychotherapy functions either as *secure-frame therapy* or as *deviant-frame therapy*. Each modality offers something to both patient and therapist, and each creates a specific set of danger situations and anxieties. For each type, the satisfactions and factors in symptom resolution are different; and each, in particular, is distinctive in the driving force that leads to meaningful communication and cure.

Secure-frame psychotherapy encompasses all those therapeutic situations in which the ideal ground rules of psychotherapy have been established. The therapist must be capable of offering and defining this particular set of ground rules, and the patient must be consciously willing to accept these tenets as his or her conditions to treatment—though protest may occur. It is not uncommon in this type of psychotherapy for patients to request the alteration of one or another ground rule. The patient should be willing, however, to explore the implications of that request, rather than insisting on immediate enactment.

Of course, the situation is different when the patient unilaterally alters the frame without the therapist's participation—*e.g.*, refuse to lie on the couch, misses or is late for a session, or completes an insurance form without a contribution from the therapist. In these instances, the patient has created a deviant-frame situation, while the therapist maintains a secure-frame attitude. Such deviations are indicators of patient-madness and can be interactionally analyzed in light of prevailing adaptive contexts. The therapist's nonparticipation places him or her in a position to analyze such material meaningfully. Were the therapist to take part in or accede to the deviation, this capacity would be greatly impaired.

The ideal frame, *i.e.*, the therapist's establishment of these validated ground rules and their proper management, is powerfully ego-enhancing for all patients—and, secondarily, for the therapist as well. In the deep unconscious system, however, the patient recognizes that the therapist's capacity to secure the frame must complement an ability to properly interpret. The absence of sound interpretations from a secure-frame therapist will lead to an unconscious split image of the therapist within the patient, and will often prompt the patient to create ground-rule issues that might not otherwise arise.

The therapist's capacity to secure the frame offers the patient:

(1) *A sense of basic trust.* This arises mainly because the therapist is fulfilling the patient's unconscious role expectations for him or her. In substance, the therapist has promised to be a therapist, and by securing the frame, has done exactly that. Trust also stems from other positive attributes of the secure frame.

(2) *Clear interpersonal boundaries* between patient and therapist, creating both appropriate distance and intimacy and thus making the relationship safe and secure.

(3) Unconscious *support for the patient's contact with reality* and his or her capacity to test reality.

(4) The foundation for a relationship that entails *a healthy therapeutic symbiosis*—the ideal treatment relationship (see Chapter 7).

(5) The basis for a mode of cure that will take place through *genuine insight,* and not entail relief through action-discharge.

(6) *A situation in which the unfolding dynamics and genetics will center on the patient's madness* rather than the madness of the therapist.

(7) *An unconscious image and introject of the therapist as having a sound identity and* an inner state of *healthy narcissistic balances.*

(8) *An image of the therapist as sane.*

(9) *A powerful sense of being held well and of appropriate containment.*

(10) A situation of *appropriate frustration* and *healthy satisfactions.*

The secure frame affords both patient and therapist a powerful sense of security, holding, and containment. The resulting sense of safety and inherent building up of ego strength helps the patient to reveal the interactional derivatives on which his or her madness is based. Similarly, the implicit support available for the therapist through his or her own capacity to secure the frame—an ability that the patient tends to respect on the unconscious level—secures his or her position, with energy available for sound listening and intervening.

At the same time, it can be shown that everything a therapist does is in some way a danger situation for the patient and a source of anxiety. A valid interpretation is dangerous because it creates an image of a therapist who is more powerful than the patient, highly attractive, and ready to take on a deeper level of meaning than is already available—one that is usually extremely anxiety-provoking for the patient. In the same way, the secure frame, despite its powerful positive attributes, creates significant anxieties for both participants to treatment. The nature of these anxieties may be summarized as follows:

(1) *Claustrophobic anxieties.* The secure frame is entrapping. It involves responsibility for all sessions, placement on the couch, (which is usually situated in a corner of the consultation room) and a sense of relative immobilization. Expression is restricted to words and feelings without active flight. In particular, the ground rules that require full responsibility for sessions and regularity of hours creates a claustrum effect.

This sense of entrapment is intimately connected with issues of death anxiety. We are all in some sense born into a claustrum from which the only exit is death. The mobilization of death anxiety is frightening for the patient—and for the therapist as well.

Paradoxically, then, the strongest hold a therapist can offer simultaneously arouses a deep sense of anxiety in both patient and therapist. Nonetheless, as these anxieties are mobilized along with the patient's adaptive and derivative responses, the related issues find expression in the patient's associations and behaviors. In this way, the underlying nature of the patient's core madness is revealed, and the unconscious factors in the patient's expressed madness become available for therapeutic insight. Indeed, it appears that the mobilization of secure-frame death anxieties is essential to sound insightful cure; such anxieties are a critical factor in all forms of core and expressed madness.

(2) The development of significant *persecutory or paranoid anxieties.* The capability of the psychotherapist to secure the frame and the more vulnerable position of the patient mobilizes the patient's unconscious persecutory perceptions and anxieties. These, too, then become available for effective therapeutic work.

(3) The mobilization of *separation anxieties.* These are aroused not only because the patient lies on the couch with the therapist out of sight, but also because the therapist does not respond directly to the patient's communications. When the therapist is attacked or challenged, asked a question, or enticed—to cite a few examples—he or she maintains a therapeutic attitude, does not respond directly, and awaits further material that will lend itself to interpretation.

(4) Paradoxically, patients experience as dangerous *the absence of pathological satisfactions and modes of relatedness, and a lack of madness in the psychotherapist.* Unconsciously, patients appear to believe that survival depends on pathological modes of interaction. These needs appear to be located in the unconscious part of the conscious system, as is a preference for mad rather than sane psychotherapy. This preference exists largely because the patient's madness tends to recede in the active presence of the therapist's madness, though if the latter is extreme (e.g., if there is physical contact or intense assault), both patient and therapist will show active expressions of madness.

With lesser forms of therapist-madness, however, the patient's expressed madness diminishes significantly. Under these conditions, the influence of the patient's madness is almost entirely *selective*—the patient's madness becomes a crucial determinant of the meanings of the therapist's mad interventions, which the patient represents and responds to. A defensive measure of relief accrues to the patient in the presence of a mad therapist, and conversely, the patient sometimes feels anxious in the presence of a sane therapist.

The meanings of transactions and inner experience tend to be more terrifying in the secure frame than they are in the deviant frame (see Chapter 8). In essence, secure-frame meaning touches on the basic human vulnerabilities of the patient and on the death-anxiety issues that are central to the traumas that have contributed to his or her core madness. Secure-frame meanings are experienced *without attendant pathological defenses*, whereas the latter defenses are operative in the experience of deviant-frame meanings, so that the patient tends to be less terrified.

In all, then, the best possible frame for both patient and therapist mobilizes in the patient the most fundamental human anxieties and issues. There is a strong resemblance between secure-frame anxieties and the basic positions defined by Melanie Klein—the paranoid-(phobic)-schizoid position and the depressive position. The secure frame sets up conditions under which the basic issues of life, death, and madness can find optimal communicative expression and analytic resolution.

The anxieties generated by the secure frame are very powerful. These anxieties exist in all patients and therapists, hence the strong pressures toward deviant-frame therapy that exist in the conscious system. In contrast, in the unconscious system, where anxiety is not a powerful determinant (the secrets of this system are inaccessible except through transformed images), the overriding need and wish for a secure frame persists. In some instances, however, the defensive needs of the conscious system prevail, and the pressures toward deviant-frame therapy are overwhelming. As a rule, such situations involve secure-frame sensitive individuals who are unconsciously convinced that they will not survive a secure-frame experience.

Secure-frame sensitive patients can often be identified in the first hour. Some show claustrophobic anxieties; others show intense and repetitive needs to move toware action-discharge and acting out (see chapter 7). Many have a history of psychotic-like moments or psychosis, or reveal the existence of psychosis in one or both parents. Others show extraordinary levels of death anxiety, and suffer from the syndrome of *overintense or premature exposure to death anxiety*. These patients have suffered a loss, major illness, or major injury in early childhood—sometimes at birth. There may be a history of abortions in the mother or in the patient, or a recent experience with death that has been highly traumatic—for example, a suicide or a fatal accident that somehow involved the patient.

These patients show an unconscious dread of the secure frame and of the derivatives that will emerge under such conditions. They reveal as well severe anxieties related to the sense of entrapment itself. In the unconscious part of the conscious system, there appears to be a significant ego defect through which such individuals are delusionally convinced that they will be destroyed under secure-frame conditions. In that regard, the secure-frame dangers are experienced as quite real, creating an extremely difficult therapeutic situation. Unilateral efforts to effect deviant-frame conditions are quite common and fiercely pursued.

The handling of patients of this kind is fraught with difficulty. Such patients often produce abundant derivatives related to their secure-frame anxieties and associated genetics and dynamics. However, the correct interactional interpretation of these derivatives in light of the secure-frame trigger that prompts them will, at times, serve only to increase secure-frame anxieties. Therapeutic efforts must be concentrated not only on these interactional derivative interpretations, but also on the patient's mistaken sense of the *reality* of the dangers he or she is experiencing (see chapter 9).

As noted the pressure to deviate is quite strong with these patients. The therapist begins to anticipate premature termination, and in some instances this concern is justified. The patient continually presses for one or more modifications in the ideal ground rules, and this may escalate to the point of an ultimatum, where the therapist is faced with the loss of the patient unless he or she accepts the deviant frame. The situation is most malignant when a secure-frame sensitive patient delivers this type of ultimatum without communicating derivative material.

In principle, under such circumstances, the therapist's basic position should remain secure-frame and interpretive. By stressing the mistaken reality of the derivative fears that emerge interactionally in the patient's material, the therapist can often help him or her to remain in secure-frame therapy. When all else fails and the patient appears certain to leave treatment, the communicative therapist may decide to deviate in the hope that subsequent therapeutic work will illuminate the patient's need for alterations in the ground rules and, in time, enable the secure frame to be restored. However, as pointed out, once a deviation has been established, meaningful therapeutic work is significantly compromised. In addition, the patient develops an unconscious image of the therapist as mad and deviant, and as inclined toward pathological satisfactions and an action-discharge mode of cure. In consequence, the deviation may have pronounced negative effects both on the patient's symptoms and on his or her attitude toward the therapist.

Typically, once a patient has obtained one deviation and has established alterations in the ground rules as a mode of symptom relief, the demand for other deviations will follow. Such therapeutic situations tend to be beyond the control and management of the therapist, especially if he or she has joined in with patient in effecting alterations in the ground rules. Therapy can become quite chaotic. None of this is surprising, because the nature of the madness of these patients is precisely that they feel a false sense of security through pathological deviation, and yet remain terrified and convinced that insight and understanding will only destroy them. These patients suffer greatly and pose a great challenge to the communicative therapist, whose skills at managing the framework and interpreting will be sorely challenged.

DEVIANT-FRAME THERAPY

Deviant-frame therapy has its own satisfactions and mode of relief, however pathological, and it, too, generates its particular measure of anxiety in both patient and therapist. In general, the relief obtained through an alteration in a ground rule always has a pathological or inappropriate component. And although relief may indeed occur, there is always the risk that a deviation will lead to a fresh symptom or to the exacerbation of an old symptom. In addition, when framework alterations become the mode of cure, one that entails action-discharge, this type of relief from expressed madness will virtually always carry over into the patient's everyday life.

Still, patients tend to rationalize this type of relief and to deny or ignore its detrimental consequences. Because of the powerful investment in the conscious system for defensive operations, no matter how pathological, there is a strong pull toward deviant-frame therapy in almost all patients and therapists. The exceptions are those patients who have been severely traumatized by prior deviant-frame therapists and those therapists who have come to understand the nature and function of the ground rules and who wish to offer the patient the best possible therapeutic experience.

There are, of course, some patients for whom deviant-frame therapy is the only form of treatment available. Patients who require hospitalization or who must be seen at a low-fee clinic are in this position. For this reason, it is imperative to understand the nature of deviant-frame therapy. The patient's unconscious and derivative responses to the alterations in ground rules will be central to illuminating the unconscious basis of the patient's expressed and core madness. In addition, most instances of deviant-frame therapy do offer the opportunity for *secure-frame moments* (see below), interludes during which the patient's secure-frame anxieties can be experienced and the relevant derivatives expressed and analyzed. In this way, whatever the limitations, deviant-frame therapy can be utilized as a fairly effective treatment modality in its own right. However, this tends to be possible only in situations where the therapist has no choice but to deviate. In those private practice situations where the therapist knowingly chooses to alter a ground rule, the effects tend to be much more detrimental than in those situations where a deviant frame is inescapable.

Let us look first at the powerful pathological defenses and satisfactions offered by any alteration in the basic ground rules. The following are most notable:

(1) *Counterphobic defenses.* Virtually all deviations entail an escape from the claustrum-like dangers of the secure frame. A deviation is an enactment of a pathological mode of adaptation. As an actuality, it has influence on the patient, his or her communications in the session and experience of the therapy and therapist, and many other qualities of the therapeutic interaction. The deviation is an action-discharge form of adaptation— a substitute for adaptation through the acceptance of the secure frame and interpretive insights.

Patients typically communicate derivatives with respect to the unconscious meanings of proposed (anticipated) or actual alterations in the ground rules. As noted earlier, these derivatives will consistently direct the therapist to maintain the frame. In situations where the frame is already broken, the derivatives also embody the implications of the alteration in the ground rules. Ideally, the therapist should respond with interactional interpretations and ground-rule securing efforts.

If the therapist merely interprets (*i.e.*, explains the meanings of the patient's material), but fails to secure the frame (*i.e.*, fails to respond to the encoded directives with respect to the ground-rule management sphere), there is an inherent split and contradiction in his or her efforts. The result is not only a split or mad image of the therapist within the patient, but also a situation in which the therapist's *denial* of the meanings of the patient's framework-management directives contradicts his or her interpretive work. The therapist's position is undermined, and often the interpretive work obtains little or no derivative validation and has a minimal positive effect on the patient.

The secure frame mobilizes major phobic anxieties, especially those related to immobilization and entrapment. An alteration in the ground rules modifies or removes these pressures so that they are no longer an issue for the patient. Often, there is an initial sense of relief, but regression may follow.

(2) *The offer of manic defenses, especially forms of blind action, denial, and fusion.* Although the counterphobic defenses offered by framework deviations tend to diminish the patient's separation and death anxieties, the patient's basic pathological defense against these issues is provided by the manic qualities of most deviations. On some level, virtually every deviation permits a pathological form of merger between patient and therapist. In addition, the deviation offers a variety of denial defenses, fundamentally the *implied delusion* that if a patient is an exception to the ground rules of therapy, he or she is also an exception to the ground rules of life—in particular, to the rule that life is followed by death.

As noted, deviations also permit the patient to pathologically set aside separation anxieties—that is, anxieties related to issues of separateness, autonomy, and independent functioning.

(3) *Pathological defenses and modes of relatedness.* All deviations involve highly satisfying, but pathological modes of relatedness. At times, a deviation may even exploit the patient, who remarkably enough, accepts the alteration in the ground rule anyhow. An increase in fee is one such deviation, though a more extreme example would be the therapist's requesting that a patient give up his or her session to another patient and wait to have his or her own hour.

Deviations also offer the patient pathological forms of defense, pathological superego sanctions, and support for his or her own tendency to use action-discharge as a mode of cure. In addition, they defensively seal off critical derivatives related to the patient's core and expressed madness. As noted earlier, deviations also generate mad images of the therapist, which the patient unconsciously exploits to curtail expressions of his or her own madness. Furthermore, all deviations actively express the psychopathology or madness of the therapist, which then becomes the central issue in the therapeutic interaction—albeit unconsciously (in most instances).

In substance, alterations in the ground rules offer pathological and ultimately maladaptive defenses against each of the basic anxieties and danger situations created by the secure frame. They relieve the patient of symptoms and pathological indicators (expressed madness) in a variety of uninsightful ways. And even though, on occasion, such relief may be lasting, clinical evidence indicates that the patient pays a price for it. Basically, such symptom alleviation requires an extension of the deviant therapeutic relationship to relationships in the patient's daily life. Ultimately, the patient insists on being the exception to the ground rules of life and society as a way of maintaining his or her fragile equilibrium.

Despite these negative aspects, deviant-frame therapy is readily sought after, accepted, and offered. Because the guiding principle for the conscious system is defensive and immediately self-protective, the conscious demand for this type of therapy is extensive. Patients have no way of knowing that their own deep unconscious system, and their own derivative communications, speak against their accession to such conscious needs and demands.

There are a number of specific negative consequences when an alteration is invoked in a ground rule. These consequences accrue to both patient and therapist, although they are stated here mainly in terms of consequences for the patient. In general, they entail the absence of the positive features of the secure frame. These consequences may be stated as follows:

(1) *The existence of a basic sense of mistrust.* The therapist who alters one ground rule is likely to alter another. It is impossible to tell where he or she will draw the line. As a result, a strong sense of persecution is generated unconsciously by every deviation.

(2) *The persecutory aspects* of the deviant frame are different from those of the secure frame, in that a deviation does in fact harm the patient and his or her therapeutic opportunity, whereas the fears raised by a secure frame—entrapment, losing autonomy, etc.—are fantasies that must be worked through. The secure frame is persecutory much in the way that being alive is persecutory simply because death is a condition of life.

There exist, then, both *secure-frame paranoia* and *deviant-frame paranoia.* Each is based on different triggers, and each is structured differently in terms of derivative perceptions and reactions to these perceptions. It should be apparent, then, that the meanings of a symptomatic response—a measure of expressed madness—will differ, depending on the conditions of the ground rules and frame. Indeed, each symptom must be analyzed for its specific unconscious structure in light of the nataure of the ongoing therapeutic interaction.

(3) *Unclear interpersonal boundaries.*

(4) *Impairments in reality testing.*

(5) *Encouragement for the use of pathological, action-discharge modes of cure.*

(6) The establishment of *pathological modes of relatedness..*

(7) The development of *pathological defenses and pathological superego sanctions.* More broadly, deviations are *pathological modes of adaptation.*

(8) An unconscious image and introject of the therapist as someone who is suffering from *identity confusion* (who promises to function as a therapist, but fails to do so) and *narcissistic disturbances.*

(9) *An image of the therapist as mad.*

(10) And finally, a specific image of the therapist as some-one who is obtaining *perverse gratification.* In this respect, it has been shown clinically that all deviations are unconsciously perceived by patients as providing the therapist with perverse forms of satisfaction.

The patient realizes most of the detrimental consequences of ground-rule deviations only in the deep unconscious system. The perceptions involved are therefore communicated almost entirely through transformed images. The patient has virtually no conscious insight into these perceptions, and he or she ex-periences little conscious need to return to a secure-frame par-adigm. Those detrimental aspects which are manifest and evi-dent are often simply denied.

It follows from this discussion that the therapist's goal should be directed toward maintaining as much of an ideal secure frame as possible. The therapist should also endeavor to interpret the patient's responses to deviant adaptive contexts, and to move to-ward securing the frame at the behest of the patient's deriva-tives. In the presence of an alteration of a ground rule, the pa-tient's derivative material will virtually always center around the issues involved in that deviation. The therapist must respond ac-cordingly.

SECURE-FRAME MOMENTS

A critical clinical finding reveals that patients in basically deviant-frame psychotherapies are capable of experiencing secure-frame interludes if the opportunity is offered by the ther-apist. Given the fact that deviant-frame patients tend to ask for additional alterations in the ground rules, the therapist's management of such requests becomes crucial to the course of the psychotherapy. At such moments, the patient's encoded derivatives will invariably direct the therapist to maintain the ground rules. Should the therapist, instead, accede to the pa-tient's conscious request and further modify the frame, the pa-tient is deprived of a *special therapeutic opportunity*—and, in addition, is faced with a therapist who has ignored the patient's derivative directives.

The deviant therapist who maintains the ground rules at such moments as directed by the patient's encoded material affords the patient a secure-frame experience. Patients are highly sensitive to such interludes, and they will find it necessary to adapt to and cope with the secure-frame anxieties that are generated in this way. As a result, the secure-frame issues that pertain to the patient's core and expressed madness will be revealed in the patient's material. The therapist typically has ample opportunity to interpret the meanings and ramifications involved. It seems likely that a truly effective therapeutic experience under deviant-frame conditions must entail secure-frame moments of this kind—and their management and interpretation.

As stated, psychotherapy is in substance a ground-rule issue experience. The therapist's development and management of the frame is therefore among his or her most crucial interventions. The therapist is well advised to keep in mind that interventions in this sphere constitute the most crucial adaptive contexts to which patients respond. They do so in ways that influence the actual vicissitudes of their expressed madness and the communication of the unconscious meanings of this madness. Whatever the compromise entails in deviant-frame therapy, consistent attention to the patient's unconscious responses to the prevailing alterations in the ground rules provides the patient with the best opportunity for insightful cure.

We may think of several types of first-hour frames, depending on the nature of the referral and the immediate conditions of treatment. With some patients, the referral is professional and the therapist offers basically secure-frame conditions. Such patients begin to experience the secure frame's claustrum effects and related anxieties early in the hour, and their derivative perceptions unfold accordingly. Prior to formally structuring the treatment, the therapist is often in a position to interpret these secure-frame anxieties—usually at a point where the patient offers a secure-frame representation, perhaps in an allusion to the quietness of the office or a passing mention of the couch. In intervening, the therapist should stress the intensity of the underlying anxieties, and the sense of conviction within the patient that the danger of entrapment and annihilation are real.

In other instances, there is a deviant aspect to the referral, but the therapist is in a position to secure the frame as the first session unfolds. This is seen, for example, when the patient has obtained some personal information about the therapist, or when the patient requires a low fee. Unconsciously, the patient will expect additional deviations from the therapist; when these are not forthcoming, secure-frame anxieties will emerge and the related material will be available for interpretation.

In still other instances, the session will begin with an understanding that deviant-frame therapy will be the basic mode of treatment. This occurs in any situation in which a deviation from the use of ideal ground rules characterizes the therapeutic relationship from the outset—for example, when the use of insurance has been agreed on in advance, or when the therapy takes place in a clinic setting, or when there has been a patient-referral.

In such instances, the patient is likely to represent the deviation in the first hour and to include selected encoded perceptions of the therapist in light of the deviant trigger. Here, too, the therapist is likely to offer interpretations before structuring the ground rules of therapy. In addition, the therapist should, to the greatest extent possible, move toward securing the altered ground rules at the behest of the patient's encoded directives. With patients in a basically deviant-frame therapy, the therapist waits for further requests for deviation, responds by maintaining the frame as guided by the patient's encoded communications, and thereby creates analyzable secure-frame moments.

The following case demonstrates a secure-frame moment in the first hour of a basically deviant-frame therapy. The material also offers us a further opportunity to study cognitive derivative validation (see chapter 4) and to see again the typical split between a patient's conscious wishes (expressions of the conscious system) and those that are derivative or unconscious (expressions of the deep unconscious system).

The patient is a young man who was referred to a female therapist by a crisis center where he had been seen briefly for mounting anxieties concerning his homosexual feelings. In accepting the referral, the therapist agreed in advance to a reduced fee. Then, in the course of the first phone call, the patient asked the therapist to confirm that she would indeed charge a reduced fee. The therapist responded that they could discuss the matter during the first session.

The patient began the hour by describing his conflicts with the staff at the crisis center. He said that he had come to the present therapist because he needed some kind of long-term treatment and his therapist at the crisis center had referred him to her. His greatest concern for the moment was the fee—a point on which he then elaborated.

The therapist indicated that the fee would be twenty-five dollars a session, as she had agreed. She pointed out that the patient had also mentioned his referring therapist. She told the patient she wanted him to know that his therapy here would be entirely private and that she would not be sending any reports back to the clinic where he had been seen.

The patient stated that that was fine with him. He then said that his throat was dry and asked the therapist if she had any water—was there any in the bathroom? The therapist said yes, there were cups for water in the bathroom.

The patient left the consultation room to get a drink of water. When he returned, he said that there were times when he had a hard time talking. In between short periods of silence, he told her that he was not very social; he tended to feel uncomfortable. He wanted people to bring him into their conversation.

When the patient fell into an extended silence, the therapist pointed out that after she had told the patient that therapy would be private and confidential, he had indicated that his throat was dry and had walked out of the office to get a drink of water. It seemed, then, that he was unable to stay because he was feeling uncomfortable and felt the need to leave. Now his discomfort seemed to be reflected in his wanting the therapist to talk and to draw him out.

The patient responded that somehow he was now thinking of something strange that had happened the previous week. He was in this bakery and had bought some delicious pastries. This woman gave him the pastries and his change. Oddly enough, the patient didn't move; he was in a trance. His mind seemed to be wandering. Suddenly an older woman came out from the back of the store and stood behind the counter. She asked him a question and he realized he was standing there transfixed, so he finally left.

The therapist's first intervention is mixed: It establishes a deviant-frame therapy, but then proposes specific aspects of the secure frame. The patient responds by leaving. This is a mini-psychotic act (see Chapter 8), which was undoubtedly stimulated by the psychotic aspects of the therapist's intervention—its inherent self-contradiction, in that it is both deviant and secure-frame in meaning.

There then follows evidence of gross behavioral resistance, and the therapist attempts to interpret the secure-frame anxieties that she believes would account for the unconscious aspects of this important indicator. The patient responds with derivative validation, revealing that he had experienced the interpretation selectively as a delicious pastry. At the same time, the gratification creates a trance-like state, and this appears to be a reflection of the patient's secure-frame anxieties and of his perception of the low fee deviation which is unconsciously perceived as a gratification that is to be forsaken by the patient lest it overwhelm him. As we have seen, it is typical for a patient to derivatively validate a secure-frame intervention and then to reveal the nature of his or her secure-frame anxieties.

Further material unfolded that is not pertinent to the present discussion. About thirty minutes into the hour, the therapist structured the balance of the therapy in secure-frame fashion. When told that he was responsible for the time, the patient asked if that meant he would have to pay when he was on vacation. The therapist indicated that this was indeed the nature of the situation.

The patient then said that something great had happened to him recently. He had a lover—a man. He was terrific and they cared about each other. They were thinking of moving in together, but the patient was uncertain. He hadn't had such a good relationship in a long time.

The added material illustrates again a measure of derivative validation of a secure-frame intervention and a continued response to the deviant conditions which continue to exist. In substance, the patient responds to the therapist's outline of the secure-frame aspects of his therapy by alluding to an extremely gratifying love relationship. The homosexual element probably touches on the perverse aspects of the single deviation—the low fee. It is a condition to treatment that is both gratifying and sexually perverse, as perceived by the deep unconscious system.

The patient's response to the overall ground rules, then, is to validate the secure-frame aspects, to suggest the perverse quality of the deviation, and to offer both cognitive and interpersonal derivative support for the therapist's efforts. In principle, even though an intervention has simply established the conditions to treatment, the therapist must attend to the patient's subsequent material for validation or its absence, and for unconscious perceptions and commentary.

To illustrate some additional secure-frame reactions, we may consider the twice-weekly psychotherapy of a woman who sought treatment because of a depressive reaction that followed the sudden death of her mother. The patient also suffered from chronic feelings of hopelessness and took little pleasure in her life. She had been in treatment on two prior occasions, including an extended period of psychoanalysis

The patient was referred to the present therapist by her physician. She was paying for treatment on her own and had been offered an ideal frame. She had, however, refused to lie on the couch. Following some interactional interpretive work related to this resistance-indicator, the patient decided toward the end of a session approximately four months into therapy that she would get on the couch in the following hour. These are some of the highlights of that following session:

The patient entered the consultation room and asked if she should simply get on the couch, but then did so without comment from the therapist. She spoke of getting a birthday card for her brother, and of wanting to be close to her sister after having felt especially distant because of the way they had fought when they were younger. The patient's thoughts then turned to her mother's funeral and to the way her sister had dominated the scene. The sister had "dropped manure" on the patient for years.

The patient had had dinner with her daughter and her daughter's husband, who was an intern and rather nice. They were able to talk openly about a lot of things, but eventually got around to the topic of suicide. A few years back the patient had fainted at a dinner and her son-in-law was concerned about her health. The patient then thought of a man whom she had once seen in a restaurant choking on food. He was saved by the waitress who picked him up and squeezed his ribs until he vomited. She had really saved his life.

The patient then recalled a dream: Her daughter is working on a project on a table. The patient messes up the project and the daughter is mortified, but the patient is able to restore order rather quickly. There is no permanent damage. The patient then goes into the next room to check on her mother, who is lying in bed, quite ill.

The patient next recalled a story about a horse who used to run about in a relatively small space surrounded by barbed wire. It seems the horse had committed suicide by cutting himself on the barbed wire and contracting tetanus. There was an odd situation going on in the patient's neighborhood, where there were many affairs and divorces. The son of one woman had gone berserk and thrown parts of her car into a ravine.

In this instance, the patient validates the positive attributes of the secure frame in her allusion to establishing a new sense of closeness with her sister. Quite soon, however, the theme of death emerges—here in the form of a reference to the mother's funeral. The images of being manipulated and having manure dumped on her may well allude to some of the inappropriate pressures the therapist had placed on the patient to accept the couch and the secure frame. They may also involve encoded expectations of how the therapist would intervene under these conditions—in part because of the abuse the patient had experienced with her previous analyst.

The patient's material continues to convey a mixture of positive and yet terrifying death-related images. There is a reference to the nice and helpful son-in-law, but the topic they discuss is suicide and an incident in which the patient fainted—a common claustrophobic symbol. There is the image of the man choking on food, another claustrum-related image, though the food provider (waitress) then saves the man's life. Clearly, there is a strong sense of danger and annihilation accompanied by a sense of salvation. Indeed, this theme is repeated once again in the dream where the patient messes up her daughter's project only to set the situation straight again. Here, too, there is an allusion to the death of the patient's mother.

When the therapist remained silent and failed to interpret the patient's secure-frame anxieties and yet hopeful expectations, more destructive secure-frame allusions emerged—the penned horse who committed suicide and the parts of the car being dropped into a ravine. Indeed, the patient later spoke in this hour of mistakes she had been making, of abandonment, and of her mother's suffering from brain damage. As noted in Chapter 3, images of this kind reflect the patient's deep unconscious awareness that the therapist has failed to respond interpretively to material that fulfills the recipe for intervening (she had begun the session with an allusion to the couch and had produced many derivative perceptions and expectations related to that particular secure-frame intervention or condition). Nonetheless, the patient's material is typical in its reflection of death anxieties mobilized after secure-frame moments and appearing alongside of positive and validating interpersonal images, which show an appreciation of the therapist's capacity to establish a secure framework for the patient's treatment.

There is always a measure of anxiety during secure-frame moments, but the ever-present positive component will also be experienced. Derivative validation of secure-frame interventions is the rule. The overall conscious and behavioral response of the patient depends greatly on the degree of his or her secure-frame sensitivities and anxieties, which are then pitted against the positive component of all secure-frame interventions. Such is the mix of valid psychotherapy—a significant measure of insight and relief, accompanied always by a greater or lesser degree of anxiety.

RECOMMENDED READINGS

Blager, J. (1967): Psycho-analysis of the psychoanalytic frame. *International Journal of Psycho-Analysis* 48:511–519.

Freud, S. (1912): Recommendations to physicians practicing psychoanalysis. *SE* 12:109–120.

Freud, S. (1913): On beginning the treatment (Further recommendations on the technique of psycho-analysis, I). *SE* 12:121–144.

Freud, S. (1914): Remembering, repeating, and working through (Further recommendations on the technique of psycho-analysis, II). *SE* 12:145–156.

Freud, S. (1914): Observations on transference-love (Further recommendations on the technique of psycho-analysis III). *SE* 12:157–171.

Greenacre, P. (1959): Certain technical problems in the transference relationship. *Journal of the American Psychoanalytic Association* 7:484–502.

Langs, R. (1982): *Psychotherapy: A Basic Text.* New York: Aronson.

Langs, R. (1984–85): Making interpretations and securing the frame: Sources of danger for psychotherapists. *International Journal of Psychoanalytic Psychotherapy* 10:3–24.

Lewin, B. (1935): Claustrophobia. *Psychoanalytic Quarterly* 4:227–233.

Strachey, J. (1934): The nature of the therapeutic action of psycho-analysis. *International Journal of Psycho-Analysis* 15:127–159.

Winnicott (1965): *The Maturational Processes and the Facilitating Environment.* New York: International Universities Press.

CHAPTER 7

Seven Dimensions of the Therapeutic Interaction

To date, the communicative approach has identified seven distinctive yet interrelated dimensions to the therapeutic experience and interaction. In theory, the therapist need not be concerned as to whether he or she will recognize the specific dimensions reflected in the patient's communications. A sound intervention—one that is built around an expressed trigger and a set of encoded derivatives—will automatically touch on those dimensions dealt with in the patient's material. Still, it is extremely useful for the therapist to trace out the vicissitudes of one or another dimension of the therapeutic interaction for a given patient. In particular, the patient's material should deal with at least two or more of the dimensions of the therapeutic interaction in order to constitute a meaningful, coalescing derivative complex. Further, there are certain dimensions that are especially related to core and expressed madness, and these ideally should appear in the patient's material before the therapist intervenes. Most important among these are the areas of ground rules and frame, communication, dynamics and genetics, and the madness or sanity of others. (Other dimensions involve modes of relatedness and cure, and issues of identity and narcissism.)

COMMUNICATION AND FRAME

These two dimensions have been discussed at length earlier in the book. Together they constitute the most critical dimensions of the therapeutic interaction.

As already stated, the therapist's management of the ground rules of psychotherapy constitute his or her most fundamental arena of intervention, and the therapist's efforts in this regard will greatly influence all of the other dimensions of the therapeutic interaction and experience. The nature of this influence has been discussed in Chapter 6 and is considered again toward the end of the present chapter.

With respect to communication, the patient's material will contain allusions to the openness of communication under secure-frame conditions and to impairments when deviations are present. Patients are exquisitely sensitive to whether or not a therapist is prepared to deal with derivative expressions, and they are very clever, albeit unconsciously, in their ways of characterizing a therapist's pressures toward nonderivative expressions. The deep unconscious system clearly recognizes those therapists who wish to gain access to its processes and contents—and those who do not.

To illustrate: A patient in psychotherapy had offered extensive derivative material in response to a therapist's acceptance of a basically deviant frame in which the patient would be seen on a different day each week. The arrangement was rationalized as necessary because the patient traveled in connection with his job. Despite this reality, the arrangement was unconsciously perceived by the patient as quite destructive to the therapeutic process.

In a session where the patient had communicated powerful derivative perceptions in this regard, the therapist intervened flatly and manifestly—ignoring the derivative aspect of the patient's associations. The patient responded by talking about his son. He said that he was aware of his son's needs for an open relationship with him, and he knew that he himself was constricting the communication between them. The patient bemoaned the fact that although he could take care of his son's financial needs, he could not respond to the son's needs for closeness, sharing, and deep contact.

Through these displaced (and therefore encoded and symbolized) derivatives, this patient was, in part, conveying his unconscious perceptions of the therapist's need to respond only to the manifest meanings of the patient's material and to ignore the deeper, emotionally charged, derivative expressions—*the point of true contact and empathy between patient and therapist.*

When patients allude to problems in communication—to not being properly heard and understood or to other types of communicative difficulties—the therapist should examine his or her recent interventions for error. Most typical among the errors represented by such allusions is the failure to intervene in the presence of a well-represented trigger and a coalescing set of derivative perceptions. Another common error involves listening, formulating, and intervening in terms of manifest contents and evident implications, so failing to properly decode the patient's material in light of activated triggers. Ironically, only the therapist who is already capable of this type of communicative effort will be able to hear the patient's derivative complaints and properly understand their unconscious meanings.

MODE OF RELATEDNESS

In the course of free associating, the patient's material will typically contain allusions to various types of interpersonal relationships. In most cases, these images characterize the patient's unconscious perceptions of the actual attributes of the therapeutic relationship. On rare occasion, the material may reflect the patient's unconscious perception of a type of relationship that the therapist is attempting to create with the patient or a relationship for which the patient wishes. Until proven otherwise, however, all such allusions to relationships in the patient's personal life *should be seen as perceptive.* Allusions to modes of relatedness after a therapist has intervened will almost always characterize the relationship implications of the intervention—and these meanings often exist beyond the awareness of both the patient and therapist.

There appear to be five possible modes of relatedness between patients and therapists: healthy therapeutic symbiosis, pathological symbiosis, healthy autism, pathological autism, and parasitism. The *commensal mode* of relatedness is the ideal mode for daily interactions, because it entails virtually equal satisfactions for both members of a dyad. This mode is uncommon, however, in the therapeutic interaction, where the ideal mode is a *healthy therapeutic symbiosis*. In the latter mode of relatedness, the patient obtains a greater measure of satisfaction than does the therapist. In therapeutic situations where satisfactions are equal, the therapist is usually exploiting the patient and the mode of relatedness is actually *parasitic*.

The following briefly defines the basic modes of relatedness seen in psychotherapy:

Healthy therapeutic symbiosis.   This mode of relatedness is represented derivatively in patient associations that involve appropriately satisfying and constructive relationships or images of appropriate intimacy and caring. For example, following a cognitively validated intervention, a patient remarked that her mother took good care of her when the going got tough.

Technically, a healthy therapeutic symbiosis is possible only when the therapist secures the ideal conditions of treatment, makes use of appropriate silence, and offers interactional interpretations and secure-frame management responses when called for by the patient's behaviors and material. All departures from efforts that meet these standards express a wish for a pathological mode of relatedness, with pathological satisfactions and defenses a prominent feature.

For the patient, participation in a healthy therapeutic symbiosis implies acceptance of the secure frame and is often reflected in the validation of interactional interpretations. Pressures on the therapist to deviate, the invocation of unilateral alterations in the ground rules, and efforts to evoke noninterpretive interventions from the therapist entail shifts away from this mode of relatedness.

In the healthy therapeutic symbiosis, the greater measure of gratification accrues to the patient, who, among other secondary satisfactions, is afforded the position of being the central figure in the psychotherapy and is offered a therapeutic attitude and space in which his or her madness and its unconscious meanings can be safely communicated. Above all, the patient is given the ultimate satisfaction of adaptive symptom relief—the resolution of his or her expressed madness.

For the therapist, there are the gratifications of an appropriate fee, the knowledge of having carried out effective therapeutic work, and a small measure of personal gain derived from the decoding of the patient's encoded ministrations at times of momentary error. Other secondary satisfactions, such as the privilege to know the conscious and unconscious secrets of the patient, are also available.

Pathological symbiosis. In this mode of relatedness, the therapist obtains excessive gratification and the patient too little. In addition, the type of gratification involved shifts toward the pathological.

To cite an example, a woman patient pressed her clinical psychotherapist (female) to reassure her that she would adequately handle and survive a pending visit with her (the patient's) family. Toward the end of the hour the therapist did offer these reassurances clearly and directly.

In the hour that followed, the patient said that she wished the therapist had gone home with her and then spoke of having been overindulged by family members, who fed her liquor and desserts. As a younger woman, she said, she had been inappropriately given the responsibility of taking care of her parents.

These images refer to inappropriate and pathological caring relationships—pathological symbioses. Typical themes are those of *overindulgence*, pressing satisfactions on others, and other destructive forms of care.

Technically, the therapist who invokes a deviation that gratifies the patient has become involved in a pathological symbiosis. In addition, all noninterpretive interventions that provide the patient with manifest satisfactions (though latent harm) are experienced unconsciously by the patient as expressions of the pathological symbiotic mode. In essence, then, every departure from validated technique that provides the patient with surface satisfaction creates a pathologically symbiotic mode of relatedness between the two participants to treatment.

Healthy autism. This mode of relatedness generates images of withdrawal and isolation that are positively toned, appropriate, and the source of reasonable self-satisfaction. Such associations often allude to moments of rest, private but creative interludes, and constructive periods of lying fallow. The patient may speak of the peace and quiet of having been alone for a day or two, or of a creative effort carried out on his or her own.

Technically, healthy autism entails an absence of meaning in the patient's associations under conditions where there is no immediate need for a derivative response. In other words, this mode of relatedness implies the absence of a meaningful representation of a trigger and/or derivative perceptions in situations where there is no immediate ground-rule or other issue activated within the therapeutic interaction. For the therapist, the situation is characterized by appropriate silence—the absence of intervention when none is called for by the patient's material.

Pathological autism. In the presence of this mode of relatedness, the patient's images involve solitude as a form of defense, retreat, or inappropriate withdrawal. Such associations allude to inappropriate abandonment, to the absence of others at a time of need, and to people who impose their own needs and fantasies on others without regard to their feelings.

Technically, pathological autism is seen in therapy when a therapist fails to intervene in response to patient material that calls for active response—an interactional interpretation and/or a framework-management intervention. Another common form of pathological autism occurs when a therapist intervenes based on his or her own fantasies, memories, and other associations to the patient's material and fails to restrict the response to the associations of the hour at hand. In this way, all nonvalidated interventions should be regarded, in part, as the autistic creation of the therapist, because they have not been correctly fashioned out of the material from the patient.

Parasitism. This mode of relatedness is always pathological. It is characterized by images of exploitation, harm, abuse, and the like. Technically, parasitism is reflected in all of the therapist's nonvalidated interventions, because these consistently entail a measure of harm for the patient. Parasitic images are especially prominent, however, when the therapist's errors and frame deviations are self-serving and openly hurtful to the patient.

MODE OF CURE

"Cure" may stem from either of two sources: from true interactional insight into unconscious meaning and the securing of the frame (insight and holding), or via relief through action-discharge and merger.

Cure through insight and holding is represented in the patient's material by allusions to situations outside of therapy in which solutions are arrived at by constructive means and conflicts are resolved in reasonable fashion. The patient's images may also allude to being understood, to being held well, and to handling a variety of situations constructively. In contrast, the action-discharge mode of cure is represented in allusions to maladaptive and inappropriate forms of action, to addictive disturbances such as alcoholism, references to affairs, and allusions to actions that are in some way dishonest and destructive.

The action-discharge mode of cure may be acted out by the patient in the interaction with the therapist. It is expressed not only through actions, but through verbal-affective communications that involve projective identification and dumping without the possibility of meaningful insight. When the patient uses language and behavior in this fashion—e.g., by directly attacking a therapist without providing concomitant derivatives—the therapist should in all instances first formulate the basis of these pathological indicators in light of an activated adaptive context and the patient's encoded perceptions. In most instances, the patient's use of action-discharge involves an introjective identification with a therapist who has himself or herself intervened in action-discharge fashion. There is an element of action-discharge to all erroneous interventions, though this aspect intensifies when the therapist has made use of ground-rule deviations and assaultive verbal interventions.

Technically, then, there is a measure of action-discharge in every nonvalidated intervention from the therapist. Efforts by the patient to alter the ground rules of treatment, to pathologically projectively identify disturbing inner contents into the therapist, and to act out in some fashion also reflect the action-discharge mode. As noted, however, such behaviors must be consistently traced to an activated trigger and encoded perceptions of the therapist.

To illustrate, a woman therapist began a session with a male patient suffering from depression by handing him an insurance form she had completed. She asked him to sign it so that she could forward it to the insurance company. The patient did not have a pen, and requested one from the therapist, who complied.

During the session, the patient spoke about his manipulation of others. He described episodes of extensive alcohol intake and alluded to times when he was out of work and allowed himself to be inappropriately supported by his mother.

Both the handling of the insurance form and handing a pen to the patient were forms of action-discharge by this therapist. The patient's material reflects encoded perceptions of the therapist's mode of cure as one that involves destructive and exploitive actions with self-destructive components. The emergence of images of this kind should alert the therapist to deviant adaptive contexts.

DYNAMICS AND GENETICS

Dynamics refers to issues of intrapsychic conflict, psychosexual development, and the vicissitudes of the instinctual drives of sexuality and aggression. Genetics involves the early life experiences that have significantly contributed to the patient's expressed madness. Allusions to each of these components of the therapeutic interaction are especially important. Dynamic issues, especially those related to the id and to instinctual drives, are a major source of core and expressed madness, and genetic factors are critical in the structure and maintenance of this madness. Both areas should be included in a therapist's interactional interpretation when pertinent references appear in the patient's material.

The communicative approach has shown that acute early life traumas that mobilize issues of death anxiety tend to form the nucleus of core and expressed madness. The role of death anxiety in psychopathology is therefore stressed by this approach, and such issues are consistently reflected in material from patients. Danger situations involving separation, bodily injury, and superego anxieties can be shown both to have meanings of their own and to be derivatives of death anxiety issues as well. Within a secure frame, these anxieties take shape around the inevitability of death as part of life; in the deviant frame, these anxieties are a response to the persecutory aspects of deviant therapy and to the unconscious perception that the deviant therapist is in some sense lost to the patient as a meaningful object—in substance, is dead as far as the deep unconscious system is concerned.

A second issue of great importance involves problems of closeness and intimacy. These two sources of danger and anxiety contribute significantly to core and expressed madness. In this regard, there appears to be an entity that we can term *therapist love*, which is expressed solely through validated interactional interpretations and frame-securing interventions. Conversely, all nonvalidated interventions disrupt appropriate intimacy and express therapist hatred. In this regard, although a therapist is often experienced consciously as warm and concerned when he or she becomes noninterpretive, engages in so-called supportive interventions, and even reacts physically to the patient, the unconscious perceptions of such a therapist always reflect the destructive nature of these interventions. For the deep unconscious system, a therapist's concern, appropriate warmth, and availability are reflected entirely through validated interventional efforts. To be appreciated in the patient's deep unconscious system, conscious empathy requires clear limitations, lest it overflow into interventional responses that are *unconsciously* perceived as a strikingly unempathic. Appropriate conscious empathy must be reinforced with empathic responses to the patient's unconscious communications. Without the latter sensitivity, surface empathy is unconsciously perceived as false and invalid. Validated interventions typically evoke images of individuals capable of intimacy and loving, whereas missed and erroneous interventions evoke derivative images of individuals who are unavailable, insensitive, and deceptive.

In most instances of nonvalidated intervention, the therapist's behavior is in some fashion similar to that of an earlier genetic figure in the patient's life and constitutes a reenactment in some form of an early genetic trauma. The patient's associations will often allude to the relevant figure and incident. To interpret such allusions interactionally, the therapist should begin with the trigger, touch on the relevant current, selected unconscious perceptions of the therapist in light of the trigger, and then trace these perceptions to the earlier figure and traumatic incidents involved. Other types of genetic connections will accrue to frame-securing interventions. Sometimes the latter will conjure up inevitable traumas, and at other times, images of supportive and constructive figures and gratifying moments will emerge. Although these earlier life experiences rarely cause patients to misperceive the therapist and therapeutic experience (see Chapter 8), such genetic issues do have a major influence on the patient's *selective* perceptions of the therapist and his or her interventions. It is the genetic basis of this selective factor that is an essential component to a complete interactional interpretation, but this element can be alluded to only when present in the patient's material in the hour at hand.

It can be shown clinically that the emergence manifestly of sexual and aggressive drive expressions either in the interventions of the therapist or in the material from the patient tends to constitute a danger situation to both participants to treatment. Defensive reactions, especially those of repression, denial, and avoidance, are common at such times. Indeed, instinctual drives and intrapsychic conflicts are a major source of madness for both patients and therapists. Because of this, the therapist should be highly sensitive to allusions to these issues and should include the relevant images when intervening. Often, a seductive or hostile prior intervention of the therapist is the trigger for such material. In such instances, the anxiety level of both participants is quite high—consciously and/or unconsciously.

IDENTITY AND NARCISSISM

In the course of free associating, patients will allude to issues of idealization, mirroring, tension regulation, object constancy, and identity. Most of these images are self-evident, because the main themes are manifest, but *it is important to monitor this material in terms of encoded perceptions of the therapist in light of activated triggers*, rather than simply confronting the patient in these areas. Many nonvalidated interventions from therapists reflect pathological needs to be idealized by their patients and to have them function as an idealizing mirror. Such interventions often reflect the therapist's confusion as to his or her own identity and role. Implications of this aspect of interventional efforts are largely overlooked—though the patient's unconscious system is highly sensitive in this respect. Truly empathic formulations take into consideration the patient's unconscious experience as well as the more readily available conscious one. A therapist can learn a great deal about the unconscious aspects of these issues by carefully attending to the material of the patient in light of activated triggers.

SANITY AND MADNESS

Sanity and madness in others and within oneself is another area of importance to both core and expressed madness. Experiences with a psychotic parent leave a lasting influence on the patient, as do unconscious perceptions of therapist-madness in light of nonvalidated interventions. Because the therapeutic interaction is designed for the understanding and cure of madness, the patient will consistently monitor the therapist's efforts for mad, insane elements. The appearance of allusions to individuals who are psychotic, grossly disturbed, out of control, and otherwise confused and dysfunctional should alert the therapist to adaptive contexts with mad implications. As has been repeatedly stated, such images should be formulated first as encoded perceptions of the therapist before attempting to understand ways in which they may also reflect the patient's perceptions of his or her own madness.

In response to a validated intervention, images of sane, stable, reliable, and intact people will often emerge. Nonetheless, the sanity of the therapist is also a danger situation for the patient, in that the deep unconscious system understands the presence of sanity in one participant of a dyad or system to bring out the madness of the other(s). When a therapist is sane, the patient's expressed madness will come to the fore; when the therapist is mad, the patient's disturbance will recede and often entirely disappear. Vicissitudes of this kind, which cannot be predicted by understanding any other dimension of the therapeutic interaction, provide strong reason for a separate study of the sanity and madness of both participants to treatment. The mad implications of nonvalid interventions is also a greatly neglected topic, yet one that is vital to a proper understanding of the patient's experience within therapy and the vicissitudes of his or her own psychopathology.

SOME FINAL COMMENTS

Rich derivative material from patients will generally include representations in three or more of the seven dimensions of the therapeutic interaction. As noted, associations that are related to communication, frame, dynamics and genetics, and sanity and madness are especially important to the vicissitudes and meanings of the patient's expressed madness. Flat material tends to exclude representations in these areas, whereas rich associations are abundant with them.

Because the state of the frame has a compelling influence on all of the dimensions of the therapeutic interaction, it is important to note that the deviant frame always skews communication so that the patient's material is mainly concerned with the deviation, thus obliterating the unconscious meanings of the patient's core and expressed madness. Furthermore, the deviant frame always involves a pathological mode of relatedness and an action-discharge mode of cure. Because of the power of a deviant-frame intervention, the patient responds by working over unconsciously the dynamics and genetics of the therapist. As a result, the patient's own psychopathology is expressed almost entirely through a selection process in which particular meanings of the therapist's errant intervention are represented and worked over. In this type of frame, the therapist is perceived to have a confused and unstable identity and to be expressing pathological narcissistic needs; he or she is also seen as mad rather than sane.

In a secure frame, the dynamics and genetics of the patient's material allude primarily to the patient, not to the therapist. The therapist is unconsciously perceived to have a clear sense of identity and a healthy state of narcissistic balance, and is seen as sane rather than mad.

The seven dimensions of the therapeutic interaction are important heuristically as well as clinically. From time to time, the therapist should pause to analyze the areas in which the patient is communicating—both in terms of the patient's manifest comments about the psychotherapy and therapist and in terms of the derivative images. The latter is often a rich source of encoded perceptions pertinent to the dimensions of the interaction. Sound interventions will touch on the issues being worked over by the patient at the moment, stimulated by the trigger of the therapist's interventions and the patient's responsive selected perceptions.

Clinical Illustrations

To briefly illustrate how the various dimensions of the therapeutic interaction are represented in material from patients, we may consider the following:

Communication. At a juncture where a therapist had missed an intervention, a patient spoke about his family. "No one ever listens to me" he said. "I can be standing next to my father, and he won't hear a word I said."

Following a validated intervention, another patient spoke about her boss. "He's a man of great sensitivity," she remarked. "When I speak, he listens. There is nothing I can't tell him."

In contrast, after a therapist had signed an insurance form, another patient spoke of how she clams up at dinner parties. Once she gets past a one-on-one relationship, she can hardly speak.

Frame. In response to a secure-frame moment, a patient mentioned some new classes in drawing that were being offered by a charitable organization to which she belongs. Allusions to play and to other creative spaces are not uncommon in response to secure-frame interventions. On the other hand, after a therapist had changed an hour for a patient, the patient began to speak about how sad she felt. Her daughter's school had become overcrowded, and they were building an addition to the present building. As a result, the children would no longer have a playground in which to play.

Mode of relatedness.   The ideal healthy therapeutic symbiosis was portrayed in derivative form in a first session after the ground rules had been proposed to the patient by her therapist. The patient spoke of her present lover as someone capable of great tenderness, as someone she could trust and really speak to. Sexual intercourse with him is gratifying, she said, but she also likes the way he holds her when they're not having sex. She really hopes nothing happens to him.

We see here the satisfying qualities of a healthy symbiosis characterized derivatively with an addendum that reveals the typical separation and death anxieties mobilized by the secure frame.

In contrast, there is the response of a young woman who was accepted into treatment by a female therapist at a low fee. When the fee had been agreed on, the patient spoke of the fact that she was still living with her mother. She wanted to get out of her mother's apartment, but the mother made it seem impossible. She gave the patient extra money, cooked for the patient, and indulged the patient's every whim. It's really sick, she said, but she had no idea how to extricate herself.

Healthy autism was touched on when a patient spoke of how gratified she feels when she can grab a moment of peace, and simply sit in her den and enter a state of quiet reverie. This is something she can do only when everyone is settled down in her house; but sitting in the den and relaxing seems to restore her soul.

In contrast, pathological autism was represented by a patient who said that whenever he has a dispute with someone at work, he locks himself in the bathroom for fear that the other person will continue to confront him.

The parasitic mode of relatedness emerged in the material from a patient who was seen in consultation by a male psychotherapist whom she knew socially. Following a passing allusion to this social contact, the patient said that her real problem was with a man at work with whom she was having an affair. She was enormously attracted to him even though he was abusive. When he got angry, he left finger marks on her flesh. During sex, he always found ways of hurting her, and once he had reached orgasm, he virtually kicked her out of bed. She needed therapy in order to fathom why she allowed herself to be used like that. (We also see here the not uncommon unconscious need to cast therapy in a mode that is identical to the very problem for which the patient seeks treatment.)

Mode of cure.   In response to a treatment situation with several deviations and frequent noninterpretive interventions from the therapist, a patient complained about her son. "He never thinks out anything," she said. "If I happen to reprimand him, he'll run out of the house and often get into more trouble than before. If something happens with one of his friends that upsets him, he's more likely to pick a fight than to try to talk it out." Now that he was learning to drive, the patient was terrified he would get into an accident and kill himself.

In contrast to this image of destructive action-discharge, a patient responded to a validated interpretation by saying that five years ago, when he was less depressed, he would deal with his anxieties by sitting down with a piece of paper, writing out his problem, and figuring out a reasonable answer. The other day at work there was a bit of that when one of the machines in the factory broke down. No one could figure out what was wrong, but the patient was able to think through the situation step by step and discover the problem. In a way, it was the first moment of satisfaction he had had on the job in years.

Dynamics and genetics.   Patients typically convey dynamics in images that involve conflict, sexuality, and aggression. It is important when formulating such material to organize it in terms of unconscious perceptions of the therapist before attempting to define the image of the patient present in the material by way of condensation.

A patient returned to a therapist with whom she had had extensive social contact following her first psychotherapy with him. Early in the hour, she spoke of a man at work who both attracted and repelled her. Like her, he was unmarried, but his coming on to her and wanting to seduce her made her feel smothered. There was also a woman at work who was always after her. The patient figured this woman was gay and wanted the patient to be her lover.

These images of heterosexual and homosexual conflict must initially be viewed as unconscious perceptions of the therapist in light of his deviant contact with the patient following their therapeutic work. The material clearly illustrates the seductive and destructive aspects of contact between patient and therapist after termination (see Chapter 5). It also illustrates the deviant-frame claustrum, the sense of destruction and entrapment that emerges when deviations reach extreme proportions. In addition to the dynamic qualities of the patient's valid unconscious perceptions of the therapist, these images also reflect her own heterosexual and homosexual conflicts. Nonetheless, in both formulating and intervening, the perceptive aspects must take precedence over the fantasied, intrapsychic dimension if valid insight is to be achieved.

Later in this session, the patient recalled an incestuous experience with her father. Here, of course, we have the genetic aspect of both the patient's selected perception of the therapist and her own psychopathology. It is critical, however, to recognize that the incestuous father does not form the basis of a distorted view of the therapist as incestuous. Instead, this early experience and its consequent memories and introjects has created an unconscious need in the patient to become involved with men who are like her father. It is because of this unconscious need that the patient helped to promote the seductive interplay between herself and the therapist, and accepted the social contact with him after the therapy.

On the other hand, the therapist has behaved in seductive and incestuous-like fashion with his extratherapeutic contact with the patient, and the patient rightfully perceives that the therapist is on some level identical to her father. In fact, the patient *consciously* spoke of ways in which the therapist was quite *different* from her father, but in her *deep unconscious system* the *similarities* between the two men are unmistakably perceived. In general, genetic images appear in sessions as a way of indicating how the therapist and the treatment situation are in some very real but unconscious fashion tending to repeat the pathogenic past. Such connections can be highly positive as well, but usually they are quite negative.

Identity and narcissism.   Following a validated intervention, a female patient spoke of another woman in her office. She is outspoken, but she knows her own mind, she said. She knows what she can contribute to the company, and she does it without a lot of fuss and bother. If someone tries to invade her space, she knows how to take a stand and assert herself. She is someone whom the patient greatly admires.

As to problems with narcissism and identity, another patient who was seen in consultation by a therapist whom she had met once at a party spoke of her confusion in relating to men. She complained of being overly seductive and said that lack of security made her feel the need to come on to all men.

Here, the manifest content alludes to the patient's conscious view of herself, but the derivative meanings pertain to the patient's selected unconscious perceptions of the therapist.

Sanity and madness.   After a validated intervention, a young male patient spoke of his grandfather. He described a summer when his family had lived with his grandparents, and said that the pressures could have driven the old man crazy. But somehow, the patient added, he managed to stay cool and lucid through it all. He never lost control and he was there for his grandson when he needed him.

In contrast, in response to her therapist's having sent a letter to her attorney with regard to a lawsuit, a patient spoke about her husband's failure to adhere to their separation agreement. "He has no sense of responsibility," she said. "He thinks he can change the world to suit his own needs. He's like a madman, running about doing this and that to get what he wants; he would squeal on his own mother if he could get something from it."

RECOMMENDED READINGS

Bion, W. (1970): *Attention and Interpretation.* In *Seven Servants* by W. Bion. New York: Aronson.

Freud, S. (1923): The ego and the id. *SE* 19:1–59.

Kohut, H. (1971): *The Analysis of the Self.* New York: International Universities Press.

Kohut, H. (1977): *The Restoration of the Self.* New York: International Universities Press.

Langs, R. (1982): *Psychotherapy: A Basic Text.* New York: Aronson.

Langs, R. (1985): *Madness and Cure.* Emerson, NJ: Newconcept Press.

Langs, R. (1985): *Workbooks for Psychotherapists: Vol. II, Listening and Formulating.* Emerson, NJ: Newconcept Press.

Searles, H. (1973): Concerning therapeutic symbiosis. *The Annual of Psychoanalysis,* 1:247–264.

CHAPTER *8*

Issues in Psychotherapy

Because the mode of listening in the communicative approach is distinctive, it has been possible to identify a number of issues that otherwise go unnoticed in the usual psychotherapy situation. The present chapter briefly considers several of these problems and the insights that have been brought to bear on them by communicative understanding.

THE NATURE OF MEANING

The communicative approach recognizes many dimensions of meaning. Meaning is embodied not only in behaviors and verbal-affective communications, but in messages that contain information, whether manifest, implied (consciously or unconsciously), or encoded (and therefore outside of awareness in the deep unconscious system).

In psychoanalytically oriented psychotherapy, manifest or conscious meaning is of some immediate interest, because it enables the therapist to understand the patient's conscious feelings, attitudes, perceptions, ways of coping, symptoms, interpersonal dysfunctions, and the like. Nonetheless, the emphasis in the communicative approach is on the illumination of *uncon-*

scious meaning, which emerges most significantly in encoded form.

Communicative studies have revealed that unconscious meaning is not a single entity. Instead, this level of meaning is shaped by the ground rules and conditions of therapy, and we have been characterizing its nature in terms of two relatively distinct categories—secure-frame and deviant-frame therapy. The meaning constellation peculiar to either therapeutic frame has a specific set of attributes and implications, whose manifestation is contingent on the prevailing triggers (frame deviations or efforts to secure the frame).

Secure-frame meaning is considerably more anxiety-provoking than deviant-frame meaning. This is especially true when patient and therapist are of the same sex. The latent homosexual issues and anxieties generated by such a relationship combine with secure-frame anxieties to produce intense feelings of danger and dread.

Unconsciously, the patient feels well held and safe within the secure frame. Nonetheless, he or she will react to these conditions with a significant measure of death anxiety and the mobilization of related early traumas and their unconscious implications.

Another factor in the dread of secure-frame meaning is the unconscious perception and introjection of the therapist as sane and constructively functioning. Patients suffer from pathological introjects and retain the memory of early traumas from hurtful parental and other figures. There is a powerful tendency—probably located mainly in the superficial unconscious system—to remain loyal to these hurtful and destructive—and often seductive—figures. This leads in part to an unconscious quest for a hurtful psychotherapist who will correspond to the earlier pathological figure and to the pathological introjects within the patient. The patient is pathologically relieved to discover this type of likeness, to which only the deep unconscious system objects—the conscious system seeks and fully accepts this type of defense.

The secure-frame therapist produces an introject that is distinctly different from the patient's pathological introjects and memories. As a result, the patient is unconsciously confronted with the damaging qualities of the introjected earlier figure, and this undermines the patient's usual defensive use of denial in respect to the hurts involved. A highly disturbing intrapsychic conflict is created, and considerable anxiety develops. The disequilibrium caused by this type of secure-frame positive introject is considerable and is, as noted, an important factor in the disturbing qualities of secure-frame meaning. In this instance, the introject mobilizes unconscious realizations regarding split-off qualities of traumatizing parental and other figures.

Secure-frame meaning is also anxiety-provoking because it is intimately connected with the basic anxieties of life and the inevitability of death. When death anxieties are the result of actual persecutory and harmful behaviors, the patient feels appropriately enraged and mobilizes resources to attack in return. On the other hand, when death anxiety arises from constructive interventions, there is a special sense of helplessness experienced by the patient.

For one thing, the intimacy of the secure-frame situation will, when pertinent, arouse images related to psychotic interactions with earlier disturbed parental and other significant figures. Furthermore, because the patient's expressed madness comes to the fore under these conditions, the relevant derivative meanings may emerge in especially intense form, creating additional anxieties within the patient. Finally, the absence of major pathological defenses (which the patient has available under deviant-frame conditions) leads the patient to feel especially vulnerable to the unconscious and derivative meanings that emerge under secure-frame conditions.

In the deep unconscious system, the therapist shares with the patient the dread of the secure frame and of secure-frame meaning. Because of this, the therapist should subject to self-analysis all situations in which there are interpretive failures with respect to secure-frame material and impulses to alter the ideal ground rules. Self-understanding is always to be preferred to enaction; however, if the pathological need for defense is enacted, it should be subjected to subsequent self-exploration and rectification in the treatment situation as permitted by the patient's material.

There appears to be a critical measure of secure-frame meaning to the core and expressed madness in every patient, and this implies that no psychotherapy is sufficiently complete unless the patient experiences, analyzes, and understands these meanings. This also implies that the unconscious meanings of madness which evoke the greatest sense of dread are also the most critical to the patient's emotional illness and therefore most in need of patient, interactionally interpretive understanding. We are reminded again that in all deviant-frame therapy situations, secure-frame moments make a special and significant contribution to the patient's cure—as long as they are effected when the opportunity presents itself, and the patient's responsive derivatives are interpreted when they emerge.

Secure-frame meaning may at times include images of safety and sound holding. However, with patients who tend to be secure-frame and death-anxiety sensitive, such images are not especially common. One such image was presented in Chapter 5, where a plumber spoke of feeling quite comfortable in the tight space where he was working. Often these images are even more positively toned. After a secure-frame intervention, another patient spoke of sitting on a chaise lounge in a corner of her bedroom with the noises of the world shut out. She described a moment of great peace and quietude.

Still another patient produced a positive (wishful) claustrum image after a series of assaultive verbal interventions from her therapist. She spoke of a time when she had retreated from the world and taken a trip to Greece. Along the shore of an island, she found a cave where she could sit by herself without intrusion. The feeling she experienced was rapturous.

As noted, most secure-frame images communicated derivatively by patients in psychotherapy have a distinctly negative component. Secure-frame meanings stem from the claustrophobic qualities of the ideal ground rules (Chapter 6), a quality that is experienced as a dangerous type of immobilization. Images of death and annihilation are not uncommon. They are often genetically connected to earlier life traumas.

A female patient responded to a secure-frame intervention by a female therapist with a dream report: She discovers her mother's dismembered body in a cupboard. Associations led back to an abortion undergone by the patient's mother, which the patient had observed. This typifies the most terrifying type of secure-frame meaning experienced by patients. Such derivative images must be interpreted in light of the secure-frame adaptive context. Meanings of this kind seldom appear in deviant-frame situations, where the death-anxiety themes are more directly persecutory and more readily defended against. Secure-frame meanings tend to be raw and especially threatening because they are not modified through defenses such as denial and enaction, which are inherently offered to the patient by the deviant therapist.

Another female patient in therapy with a female therapist responded with a similar image to a secure-frame intervention that maintained the patient's responsibility for all sessions. She recalled a fatal automobile accident in a car driven by her uncle: the patient had been scheduled to be in the car, but at the last minute took a ride with a different relative. The patient's associations stressed her dread of entrapment and helplessness in the secure-frame situation. Threats of this kind are seldom seen under deviant-frame conditions, where images of direct pursuit and assault tend to prevail.

Deviant-frame meaning is stimulated by and constitutes an adaptive reaction to a ground-rule alteration in which the therapist has usually participated—at the very least, by acting as a passive victim of a deviation by the patient. As a result, the patient experiences both the alteration in the ground rule and a sense of the therapist as either helpless or in error. Unconsciously, the patient perceives therapist-madness and a need in the therapist for pathological satisfactions and defense.

Quite willingly, though often with anxiety, patients will explore and work over the implications of a deviant adaptive context. The meanings involved center on the therapist's madness as selectively perceived by the patient in terms of his or her own madness. This indirect way of working over encoded or unconscious meaning is far more comfortable than one in which the patient's madness is to the forefront and its implications are being communicated directly. Thus, as a rule, deviant-frame meanings have a lesser impact on the patient than meanings that occur in the secure frame.

The deviant frame provides the patient with pathological defenses. These modify the meanings of the derivatives that emerge under such conditions. Deviation implies action and *denial*, so that even if derivatives emerge and are correctly interpreted, the interpretations will obtain little or no derivative validation from the patient. Instead, supported by the therapist's participation in the deviation (which inherently denies the destructive meanings of the altered ground rules), the patient invokes his or her own denial defenses and reinforces them through unconscious introjections of the therapist's use of similar defensive operations.

Under deviant-frame conditions, death anxiety is usually mobilized, though it generally has far less impact than it does under secure-frame conditions. Under deviant conditions, death-related images serve mainly to portray the death or loss of the therapist, who becomes partially or entirely unavailable as a meaningful object and as a functioning psychotherapist because of the alteration in the ground rule. Further, when the deviation is extreme and especially destructive, deviant-frame claustrum images and deviant-frame death-related images will emerge that pertain to the destruction and death of the patient as a consequence of the therapist's persecutory interventions (qualities that are usually overlooked by the therapist). However, because the perceptions involved are justified, the patient's level of anxiety is not as great as it is under secure-frame conditions.

Moreover, the range of derivatives communicated by the patient under deviant-frame conditions is significantly restricted, which accordingly constricts the range of unconscious meanings available for experience and interpretation. When an alteration in a ground rule is invoked, it becomes the critical, wounding trigger for the patient's adaptive and derivative communications. The patient works over the implications of the deviation in light of the sensitivities of his or her own madness. In this way, some measure of the patient's own psychopathology is indeed available for interpretation and understanding. However, clinical evidence strongly indicates that the links between these issues and the unconscious meanings of the patient's core and expressed madness are greatly weakened and sometimes entirely broken. That is, under deviant-frame conditions, the most critical and compelling derivatives as they illuminate the nature and unconscious structure of the patient's madness tend not to be available for effective interpretation.

The alteration in meaning created by modifications in the ideal ground rules has not been considered in the psychotherapeutic literature because of the failure to distinguish between manifest contents and implications on the one hand, and encoded meaning on the other. Only attention to derivative communications in light of their interactional triggers will give a therapist access to the distinctive aspects of meaning described here.

Technically, the therapist's goal is to interpret those interactional meanings that are available in the patient's material. However, *the therapist must also strive to rectify all frame deviations* that can be corrected at the behest of the patient's derivative material. In addition, it is critical that the therapist provide the patient with secure-frame opportunities in the presence of unmodifiable alterations in the ground rules. This is the best he or she can do until fresh clinical investigations help us to further clarify the situation.

Deviant-frame meanings center on the inherently destructive qualities of the deviation, rather than on its surface gratifications, which tend to be restricted to manifest-content and conscious system responses. For example, a female patient who consciously and directly expressed her gratitude when her therapist signed an insurance form immediately thought of an abortion she had undergone several years earlier. This proved to be a derivative perception of the therapy, therapist, and effects of the deviation on the patient—all destructive and murderous. It is typical of deviant-frame meaning to be coated with denial when the therapist has particpated in the deviation. This occurs because the deviant therapist is unconsciously perceived as denying the destructive implications of such interventions. The result is a split image of the therapist, consciously positive and unconsciously negative. This type of splitting between the conscious and unconscious system does not appear in secure-frame situations.

Another female patient was in psychotherapy with a male therapist who was secretly recording her sessions with a tape recorder placed in his desk drawer, which was left partially open. Although the patient expressed no conscious awareness of the tape recordings, she entered a session soon after this practice was begun by stating that she must be losing touch with reality. She had been taking a shower and was convinced that she had heard an intruder in her apartment. She searched the apartment and thought that certain items had been moved about, but could find no clear evidence of a break-in. She went next door to a male neighbor who also inspected the apartment but could not be certain that someone had indeed been there. Throughout that night, the patient had remained terrified that the intruder would return and murder her.

Although the particulars of each deviation help to shape the specific selected images to which the patient alludes on the derivative level, there are certain general attributes to deviant-frame meaning. These include images of persecution, intrusion, murder, destruction, and madness. In addition, deviant-frame meaning often involves impairments in reality testing and mini-psychotic qualities. Many deviations are constituted as mini-psychotic acts of the therapist in defense against his or her own death anxieties, a topic to which we may now turn.

THE ROLE OF DEATH ANXIETY

Freud offered psychoanalysts two major defenses: (1) *the concept of "transference"*, through which the therapist could deny his own contribution to the patient's madness, and instead account for such experiences entirely through the intrapsychic state and genetics of the patient; and (2) *the denial of death anxiety*. Freud claimed that whereas it is possible to experience separation, loss of love, bodily anxiety, and super-ego anxiety, it is impossible to conceptualize one's own death.

A growing body of literature, however, indicates that death anxiety plays a critical role in life choices and in madness. It is the specific contribution of the communicative approach to identify death anxiety as a central source of emotional danger and, in particular, as a major factor in the *unconscious meanings* of madness. Surface considerations of death anxiety limit our understanding of its ramifications. However, an understanding of the influence of death anxiety on the patient's derivative responses to triggers greatly widens our insight.

All human beings experience death anxiety, and death anxiety is a central factor in the development of core and expressed madness. Death anxiety arises mainly in response to experiences (both early and later) of abandonment, separation, and loss, as well as to incidents of illness, injury, and other major traumas that in some way threaten life or bodily integrity. The anxieties, unconscious perceptions, unconscious fantasies, and unconscious memories created by such experiences have a strong influence on both the deep unconscious and conscious systems, and on the patient's emotional adaptational resources.

It has been possible through a study of patients in the clinical situation to identify a critical syndrome in this regard—*the premature or overintense exposure to death-anxiety issues.* The syndrome may evolve from early traumas of the type just identified, or as a result of later-life, highly traumatic incidents with death and injury—the loss of a body part, the experience of a fatal illness, the suicide of someone close, involvement in a fatal accident, and such. Patients who suffer from this syndrome show extremely intense anxieties with respect to derivative communication as such and to the secure frame as well. The deep unconscious system of these individuals contains images and schemata so unusually primitive and terrifying that the patient fears the escape of any derivative expression of the related themes. The unconscious meanings and images contained in the deep unconscious system of these patients are treated as powerful and real, and there is an evident unconscious conviction within these patients that any measure of actual derivative expression of these meanings will cause annihilating anxieties and actual psychic disintegration.

Technically, then, the therapist is faced with a serious dilemma: On the one hand, to avoid the interpretation of death-related derivatives that do find expression is unconsciously perceived by the patient as reflecting a dread within the therapist of the patient's unconscious experience and meaning; on the other hand, the most tactful and sensitive interactional interpretation of these derivatives as they emerge in response to triggers within the therapeutic interaction increases the patient's anxieties. He or she dreads not only the decoded meanings of these encoded expressions, but the potential emergence of new derivatives and new decoded meanings. Although the patient does find a measure of strength in the therapist's capacity to understand, contain, and interpret these meanings, the level of anxiety is, as a rule, so intense that there is a continuous risk of premature termination. It is therefore crucial that the therapist proceed slowly with such patients, and that interpretive attention be paid to the death-sensitive patient's enormous dread of meaning and its underlying causes.

The dread of the secure frame in these patients is extraordinary because the secure frame becomes a claustrum in which the patient is unconsciously convinced that the earlier trauma will be repeated—this time, with a fatal outcome. This experience has the qualities of an unconscious neurotic delusion (*i.e.*, it is not a fixed conviction immutable to surface reality testing) and reflects the patient's belief in the reality of the unconscious images contained in the deep unconscious system. It is not uncommon to obtain a dream of mutilated bodies in a closed space under these circumstances.

For the therapist, the dread of the secure frame involves a fantasy; for the patient, a reality. To illustrate, a female patient told her male psychotherapist about a hospital visit to a former lover who was seriously ill. The doctor at the hospital had assured the patient during her visit that the man would soon recover and be able to go home. But one look at her former boyfriend, and the patient knew for certain he was going to die. The doctor didn't believe it was going to happen, the patient complained, but she knew it would. The patient's friend did indeed expire one week later.

These communications were a response to efforts by the therapist to secure aspects of a deviant-frame psychotherapy. In her images, the patient was unconsciously conveying her conviction that she would be destroyed within the secure frame, even though the therapist thought otherwise. It is important to interpret convictions of this kind to the patient when they appear in the derivative material. In this instance, the therapist made a suitable interpretation, which did not obtain derivative validation, however, until he later added his impression that the patient's beliefs about the consequences of securing the ground rules were absolute certainties and realities for her. With that comment, derivative validation followed, and the patient was able to remain in treatment and to continue to work over the recently mobilized secure-frame issues.

As we have seen, death anxiety takes two forms: secure-frame death anxiety and deviant-frame death anxiety. In the first situation, the patient unconsciously experiences the danger of repeating earlier death-related experiences, and expects that this time he or she will be annihilated. In addition, all patients experience a measure of death anxiety in the secure frame, because its boundaries create a claustrum that raises existential terrors: There is but one exit from the space of life. Deviant-frame death anxiety, in contrast, arises from the persecutory qualities of deviation. The patient unconsciously perceives the demise of the therapist as an effectively functioning figure when he or she deviates, and experiences other meanings related to the destruction of treatment under such circumstances.

In the course of each psychotherapy, then, it is expected that death-anxiety issues will be mobilized in some fashion, will evoke derivative responses to therapeutic triggers, and will lead to interactional interpretations that include an understanding of the genetic component. In addition, death-anxiety issues will inevitably arise in response to the therapist's management of the ground rules, whether deviant or secure; these interventions create critical triggers for the patient's experience and communicative response. In a truly effective psychotherapy, the analysis of death-anxiety issues is as inevitable as death itself.

PSYCHOTIC EXPRESSIONS IN NONPSYCHOTIC PATIENTS

It is well known that psychotic patients will communicate primitive and psychotic images with some frequency, whereas nonpsychotic patients do so, if at all, mainly in their dreams. We may define a psychotic communication as any expression—association or behavior—in which there is a break with reality, an inherent contradiction, a primitive quality, an extreme act (*e.g.*, a brutal murder or a blatantly inappropriate seduction), and otherwise irrational imagery. Such expressions, particularly in nonpsychotic patients, are often dismissed by therapists as merely part of a dream or as an innocent slip of the tongue or a lapse. Communicative studies have, however, revealed that these communications have special importance and meaning.

Psychotic lapses may involve delusions and hallucinations that represent a relatively significant break in overall contact with reality. The false belief is maintained with considerable intensity and often over an extended period of time—though there may be lucid intervals as well. These would be termed psychotic breaks with reality.

There are also borderline and neurotic breaks with reality. *Borderline lapses* involve a false belief, perception, or experience that is less intensely maintained than in the psychotic situation and which alternates with clear and often extended lucid intervals. Such lapses tend to occur under stress and to eventually be brought under control.

Neurotic breaks with reality are short-lived and, on examination, entirely modifiable. Also, they occur in the absence of other disturbances in ego functions that are generally present to some degree in the borderline lapse and to a significant degree in the psychotic lapse.

The lapses with which we are concerned may be considered *minipsychotic acts* and *momentary breaks with reality*. They occur in otherwise well-functioning patients, and take the form of slips of the tongue, an unexpected misperception, or a mistaken type of behavior. A patient may sit in the wrong chair in a first session when the patient's chair is self-evident, or leave the therapist's consultation room by the wrong door. In everyday life, such occurrences as locking one's keys in a car, forgetting an appointment, going to the wrong place, mishearing and misunderstanding someone else's words, and the like, are typical of minipsychotic acts and expressions. In all instances, there is a momentary break with reality, then contact is quickly restored.

In addition to minipsychotic acts in nonpsychotic patients (and therapists), virtually everyone will experience psychotic or minipsychotic communication. As noted, such moments involve any image contradictory to reality and actuality. Thus, a patient may dream of flying or dream that someone who is dead is still alive. He or she may misremember the time of the session or incorrectly calculate the fee owed to the therapist. Psychotic communications of this kind are not uncommon in the course of a psychotherapy—nor in everyday life.

There are several factors that contribute to the emergence of this type of expression. Psychotic communications are an indication of *psychotic anxieties*, regardless of the character structure and basic diagnosis of the patient. As such, these images emerge at moments of extreme distress, and in the presence of disorganizing and annihilating issues. Primitive responses to death anxiety, psychotic communications from others (including the therapist), and extremely traumatic triggers all contribute to such expressions. This type of response can occur with secure-frame interventions, but such expressions are especially characteristic of highly charged unconscious perceptions of mad and self-contradictory interventions from the therapist.

Of special note in this regard are manifestations of splitting in the therapist, such as when he or she secures the frame but fails to offer valid interactional interpretations. Similarly, these reactions are not uncommon when a therapist alters a particular ground rule and yet reveals to the patient his or her capacity to understand and interpret derivative expressions. The unconscious system of the patient recognizes these contradictions, perceives the therapist as mad, and often responds with psychotic anxieties and communications.

Expressions of this kind have special importance for technique. In response to a given trigger, a patient will often communicate a mixture of psychotic and nonpsychotic images and derivatives. As a rule, only the nonpsychotic material will prove to be interpretable interactionally and to evoke derivative validation. Patients have an enormous dread of psychotic expressions—both as derivatives and as a means of access to highly charged and primitive perceptions and fantasies. They fear being overwhelmed by anxiety and they fear the possibility of annihilation when material of this kind is interpreted to them. Rather than validation, the response to interventions based on such material is often strong denial and negation of meaning.

At times, however, it may be possible to interpret some elements of this type. Such interpretations should be made mainly when the patient's derivative material makes it feasible to also interpret the patient's enormous dread of these communications and their manifest and underlying meanings. Such work is quite difficult, because expressions of this kind often evoke psychotic anxieties in the therapist as well. Although these anxieties and the therapist's own unconscious perceptions of the patient and his or her material are often outside of awareness, they have a powerful unconscious influence on the conscious system, which automatically invokes defensive denial and avoidance. It is therefore incumbent on the psychotherapist to be especially alert to this dimension of the patient's material.

Earlier in the chapter, we considered a vignette in which a female patient's sessions were being secretly tape recorded. Certainly this is a minipsychotic act on the part of the therapist; in fact, it may have even more serious implications—that is, it may constitute a truly borderline or psychotic form of abberant intervention. The patient responded by believing that her apartment had been broken into, though no evidence of a break-in could be established.

Minipsychotic acts and communications tend to occur in patients after acute breaks in the frame. This occurs, in part, because many deviations are unconsciously perceived by the patient as acts of madness in the therapist. On rare occasion, the secure-frame sensitive patient will react to a secure-frame intervention with a minipsychotic lapse. Such was the case with a male patient who was a twin. His twin brother had died soon after birth. On leaving the first hour with a male therapist, the patient mistakenly entered the therapist's closet rather than the door to the corridor. In a later session he reported a dream of being under water struggling to reach the surface for what seemed like an eternity—at least an hour. Dreams that defy reality must be understood as psychotic communications and related to pertinent adaptive contexts—here, the dangerous claustrum of the secure frame.

A male therapist agreed to change the time of his female patient's session, whereupon the patient appeared for her next hour at the wrong time. This minipsychotic act, which was subjected to immediate reality testing and the patient's realization of her mistake, involved an unconscious perception and introjection of an unconsciously perceived lapse in the therapist—his compliance with the change in the hour.

In the deep unconscious system, the patient believes there is only one time slot for his or her session. When the therapist renders it otherwise, reality becomes uncertain and the patient behaves accordingly. Another therapist offered his patient telephone contact during an absence caused by a surgical procedure. The pateint responded with a psychotic dream in which her dead brother was alive, and another dream in which a friend wanted to murder her. Most minipsychotic acts and psychotic communications involve a significant input of therapist-madness. They are also more likely to occur in otherwise nonpsychotic patients who are vulnerable to psychotic lapses. It is therefore critical in interpreting such behaviors and communications to do so in light of an activated adaptive context and the patient's *selected* unconscious perceptions of the therapist.

THE CONCEPTS OF TRANSFERENCE, COUNTERTRANSFERENCE, AND INTERACTION

It has been possible in the present volume to clearly define the nature of the conscious and unconscious therapeutic interaction without reference to the term "transference." For the term "countertransference," the concept of "therapist-madness" has been substituted. In addition, communicative techniques require the consistent monitoring of the patient's unconscious perceptions of the therapist. As a result, the detection of therapist-madness and its expression is an integral component of the approach.

Whatever its function and usefulness, the concept of transference has outlived its clinical utility. The term is defined theoretically in at least a dozen different ways, and its clinical referents are poorly defined if at all. Transference implies a distorting intrapsychic influence from the patient, and acknowledges only minimal or no contribution from the therapist or analyst. This assumption—that the patient's *fundamental response* to the therapeutic situation and therapist is both distorting and essentially founded on an overriding genetic influence—is clinically untenable. No complex animal, humans included, could survive if perception were so easily distorted.

This erroneous conception must be replaced by a formulation that takes into account both stimulus and response—the trigger of the therapist's intervention (the external or reality determinant of the patient's therapeutic experience and material) and the patient's full range of reactions (the intrapsychic component). This can be done only by taking into account the patient's perceptions (conscious and unconscious) of the therapeutic interaction and his or her reactions to those perceptions—including occasional distorted views of the therapist.

Rather than transference, there is an intrapsychic influence which determines behavior and serves as a selective guide in unconscious communication and experience. Overly intense intrapsychic fantasies, memories, and other propensities may in extreme situations contribute to exaggerated and overstated responses, both in terms of derivative communication as well as in terms of symptoms and behaviors. The concept of transference as an essentially distorting factor should be discarded.

Also, instead of referring to the entire relationship between patient and therapist as "the transference," or using the term to characterize the unconsciously distorted aspects of that relationship, it is far more precise to speak simply of the therapeutic interaction and of the patient's relationship to the therapist. It is then the therapist's job to analyze the material from the patient for its conscious and unconscious elements, both perceptive and distorted.

Transference was basically defined by Freud as a phenomenon of an *unconscious* fantasy/memory system that led to misperceptions of and inappropriate reactions to the therapist based on earlier genetic experiences. It can be shown, however, that the deep unconscious system does not distort, but almost always perceives accurately and soundly. Conscious distortions of the therapist's words and actions do occur, but they are rare in a well-run psychotherapy. However, this type of distortion is mainly an indicator of madness and a dysfunction of the conscious system. As such, the perceptions involved must be carefully evaluated by the therapist. This type of distortion seldom carries derivative meaning, though it is based on unconscious factors which themselves can be revealed only through additional derivative material. Furthermore, as indications of madness, these conscious distortions always have contributions from both participants to therapy. True distortions of this kind involve minipsychotic moments and their ramifications.

Although the concept of transference has been discarded in the communicative approach, the important role played by intrapsychic determinants within the patient and by his or her genetic history in both the therapeutic interaction and in symptom formation have been retained. The communicative approach simply insists on the validity of the finding that almost all of the patient's associations and behaviors in the therapy session are to a significant degree adaptive responses to the therapist's interventions, and that furthermore, the critical unconscious meanings of all madness, whether in patient or therapist, are revealed solely through encoded or derivative (transformed) expressions.

The term "therapist-madness" is to be preferred to "countertransference" largely because the literature on the latter subject tends to be manifest-content oriented and naive, and because therapists should avoid intellectualized terms when alluding to emotionally charged issues. The best guide for the discovery of expressions of therapist-madness is the nonvalidating responses of patients to therapeutic interventions, and the patient's encoded perceptions of the therapist. *Unconsciously, the patient automatically functions as supervisor to the therapist*, making use of the enormous wisdom of the deep unconscious system to detect expressions of therapist-madness. In addition, *on the derivative level*, the patient will also offer general interpretations as to the unconscious factors in the therapist that relate to his or her disturbance.

In the presence of indications of therapist-madness, the therapist should engage briefly and quickly in an effort at self-analysis while listening to the continuation of the patient's material. Following such an hour, during a quiet period, the therapist should free associate before attempting to analyze and understand the basis of the difficulty. Efforts at direct detection either fail or are extremely limited. On the other hand, the use of free association opens up the communicative network and allows the therapist an opportunity for derivative expression. This creates communicative material that can be analyzed subsequently in terms of triggers, derivative perceptions, genetic connections, memories, and the like. In this regard, it is especially useful to *identify the material from the patient that prompted the nonvalidated intervention*, because these antecedents often reveal the area of vulnerability within the therapist that has contributed to the problem.

The therapeutic interaction is structured in such a manner that there is an extremely high likelihood of expressions of therapist-madness. As noted in Chapter 2, the therapist's responsibility to integrate the patient's material into an interactional interpretation and to maintain the secure frame arouses major anxieties that create extraordinary pressures toward pathological interventions. The psychotherapist is involved in a situation where his or her greatest vulnerabilities and psychotic anxieties are certain to be evoked from time to time. Because of this, a measure of error—an expression of madness—is inevitable. Realistically, the goal is to keep these errors to a minimum and for the therapist to develop a capacity to identify almost all lapses within the session in which they occur so that corrective work can be undertaken in the same hour—though always, entirely in terms of the patient's available material.

The inevitable guilt that arises after an expression of therapist-madness typically creates an intense need for reparation. This often leads to premature interventions, which then constitute further expressions of therapist-madness rather than a shift to sanity. Despite the intensity of internal pressures, during moments of error and madness it is all the more vital that the therapist adhere to the validated principles of communicative technique and allow the patient to create the necessary moment of repair, rectification, and reparation. Virtually always, patients will unconsciously rescue or redeem the therapist in this fashion. There is no substitute for *faith* in the patient in respect to his or her wishes to be emotionally sound—and to help the therapist be emotionally sound as well.

Finally, we need no longer debate the issue of whether the hardest part of analysis and psychotherapy is the management of "transference" or "countertransference." Here, we might state the question in terms of the patient's selected unconscious perceptions of the therapist as compared with the therapist's reactions to the patient. It is, however, immediately apparent that patient- and therapist-madness are intertwined, and that properly managing or interpreting the patient's communications require a strong degree of self-understanding and sanity within the psychotherapist. Therapist-madness is evoked by the triggers of the patient's behaviors and material and, as such, is always a result of two factors: the nature of the trigger and the therapist's own intrapsychic propensities. The successful interactional interpretation of the patient's material and the development of a secure-frame treatment experience is possible only in the hands of a psychotherapist who is by and large quite sane and, in addition, able to identify, manage, and rectify his or her inevitable expressions of madness.

Clinical Material

We may turn now to a dramatic deviation that led to a powerful and rather typical response in a patient. The material illustrates many of the ideas discussed in the present chapter. The situation is drawn from the intensive psychotherapy of a thirty-one-year-old single woman who sought therapy beause of intense feelings of hopelessness and depression, and a tendency toward extreme withdrawal from others. Three months into treatment the patient required hospitalization for an exploratory operation made necessary by what appeared to be a uterine fibroid. When the patient asked about responsibility for the four sessions she would miss over the ensuing two weeks, the therapist suggested that the patient remain responsible for her hours. He then proposed that he would be available by telephone so that the patient could call him from the hospital, or from her home, where she planned to recover. The patient was pleased with this arragement, which was made two sessions before her hospitalization.

In the next hour, the patient began by asking the therapist to change the time of this particular session, because she was finding it a rush to get to work afterward. She then went on to speak briefly of her pending hospitalization and the relief she felt that her therapist would be available by telephone.

She recalled two dreams. In the first, she is in a theater, in the audience, and her brother Al [who had died in an automobile accident when the patient was thirteen years old] is on stage. He had come back from the dead. He told everyone, "You're better off being dead, but maybe I died too early." It seemed to be a strange setting for him to be saying that.

In the second dream, the patient is with a friend, Mike. They are in a cabin, and Chet, another friend, goes crazy and tries to rob and kill them. They receive a telephone call from Chet and he seems normal, but then Chet's father calls and says that Chet went crazy and is coming to kill them. The patient tells Mike they should leave the cabin and they do. Chet comes, goes into the cabin, lies in the patient's bed, and then leaves. The patient and Mike run off, and Chet chases them.

The trigger for this material is clearly the therapist's offer to be available by telephone to the patient while she is in the hospital and recovering. This is a major deviation and violation of the ground rule that states that psychotherapy takes place in a single setting, the office of the psychotherapist. How then did the patient respond to this adaptive context?

On the conscious level, as an expression of the conscious system, the patient was pleased and accepted this proposal. It appears, however, that the therapist's offer of a deviation became a model of cure for the patient, in that she began the following hour by requesting another deviation, a change in the time of her session. As a rule, one deviation does beget another, and deviant-frame gratification becomes the action-discharge mode of cure for both the patient and therapist.

Without citing the patient's additional associations, we may suggest that the first dream reveals an unconscious perception of the therapist in light of his proposed deviations as someone who has a need to deny death—here, the temporary loss of the patient and the possibility of some fatal outcome to her surgery. The patient offers a model of rectification, which suggests the idea that the therapist would be better off dealing with his death anxieties rather than avoiding them.

In substance, the dream suggests that the patient's perceptions are both veridical and selective. They are based on her own unresolved death anxieties, whose genetic aspect involves not only the death of her brother, but also a series of miscarriages experienced by her mother when the patient was six years and younger. In addition, the patient unconsciously characterizes the telephone contact as an extreme or psychotic maneuver—in substance as a psychotic form of denial. As noted, intense experiences of death anxiety lead to minipsychotic acts and psychotic communications in patients and therapists alike. In this instance, the patient perceived the deviation as this type of expression.

In essence, the second dream extends the patient's unconscious view of the deviation as crazy, as robbing her (probably in the sense of depriving her of an important therapeutic opportunity), and as an attempt at murder—the destruction of the therapy and of the patient. Quite eloquently, the patient suggests through her derivatives that the suggestion *seems* normal (*i.e.*, as per the view of the conscious system), whereas it is *actually* an insane attempt at murder (the view of the deep unconscious system). The deviation also invades the patient's space and moves the therapist into the patient's bed. In addition, it is a form of pursuit.

We can see, then, that the conscious system accepts and attempts to exploit and extend deviant interventions. In contrast, the deep unconscious system perceives the defensive, psychotic, and destructive qualities of the deviation, and voices a clear, encoded, protest. The vignette illustrates the ways in which all deviations involve some form of perverse sexual gratification, notably interfere with contact with reality, generate an image of a mad therapist, and function as a defense against death anxiety (see Chapter 6). In this instance, mainly because the deviation is sudden and extreme, the patient's response includes expressions of her own core anxieties and madness, though these serve mainly as a guide for her selective perceptions of virtually identical anxieties in the psychotherapist.

It seems likely that the patient has unconsciously perceived the therapist's need to deviate as a basic manic-fusion-denial defense against his own anxieties related to loss and death. These, of course, correspond to the patient's own anxieties, and using the therapist as her model, the patient attempts to use a deviation to diminish her own—and the therapist's—sense of dread and the attendant unconscious perceptions and fantasies. Nonetheless, based mainly on the response of her deep unconscious system, which consistently seeks the secure frame and the use of healthy defenses, the patient does offer an implied protest in both dreams.

We may note, too, the emergence of a psychotic communication in the first dream—that the brother came back from the dead. This psychotic communication in a patient who has been clearly nonpsychotic was stimulated by the patient's unconscious perception of the psychotic aspects of the therapist's proposed deviation. These aspects are not a quality of his interventions at the conscious level, because for the conscious system, the means and place of contact between patient and therapist can vary in what appears to be a logical and acceptable fashion. Not so for the deep unconscious system, where a model of the ideal conditions of treatment is maintained and seeks concrete existence.

We see here an instance in which the conscious system sees no contradiction—the therapist can either hold a session with the patient in his office or talk to her by telephone. But the deep unconscious system has a different view: Treatment can take place only in the therapist's office and cannot occur by telephone. Telephone contact is unconsciously perceived as a break in the boundaries that denies absence and brings the patient into contact with the therapist under forbidden or impossible conditions. Ultimately, such contact is seen as bringing the dead back to life—the image portrayed in the patient's dream. As such, telephone contact is a minipsychotic act for the deep unconscious system. It is also an impossibility—that is, therapy cannot take place under those conditions.

The deep unconscious system was first crudely conceptualized by Freud (1900) in terms of primary process thinking. Freud believed that there were no contradictions at this level of thought—that is, that all opposites are tolerated. The communicative approach, by separating manifest from derivative images, has shown that primary process thinking (the deep unconscious system) actually does have its own set of contradictions and negations, which are distinct from those that exist in the conscious system. Thus, for this patient, the conscious system would argue that she cannot be in the hospital and in the therapist's office at the same time. The telephone contact is an attempt to deny this particular conscious premise. This sort of denial always involves a major or minor break with reality—often a minipsychotic act.

In the deep unconscious system, as noted, therapy can take place in only one setting and under only one set of conditions. In this system, telephone contact cannot be therapeutic. The absence of the patient from the therapist's office precludes a psychotherapeutic experience.

The proposed deviation, then, is unconsciously perceived by the patient as a minipsychotic act of the therapist. Given the patient's own intrapsychic anxieties and vulnerabilities, this then leads to a psychotic dream communication—one clearly connected with issues of death anxiety. Were this patient more ill and inclined toward acting out, she might have reacted by engaging in an actual minipsychotic act of her own—for example, a failure to return to her sessions when she was well, because she forgot the time of her hour.

In the second dream, the psychotic qualities of the deviation as selectively perceived by the patient are reflected in the image of the friend who goes crazy and tries to rob and kill the patient and her other friend Mike. Whereas the first dream appears to reflect the patient's unconscious perceptions of the therapist's secure-frame death anxiety and his need to deny these anxieties through the deviation, the second dream seems to portray the destructive and death-related aspects of the therapist's proposed deviation.

Finally, it is to be stressed that in dealing with this type of material the therapist must always begin with an adaptive context constituted by one or more of his or her interventions (which will usually be frame-related). From there, he or she should turn to the patient's selected and valid unconscious perceptions before identifying the intrapsychic issues within the patient that have helped to shape these perceptions. In most of these situations, the therapist himself or herself is dealing with psychotic anxieties, death-related issues, and minipsychotic defenses. He or she will therefore be strongly motivated unconsciously to avoid or deny the patient's unconscious perceptions, and to dump the issues into the patient—holding him or her accountable for the pathological component. An intervention of this type can only intensify the patient's sense of unreality and psychotic anxieties, and is to be avoided at all costs.

RECOMMENDED READINGS

Becker, E. (1973): *The Denial of Death*. New York: Free Press.
Bird, B. (1972): Notes on transference: Universal phenomenon and the hardest part of analysis. *Journal of the American Psychoanalytic Association* 20:267–301.
Freud, S. (1912): The dynamics of transference. *SE* 12:97–108.
Gill, M., & Hoffman, I. (1982): *Analysis of Transference, Vols. 1 & 2*. New York: International Universities Press.
Greenson, R. (1967): *The Technique and Practice of Psychoanalysis*. New York: International Universities Press.
Grotstein, J. (1977): The psychoanalytic concept of schizophrenia; I, The dilemma. *International Journal of Psycho-Analysis* 58:403–426.
Grotstein, J. (1977): The psychoanalytic concept of schizophrenia: II, Reconciliation. *International Journal of Psycho-Analysis* 58:427–452.
Langs, R. (1984–85): Making interpretations and securing the frame: Sources of danger for psychotherapists. *International Journal of Psychoanalytic Psychotherapy* 10:3–24.
Langs, R. (1985): *Workbooks for Psychotherapists: Vol. II, Listening and Formulating*. Emerson, NJ: Newconcept Press.
McLaughlin, J. (1981): Transference, psychic reality, and countertransference. *The Psychoanalytic Quarterly* 50:639–664.

CHAPTER **9**

The Communicative Model
of the Mind

Topographical models—maps of the mind—have fallen into disfavor in psychoanalysis. Freud himself rejected his main topographic model, wherein he had distinguished the systems CS (Conscious), PCS (preconscious), and UCS (Unconscious), when he discovered that defenses which, according to his model, should have been located in the system CS were actually unconscious. He did reserve the terms "conscious" and "unconscious," however, for qualities of thought and experience.

The very nature of Freud's topography has been a problem for analysts. Freud postulated a simple stimulus-response sequence of events—conscious registration occurring before unconscious processing, and an essentially stepwise progress of the information from the UCS to the PCS to the system CS. The model implies the existence of censorship or defense at both the receptor and motoric ends of the sequence, a conception that Freud could not justify clinically.

Furthermore, Freud did not expect neurophysiologic correlates of his model. He regarded the distinctions proposed by the model, such as the differences between primary and secondary process thinking, as a matter of energics rather than location. Freud eventually replaced his topographic model with the structural hypothesis, which divides the mind into id, ego, and superego, and offered a hypothetical diagram of these structures as the scene of conflict and adaptation.

It has emerged, however, that there are, in fact, as Freud originally postulated, two distinctive modes of *thinking*. This finding was undoubtedly Freud's greatest discovery. Through the communicative approach, this postulate has been extended to the areas of *communication, experience,* and the *schemata through which we process incoming information.* In each area there are two distinct modes of operation—conscious and unconscious.

By crystallizing the relevant clinical findings into a new model of the mind, we can capture visually how the mind processes and deals with emotionally charged information and meaning. The great value of togopgaphic visualization is that it enables us to shift from the linear word-and-thought processes that may be characteristic of the left brain, which are a relatively limited means of ordering and comprehending information, to the wholistic processing said to be a function mainly of the right brain, which is considerably more efficient. (These brain characterizations are now in dispute.) One might consider the difference between verbally describing a large room full of people and taking it all in at a glance. By shifting from "left brain" to "right brain" thinking—from conceptualizing the therapeutic interaction and madness in terms of words and ideas to embodying aspects of these issues in visual terms—we can ultimately generate fresh verbal formulations and new understanding that can be applied directly to therapeutic technique.

THE BASIC MODEL

Figure 9-1 presents the apparatus, schemata, and systems with which we process incoming emotionally charged messages and information.

Incoming information is first received at a sensory receptor site—the eyes, ears, skin, etc. From there, it is forwarded to a synthesizing center, which passes the information on to the message analyzing center. The message analyzing center is a point of choice: Each component of a message—manifest con-

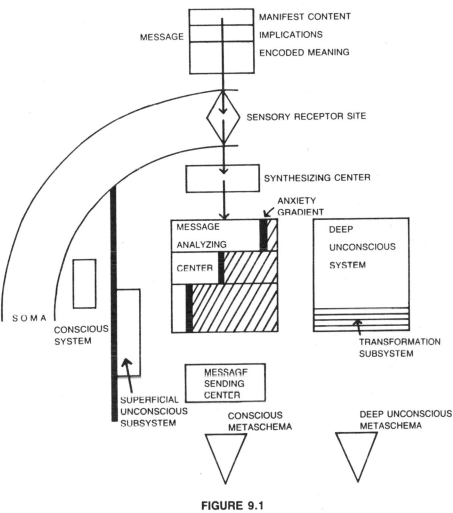

FIGURE 9.1
The Mental Systems for Processing
Emotionally Charged Information

tent, implications, and encoded meaning—is analyzed and as-
signed to different sites for further processing.

For each aspect of meaning, one of two fates is possible. On
the one hand, when the anxiety gradient is high, so that the
measure of anxiety experienced is low, the meaning is viewed
as acceptable to conscious awareness. Such meanings are for-

warded directly to the message sending center. The conscious system scans all messages available in the message sending center and selects for representation those, basically, for which it has a preference. What does not become directly conscious becomes part of storage in the superficial unconscious subsystem of conscious awareness. Obviously this processing system is more complicated than the latter explanation would imply. Certain aspects of its operation have been omitted for purposes of simplification. The particular sequence just described, in which a meaning is ultimately experienced consciously on its own terms, directly and without disguise, is presented in Figure 9-2.

It can be seen that all of the processing takes place unconsciously (without awareness) up to the point at which a processed message meets halfway the hypercathexes of attention. Furthermore, this processing is under the influence of a conscious metaschema. This metaschema contains the premises, guiding principles, and mode of operation that pertain to the entire conscious system, including its superficial unconscious subsystem. Freud attempted to characterize this metaschema in terms of the principles of secondary process thinking—its use of direct meaning and logic, delay of discharge, and contact with reality—concepts that are correctly formulated as far as they go, but very much in need of revision (see below).

We may illustrate this type of processing and its aberrations with several brief examples. As the therapist listens to the patient's manifest associations, in most instances, all of the manifest content is allowed immediate access to awareness. On occasion, an image will be missed or a word will be misheard. This happens when the communication has evoked a relatively high level of anxiety during the extremely rapid analysis carried out by the message analyzing center. We may assume that this anxiety-provoking information has been forwarded to the deep unconscious system. In addition, when trying to recall a session, a particular image may not be recalled, because that conscious information has been stored in the superficial unconscious subsystem. Most of this information can be readily retrieved by awareness; however, when there is a notable emotional charge and anxiety factor, repression may occur. Such repressed information is probably forwarded for storage in the memory bank and schemata of the deep unconscious system.

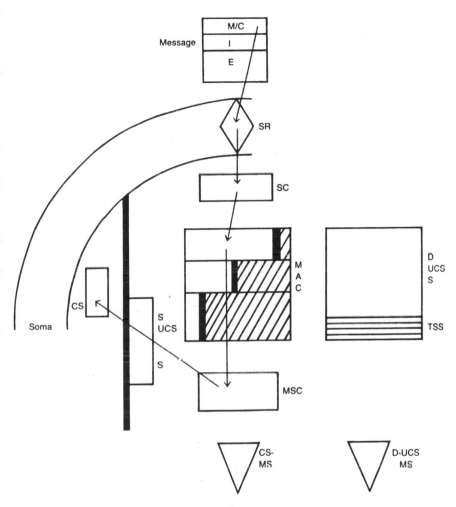

FIGURE 9.2
Steps in Processing Conscious Information

For example, a therapist thought she heard her patient say, "I'm going to have a celebration"; but further associations revealed that the actual words were, "I'm going to have an operation." The therapist was herself at the moment debating a question of elective surgery and had misheard her patient.

In terms of the model of the mind, the incoming message was considered by the message analyzing center to be too charged with anxiety for direct conscious awareness. The message was therefore deflected to the deep unconscious system. In the meantime, the message sending center had to fill the void. The word "celebration" was substituted for the word "operation," suggesting the use of a manic defense and wish-fulfilling denial. It may well be that some aspect of the superficial unconscious subsystem provides a substitute word, which then becomes accessible to consciousness. The therapist was able to discover her error only by realizing that the word she had heard did not fit with the patient's subsequent associations. It appears likely that defensive operations can take place at every level at which a message, conscious and otherwise, is processed.

The processing of manifest information becomes important in psychotherapy primarily when there is a misperception or falsification of a manifest message. This type of experience in the patient becomes an *indicator*—a sign of madness—and the unconscious basis and meaning of the processing dysfunction can then be discovered from the patient's additional associations. In virtually all instances, there will be a trigger and encoded perceptions available in the patient's material to illuminate the difficulty. Disturbances in information processing are one facet of madness and are, as would be expected, maladaptive reactions to dangerous triggers and anxiety-provoking encoded perceptions—and reactions to these perceptions.

PROCESSING THE IMPLICATIONS OF MESSAGES

As we have seen, some implications that can be extracted from a manifest message will become conscious, whereas other implications will fail to reach awareness directly. When we speak of *conscious implications*, we mean those implications that the message analyzing center processes toward *direct* (immediate or delayed) awareness. Thus, a conscious implication may be accepted into awareness at the very moment a message is received, or realized later through subsequent analysis—that is, retrieved from storage in the superficial unconscious subsystem. Information that is stored in that subsystem is directly accessible to the hypercathexes of attention when it is sought out.

In substance, implications fated for awareness (*i.e.*, conscious implications) are processed much like manifest meanings, which are directly accessible to consciouness. It appears, however, that the component of the message analyzing center which unconsciously sorts out implications of messages—a remarkable unconscious feat that is carried out with enormous intelligence and speed—has a somewhat different anxiety gradient than the component that deals with manifest contents. To state this in clinical terms, most manifest meanings, because they are directly conveyed to awareness, are made immediately available to the conscious system—even when they are a source of notable *conscious anxiety*. Implications, on the other hand, seem to be a source of greater anxiety, and those that are threatening—in part, because of *unconscious anxiety*—are more readily repressed and forwarded to the deep unconcious system.

Thus, whereas virtually all manifest information is forwarded directly to consciousness, a far smaller proportion of inherent implications reach direct awareness. To some degree, of course, each of the processing centers is influenced by the patient's memory systems, psychopathology, assets, ongoing relationship with the message sender, broader factors in the immediate interaction, and a host of other vectors. There is clinical evidence, too, that these influencing systems are quite different at each level of processing—in other words, that the message analyzing center is influenced by one constellation, the deep unconscious system by another, and the superficial unconscious subsystem by still another. There is much to be explored and discovered in this regard.

Of great importance clinically then is the realization that some implications of a message are forwarded to the conscious system, whereas other implications reach the deep unconscious system. When we speak of a sensitive individual, we mean, for one thing, a person who is aware of an unusually large number of implications in the messages sent by himself or herself and others.

To illustrate, again, the difference between conscious and unconscious information processing, a female therapist directly reassured a female patient, who was about to make a trying visit to her family of origin, that she would be able to handle the situation. The patient thanked the therapist for her reassurance, and consciously saw the therapist as empathic and concerned about her. These, of course, are the meanings that the patient extracted directly from the therapist's intervention, or message. They involve some of the *conscious implications* of the message for the patient.

In the next session, the patient said that her father was always trying to control her and telling her what to do. He would offer gratuitous advice when the patient needed none, because she knew full well the nature of the issues.

In this brief fragment of material, we can readily see that the patient's displaced and symbolized reaction to the therapist's intervention was quite different from her conscious reaction. In substance, the conscious implications were positive, whereas the unconscious implications appraised the situation quite negatively. These negative meanings can also be extracted from the manifest message, but they were not allowed access to direct awareness, and were instead forwarded to the deep unconscious system. It is evident that conscious and unconscious processing are quite different in character and that their design leads to diametrically opposing conclusions.

THE PROCESSING OF INFORMATION RELEGATED TO THE DEEP UNCONSCIOUS SYSTEM

Figure 9-3 diagrams the processing of information that is directed toward the deep unconscious system by the message analyzing center. As noted, information of this kind is never sent directly into consciousness; on the contrary, information forwarded to the conscious system does not reach the deep unconscious system at all.

In response to a given message, the manifest content may well be sent immediately to the conscious system, as will certain implications. Other implications will be forwarded to the deep unconscious system, as will almost all of the encoded meanings. Tracing each element of meaning separately supports the concept that the type of information processed in the deep unconscious system is different from the type of information

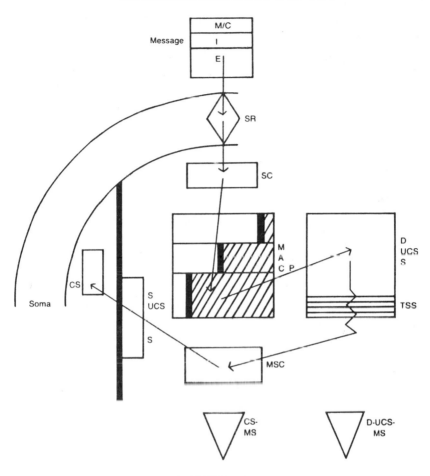

FIGURE 9.3
Steps in Processing Unconscious Information

processed in the conscious system. This finding makes additional sense, given that each system has its own way of processing the information, and that the nature of their aims are often opposed. Clearly, it would make little sense to process a given meaning simultaneously in two opposite directions. Chaos and madness would follow such an effort. It remains to be seen as to whether any form of madness does in fact eventuate because of this type of malfunction in the information-processing system.

The processing of unconscious implications is similar to the processing of encoded meanings, although there is clinical evidence that encoded meanings touch on somewhat more primitive images and issues in the deep unconscious system than do most implications. As can be seen in Figure 9.3, an unconscious implication or unconscious encoded message is given meaning in the synthesizing center and then subjected to analysis in the message analyzing center, which determines its fate and characterization.

The anxiety gradient for encoded meanings is quite low, in that virtually all encoded meanings are relegated to the deep unconscious system. Clinical evidence suggests that encoded meanings are a source of great anxiety for both the message sender (who, of course, has found it necessary to encode the perception or fantasy that he or she is imparting) and the receiver (who in most instances is in dread of all messages that are encoded). Encoded meaning touches on the realm of the deep unconscious, and all information processed in that system is affiliated with or surrounded by extremely intense anxieties and dread. It is these enormous anxieties which lead to the deep unconscious processing in the first place.

Analysis of clinical data reveals that there are several important and distinctive attributes to the processing of information directed from the message analyzing center to the deep unconscious system. Collectively, these attributes account for *unconscious experience* of the world, which is quite different from *conscious experience* of the world.

The first of these attributes involves the form in which information is forwarded to the deep unconscious system. Such information is restructured or coded according to principles or *premises* that are different from those that exist for processing conscious information. This coding is one of the distinctive aspects of what Freud termed primary process thinking (which he believed to be fluid, based on displacement and symbolization, out of contact with reality, interested in immediate discharge, timeless, and without contradictions). Clinical data indicate that much of our psychoanalytic thinking in this regard requires revision.

The deep unconscious schemata subjects all information to the following premises: Parts equal whole, possessions equal the possessor, what happened before will happen again, symbols are real, and so forth (the list is undoubtedly incomplete). This manner of thinking or processing information may be characterized as primitive (and it may be characteristic of nonverbal thinking), but it also represents a valid way of experiencing, because on the symbolic level, all of these premises are highly sensitive and accurate.

Though Freud saw primary process thinking as entirely illogical, the deep unconscious system clearly operates with considerable logic and knowledge. The schemata of the deep unconscious system—and the influencing unconscious systems to which it has access (memories and the like)—are considerably more informed in the emotional realm than the conscious schemata. Indeed, the *I.Q.* of every individual, a reflection of conscious processing, is far inferior to the *I.Q.*, which reflects the deep unconscious system's enormous sensitivity to and capacity to store emotionally charged information that is unconsciously received, processed, and maintained. It may well be that the complexity of the meanings we render unconscious is far greater than the complexity of conscious information, thereby requiring a processing system equal to the nature of such meanings.

The deep unconscious system appears to process information quickly and silently throughout the day and night. The rapidity of this type of processing becomes appareant in psychotherapy when there is a traumatic deviation in a particular session. As a rule, the patient is quick to respond with a narrative that contains valid encoded perceptions of that deviation. The narrative is clearly the product of inputs from both the conscious and unconscious systems, and the validity of the unconscious meaning contained in these perceptions attests to both the rapidity and high intelligence of the schemata of the deep unconscious system.

A critical feature of the deep unconscious system is its *transformation subsystem* (see Figure 9.3), which serves to modify the results of deep unconscious processing for output. The information so derived is transformed through the fundamental mechanisms of displacement, symbolization (disguise in its broadest sense), and condensation.

In substance, then, no message emerges from the deep unconscious system unless it has been subjected to the processes of transformation—of encoding, or disguise. Thus, the workings and intelligence of the deep unconscious system are never available to consciousness directly, but only through transformed images. Initial clinical research indicates that transformation is a basic psychic modulating function which helps to protect the individual against pathological expressions—emotionally founded symptoms, somatization, and blind acting out.

The deep unconscious system can process information without creating overwhelming anxiety—despite the overload of anxiety that adheres to the information being processed—largely because its workings are not known consciously to the individual. In other words, we are capable of processing and comprehending emotionally charged truths only so long as we do not have any direct awareness that such processing is taking place—and do not know its contents and outcome.

We pay an enormous price for this safeguard against anxiety. We lose much of the great wisdom of the deep unconscious system. Because the processing carried out in this system is never known to us directly, it cannot be utilized directly in decision making and overt behavior as a reality–oriented adaptive tool—for which conscious choice is a vital and essential feature. We have a situation of pervasive unconscious influence and inner adaptation without conscious choice.

This sort of situation is most readily seen in the case of subliminal advertising. When the words "eat popcorn" were flashed subliminally on screens in movie theaters, popcorn sales increased considerably, although the individuals involved could not consciously explain why they had felt a sudden impetus to buy. There is considerable evidence that subliminal stimuli do indeed enter the deep unconscious system, which then processes the information.

Such experiments illustrate the nature of an output system that does not permit direct access to its basis of action. Indeed, the only means of gaining this access to the deep unconscious system is by decoding this output in terms of activating triggers—either in therapy or through a meaningful communicative self–analysis. Thus, a therapist can meaningfully interpret deep unconscious meanings only when the patient actually provides encoded output, thereby opening the system to the therapist's influence.

Freud himself (1915) conveyed this insight when he doubted the extent to which an analyst could influence the unconscious part of the mind, except by way of derivatives. Clearly, the only way a patient or therapist can make use of the enormous wisdom of the deep unconscious system is through interactional decoding. Even so, the conscious system abhors realizations from the deep unconscious system. As a result, the half-life of any insight into deep unconscious expressions is brief indeed. True insight is fleeting with respect to conscious understanding. Nonetheless, such a moment of insight greatly influences the conscious system and sets into motion a very significant unconscious process which ultimately modifies the patient's expressed—and perhaps core—madness.

To summarize, unconscious processing is distinctly different from conscious processing; each accounts for a different way of experiencing messages, meaning, self, and the world. When the message analyzing center experiences a particular meaning—manifest, implied, or encoded—as too anxiety provoking for unmodified acceptance into the conscious system, the message is transmitted to the deep unconscious system and processed in terms of a distinctive set of root ideas. It is to be emphasized, however, that the premises deriving from these root ideas do not distort or falsify information. On the contrary, they form the basis for a singular but accurate reading of the unconscious meaning that has been communicated.

Within the schemata of the deep unconscious system, incoming messages are treated with utmost logic. The deep unconscious system is highly sensitive to the unconscious dimension of reality, just as the conscious system is attuned to the manifest and conscious aspects. Because unconscious meaning and conscious meaning are often diametrically opposed, the wisdom and responses of the two systems—unconscious and conscious—are often at odds. These differences are accentuated by the guiding metaschema for each system —in substance, the conscious system is geared in the emotional sphere for defense at all costs, whereas the unconscious system is designed for the pursuit of truth, especially as it pertains to unconscious communication and meaning (see below).

Both the conscious and unconscious systems are adaptive resources and constitute efforts to identify, understand, and cope with incoming messages and their meanings. The goal is an adaptive, satisfying, self-protective, and at times helpful and compassionate response. Though each system carries them out differently, such functions are basic to the operation of the human mind.

The adaptive processing of information in the deep unconscious system is powerfully safeguarded by means of the *transformation function*. That is, the unconscious system processes information and meaning silently and without awareness. It appears designed mainly to work over extremely terrifying information, and deals with meaning of dreadful proportions. Awareness of these meanings would overwhelm the conscious system and create panic states and experiences of psychic annihilation. Furthermore, insight into the information processed in the deep unconscious system—for example, that a loved one wishes to commit incest or to murder or to dismember—is often so chaotic, psychotic, and disturbing, that the mind would falter and the patient would be overwhelmed and without effective recourse. The capacity to process this type of information in safe fashion without access to consciousness and action is of utmost necessity. And even though the transformation function—displacement and symbolization—precludes the use of deep unconscious knowledge for direct and conscious adaptation, we are provided with a safe means of working over terrifying information in silent fashion.

The deep unconscious system sends transformed images to the message sending center, which passes them on to the superficial unconscious subsystem or, when met half-way by the hypercathexes of attention, to direct conscious awareness. The manifest meanings are then stored in the superficial unconscious subsystem, while the unconscious meanings go unrecognized.

WHY TWO SYSTEMS?

The conscious system is designed to enable the individual to safeguard and satisfy basic needs for safety, self-defense, food, shelter, and companionship. With the satisfaction of these needs assured, the system also fosters procreative needs, sexual satisfactions, and other needs and pleasurable activities. The conscious mind, therefore, must be attuned to direct information and surface meanings, without being distracted by ambiguity and symbolism. The conscious system adapts by making choices, and choices require a concrete assessment of facts relevant to achieving a desired goal. Furthermore, this system must assure the individual not only of physical safety, but of emotional, or psychological, safety as well. To this end, the system evokes a wide range of behavioral and psychic defenses—repression, denial, flight, avoidance, and the like. Most of these defenses are in fact directed against unconscious and encoded meanings, because these elicit both anxiety and confusion, which interfere with smooth conscious functioning.

There is, however, another side to survival that does involve ambiguity, symbolism, highly charged emotional needs, and emotional inputs and responses from others. It is hardly possible for the same set of schemata to proceed toward the goal of accessibility to unconscious meaning at the same time that it is taking flight from and obliterating this meaning. A system that is sensitive to unconscious meaning protects the individual emotionally—even though the incoming messages do not reach conscious awareness.

THE CLINICAL RELEVANCE OF THE MODEL

Though relatively new, this model of the mind has already clarified many clinical issues, pointed to fresh problems, and provided some initial solutions. For example, the model demonstrates that the psychotherapist who wishes to be in touch with, understand, and interpret unconscious meaning must be highly sensitive to the premises, attributes, and functioning of the deep unconscious system—to a second *voice* embedded in the patient's conscious flow of words, affects, and images. Narratives and dreams are not themselves processing vehicles, but already-transformed reports that inform us of the ongoing processes within the deep unconscious system.

The failure to distinguish between these conscious and unconscious realms of experience, as well as the failure to understand that it is only the deep unconscious realm that entails repressed unconscious meaning, has led to much confusion in clinical technique and theory. Furthermore, since the conscious system is made anxious by the deep unconscious system, the therapist must overcome natural defensive tendencies to avoid transformed derivatives, unconscious meaning and experience, and everything associated with the deep unconscious system. Therapists prefer to work with the conscious system and its superficial unconscious components, where meanings are direct, relatively anxiety-free, and easy to recognize. There is, then, a basic fear of getting in touch with the deep unconscious system in any conceivable form.

What, then, does the model tell us about the nature of psychopathology or madness? Initial observation indicates that there are contributions to patient-madness from both systems of the mind—conscious and unconscious. The deep unconscious system contributes the unresolved and raw unconscious memories, perceptions, and fantasies on which core and expressed madness are founded. When these constellations are extremely traumatic and when the schemata themselves have primitive and other dysfunctional attributes, material processed within this system is an especially significant factor in madness. The transformed images that emerge from this system are imbued with anxiety and dread, and tend to evoke extreme and unusually defensive reactions in the conscious system.

Within the conscious system, there may well be a contribution to madness due to pathological denial and repression that operates within the framework of the superficial unconscious system. In addition, the conscious system is so deeply committed to defensive responses to anxiety-provoking triggers and derivative communications that it will resort to extreme and pathological defenses, thereby precipitating symptoms and other emotional dysfunctions.

Much appears to depend on the functional nature and capacities of, and influences on, each of these systems. In schizophrenia, there are major disturbances in the conscious system, which help to account for the breaks with reality, but there is also evidence of a major disturbance in the transformation function. This results in the emergence into consciousness of primitive images that reflect processing by the deep unconscious system—images that are usually expressed entirely in derivative form. With borderline patients, these dysfunctions are more intermittent and less extreme. It is likely that psychopathology involves rather selective dysfunctions of the systems and subsystems of the unconscious mind. It can be expected that fresh clinical research will clarify these issues.

One way of conceptualizing the development of expressed madness is to think of a symptom as a process that emerges when the information-processing systems of the mind are overloaded and unable to effectively cope with and adapt to incoming traumatic messages. A mad symptom has contributions from both the conscious and unconscious systems, and is, in part, a special type of encoded message (one that is incompletely transformed?), which is difficult to decode without narrative associations. It follows, then, that a derivative and a symptom share a basic structure—a point made by Freud as early as 1900. We may postulate that a high level of trauma and anxiety, along with internal dysfunctions of the systems themselves, result in an overloading of the information-processing schemata, thus precipitating a shift from derivative image to symptomatic expression.

The model suggests that adaptive cure is effected not only by interpreting the unconscious meanings of the patient's madness, but the guiding premises and needs (the deep unconscious metaschema) that serve to maintain it.

Interpretations that touch on manifest contents and conscious implications, without considering interactional derivatives, deal exclusively with the conscious system and fail to consider the deep unconscious system at all. Such interpretations tend to be clichéd and self-evident, often involving the identification of unnoticed patterns, the introduction of intellectualized formulations, and the further introduction of genetic connections that are held accountable for the patient's madness—to the exclusion of contributions from the therapist. As such, they may enable the patient to consciously recognize certain propensities and to consciously decide to alter his or her behavior. Nonetheless, such a patient will maintain a strong unconscious perception of the therapist as unknowledgeable (and often, as frame-deviant and interested only in nonderivative expressions). Such perceptions also have an influence on the patient.

Properly formulated interactional interpretations bring the thinking and insights of the deep unconscious system into the conscious system. As noted, this type of intervention is consistently followed by derivative validation, though the resultant conscious understanding is, in almost all instances, quickly dissipated, because the conscious system finds unconscious meaning almost intolerable. Nonetheless, as stated, there is clinical evidence that an important unconscious process is set into motion at such junctures, which leads to eventual, adaptive symptom alleviation.

Psychoanalytic work in general has been fashioned largely in keeping with the unconscious defensive needs of the conscious system of the therapist or analyst. Indeed, the most common error made by the noncommunicative therapist is a failure to attend to and understand the many implications of his or her own interventions. For the communicative therapist, the most common form of error is an unconsciously motivated avoidance of those derivatives from a patient which touch on active issues within the therapist—a defense invoked by the conscious system against the mobilization of anxiety-provoking derivatives stemming from the deep unconscious system.

THE PREMISES AND METASCHEMA
THAT GUIDE EACH SYSTEM

The guiding metaschema for the conscious and unconscious systems are also distinctive. Operations in the conscious schema are guided, above all, by the need for defense and self-protection at any price. Of course, patients differ in the means by which this defensive need is expressed—lying, denying, splitting off, taking flight, acting out, cheating—but they share it in common with one another and with their therapists as well. And despite Freud's contention otherwise, it is the conscious system that is designed for immediate discharge because of its tendencies toward defense, flight, and action. In contrast, the deep unconscious system speaks for delay because it can tolerate anxiety-provoking unconscious meaning, safeguarded by the realization that none of this disturbing meaning will emerge into awareness without protective transformations.

The basic guiding principle for the unconscious system is a quest for unconscious truth no matter how great the potential terror. Whereas the internal processing of the conscious schemata may involve many moments of defense, the unconscious schemata appear to be open and without defense, protected by the absence of direct output.

Because the conscious and unconscious schemata are distinctive ways of experiencing, the dimensions of meaning are processed quite differently in the deep unconscious and conscious realms. In brief, the deep unconscious system is exquisitely sensitive to ground rule/frame issues, whereas the conscious system is inconsistent and often insensitive to such concerns. In addition, the deep unconscious system consistently expresses the wish for and wisdom of the secure, or ideal, frame, whereas the conscious system in most instances wishes for and actually seeks out deviations.

Communicatively, the conscious system stresses the *differences* between two individuals, objects, or situations. In contrast, the deep unconscious system picks up and stresses the *similarities*. Furthermore, each system prefers expressions in its own mode. Thus, the conscious system values nonderivative expressions and the direct, nonsymbolic experience of meaning. On the other hand, the unconscious system prefers derivatives and symbols as a medium of expression.

As for mode of relatedness, the conscious system seeks out pathological modes, whereas the unconscious system seeks healthy forms of relatedness. It would appear that the pathological mode provides the conscious system with important pathological defenses and satisfactions which enable it to adapt to pathological introjects. The deep unconscious system, seeking the truth, has no such concern and maintains a quest for ideals.

As noted, the conscious system typically seeks action-discharge or pathological merger, whereas the deep unconscious system is truly invested in insight into unconscious meaning. Similarly, the conscious system, mainly in the realm of the superficial unconscious subsystem, prefers madness in others, whereas the deep unconscious system seeks out sanity. As can be seen, in virtually all of these situations the two systems take opposing positions and process information toward distinctly different goals.

This model of the mind suggests that dysfunctions may occur on many unconscious levels and in each of the systems within which emotionally charged information is processed. For example, the message analyzing center may overempasize a particular encoded meaning at the expense of others. This type of selectivity would, of course, be influenced by intrapsychic conflicts, memory systems, and other factors. The message analyzing center is open to dysfunctions with respect to the level of anxiety at which information is forwarded to the deep unconscious system. It has been discovered clinically that the latter system is vulnerable in at least three ways: first, by being prone to overidealization in the presence of traumas that create extremes of death anxiety—a form of deep unconscious denial. Secondly, in response to frame-securing efforts and meanings, the system is prone to exaggeration and, at times, to unconscious distortion. A third cluster of dysfunctions accrue to the transformation function, which may either fail to operate or become overly defensive so that critical transformed images are barred access to the message sending center.

The message sending center itself has proven to be a critical part of the unconscious information-processing system. It may malfunction by overemphasizing either conscious or unconscious inputs, thus failing to produce a balanced, compromised, outgoing communication. Furthermore, it is this system that appears to be especially vulnerable to the influence of the many other systems that play a role in communication, behavior, and symptom formation.

It should be noted that the present chapter has focused on the basic system with which we process information toward immediate conscious or unconscious registration. There are, however, additional systems that are called into play that more fully account for behaviors and symptomatic formation. They have been omitted from the present work for purposes of simplification.

In brief, it would appear that there are at least four interacting, largely sequential processes that are involved in the total response to incoming emotionally charged information:

(1) The information-processing system described here, which also helps to account for the creation of conscious and unconscious short-term memory units.

(2) A decision-making system, conscious and unconscious, through which the information in each sector is considered, worked over, and decisions are made as to how to evaluate and respond to the incoming information. An internal message generating center is a crucial component of this system.

(3) A second-level response system that involves a choice of expressive channel. The main possibilities are those of thought, image, affect, symptom, and behavior.

(4) Long-term storage, conscious and unconscious, which includes the recording of events, the creation of introjects pertinent to the individuals involved in the emotionally charged situation, and the registration of meanings.

The interactions described here involve harmonies and conflicts within the separate realms of the conscious and unconscious systems, and between these two systems as well. Among the more interesting clinical problems raised by elaborations of this model, there is the discovery of major discrepancies between unconscious realizations and conscious decisions regarding behaviors. For example, not infrequently, a patient will unconsciously register and recognize the destructiveness of an intervention from a therapist, and yet the verbal/behavioral response involves affirmation of the psychotherapy. There is much to be explained here on both the clinical and research levels.

RECOMMENDED READINGS

Arlow, J., & Brenner, C. (1964). *Psychoanalytic Concepts and the Structural Theory.* New York: International Universities Press.
Basch, M. (1976). Psychoanalysis and communications science. The Annual of Psychoanalysis 4:385–421.

Basch, M. (1976). Theory formation in chapter VII: A critique. *Journal of the American Psychoanalytic Association* 24:61–100.

Basch, M. (1981). Psychoanalytic interpretation and cognitive transformation. *International Journal of Psycho-Analysis* 62:151–175.

Freud, S. (1900). The interpretation of dreams. *SE* 4-5:1–627.

Freud, S. (1915). The unconscious. *SE* 14:159–204.

Galatzer-Levy, R. (1978). Qualitative change from quantitative change: Mathematical catastrophe theory in relation to psychoanalysis. *Journal of the American Psychoanalytic Association* 26:921–935.

Gill, M. (1963). *Topography and Systems in Psychoanalytic Theory, Psychological Issues.* Monograph 10. New York: International Universities Press.

Goleman, D. (1985). *Vital Lies, Simple Truths.* New York: Simon & Schuster.

Holt, R. (1967). The development of the primary process: The structural view. In R. Holt (ed.): *Motives and Thought, Psychological Issues.* New York: International Universities Press.

Langs, R. (1986). Clinical issues arising from a new model of the mind. *Contemporary Psychoanalysis* 22:418–444.

Noy, P. (1969). A revision of the psychoanalytic theory of the primary process. *International Journal of Psycho-Analysis* 50:155–178.

Palombo, S. (1978). *Dreaming and Memory: A New Information-Processing Model.* New York: Basic Books.

Peterfreund, E. (1971). *Information, Systems, and Psychoanalysis, Psychological Issues.* Monograph 25/26. New York: International Universities Press.

CHAPTER **10**

Safeguarding the
Therapeutic Experience

We return now to the clinical situation and to matters of technique, closing our condensed study of the therapeutic interaction by identifying a number of clinical precepts that safeguard the therapist against common errors and failings.

(1) Perhaps the most difficult task required of the therapist is to recognize all of the critical implications of his or her interventions. The therapist may judiciously monitor the patient's material toward this end, largely because the patient will represent in encoded form those implications of the therapist's efforts that have meaning in light of the patient's own madness. In addition, patients often encode those implications of an intervention which are threatening to both parties to treatment.

(2) The therapist should treat the implications of his or her interventions as *actualities with unconscious meaning*. The patient's response to these implications is not a matter of fantasy, but a matter of perception. For too long now, therapists have acknowledged some type of unconscious meaning in the material from patients (however erroneously formulated), while believing that their own interventions should be taken at face value. Such a position is untenable and highly defensive for the therapist.

(3) Listening should center around triggers, and all formulations should begin by defining valid, encoded (transformed) selected perceptions of the implications of the therapist's interventions. Since the patient's perceptions are often geared toward therapist-madness and error, the therapist will adopt natural defenses and avoidance in this regard—mainly because he or she operates in terms of his or her own conscious system. In order to counteract the defensive tendency to avoid formulating the patient's perceptions, the therapist should consistently regard each image from the patient as veridical and perceptive until proven otherwise. There is a tendency among therapists to either avoid formulating perceptions entirely, or to begin with a perception and then to consider subsequent images, which are often highly negative and disturbing, as reactions to these perceptions. In principle, every single image should be treated as a perception before all other considerations.

(4) The central issue in therapist-madness involves residuals in the deep unconscious system that are activated by the triggers of the patient's material. When the patient's conscious and unconscious perceptions are unflattering and disturbing, and when the patient's derivatives touch on conscious and unconscious issues within the therapist, misunderstanding, avoidance, and especially misinterpretations are likely to ensue. The therapist should therefore know his or her recent emotional traumas, anniversary reactions, long-standing vulnerabilities, and other emotionally charged issues so that he or she can safeguard against either defensive avoidance or misinterpretation.

(5) In addition to interventions missed because of unconscious defensive needs, the main communicative error in intervening involves holding the patient solely accountable for a mad symptom. Whenever a patient is provocative or regresses unexpectedly, the therapist may be inclined toward anger at the patient. Such anger is expressed most often through erroneous confrontations and mistaken interventions in which the patient is given virtually all of the responsibility for the emotional disturbance. By consistently beginning an intervention with an adaptive context and encoded perceptions, that is, with the therapist's accountability, such a tendency may be shortcircuited.

(6) The therapist should be sensitive to all alterations in the ground rules, even those that are seemingly minor. The deep unconscious system is extremely sensitive to such interventions, and derivative response is virtually inevitable. However, because of the guilt that is often evoked within the therapist when he or she deviates or makes an active interventional error of some other kind, there is often a powerful unconscious need (within his or her conscious system) to pass over the deviant intervention. At times, this leads to an especially destructive and functionally psychotic position in which a therapist will intervene in terms of a frame-securing adaptive context, when the patient is actually reacting to a frame deviation. In the deep unconscious system, deviations take precedence over all other types of stimuli for processing and informing. The therapist's listening and formulating should reflect this realization.

(7) In intervening, it is important to remember to explain the unconscious basis of all indicators—symptoms and resistances. Some interventions may be made in the absence of indicators, as when the therapist has modified a ground rule. Nonetheless, it is important to remember that in most sessions, the therapist's goal is to explain the unconscious basis of an immediate symptom or resistance in light of a trigger, selected encoded perceptions, and reactions to these perceptions.

(8) When patients act out in their daily lives, unilaterally alter the ground rules of treatment (*i.e.*, express gross behavioral resistances), or press the therapist to deviate, the trigger for such mad expressions is almost always an alteration of the ground rules in which the therapist has already participated. More rarely, a secure-frame intervention will evoke a measure of anxiety and efforts to alter the ground rules, though it will rarely precipitate the use of action-discharge by the patient. Deviations express a measure of action-discharge by the therapist, and unconsciously encourage the patient to behave in similar fashion. The secure frame holds the patient and encourages insight rather than action; as a result, patients seldom act inappropriately in response to that type of intervention. On the other hand, secure-frame sensitive patients will validate secure frame interventions on a derivative level, only to subsequently attempt to

engage the therapist in some type of modification in the existing ground rules.

(9) The therapist should develop an ear for the expressions of the deep unconscious system. As we have seen, the conscious system speaks for survival in the everyday world, stresses defenses, prefers a manifest–content type of interaction with the therapist, tends to seek a deviant frame, wishes for pathological modes of relatedness, often turns to action-discharge and denial, and searches for madness in others—which it then minimizes as a rule. In addition, the conscious system tends to emphasize the differences between people and situations, thereby blurring similarities, which are then relegated to the deep unconscious system. And although some patients are indeed consciously preoccupied with death, in most instances the conscious system tends to minimize death anxieties and related issues.

In contrast, the deep unconscious system is highly sensitive to frame issues, seeks out derivative relatedness, prefers a healthy type of relationship and genuine insight, and shows a strong preference for sanity in others. Moreover, issues of death anxiety and psychotic forms of communication are central to its mode of experience. The deep unconscious system stresses the similarities between people and incidents, especially when the situation is emotionally harmful. Where the conscious system defensively tries to overlook, the unconscious system is painfully in touch. Finally, the conscious system has a limited and defensive view of reality and remains unaware of various dimensions, which are relegated to unconscious perception. It is, of course, the deep unconscious system that responds to these unconscious implications of reality and to realities that are expressed through encoded messages. In general, the realm of experience available to the conscious system is far more circumscribed and concrete than the kind of experience available to the unconscious system.

(10) Throughout this book, we have identified a variety of factors in symptom formation. Broadly, symptoms are responses to traumas and danger situations that evoke anxiety and dysfunction—the macrogenesis of symptom formation. Early life traumas that evoke death anxiety play a central role in the etiology of mad disturbances. Later traumas that mobilize these

earlier anxieties and issues—and the unconscious memories, fantasies, and perceptions pertinent to them—are a major cause of fresh symptom formation.

Symptoms can also arise from dysfunctions of the systems that process emotionally charged information—the microgenesis of symptom formation. Expressed madness may arise from the overuse of defenses in the conscious system, or from dysfunctional processing by the schemata of the deep unconscious system. A critical role in symptom formation appears to lie within the transformation subsystem of the deep unconscious system. Disturbances in this function appear to be a major determinant of whether a particular trauma is processed through communicative derivatives or communicative symptoms.

Another critical factor in symptom formation involves the vicissitudes of other unconscious systems during the course of a psychotherapy (see Chapter 9). It can be shown clinically that the patient's symptoms and their alleviation correlate closely with the therapist's management of the ground rules and frame, and his or her interpretations in this area. In general, frame deviations tend to produce symptomatic disturbance, though gratifying and defense-offering deviations may also offer a measure of symptom relief. On the other hand, frame-securing interventions tend to be a major source of cure, especially when accompanied by appropriate interpretive work. Paradoxically, unexpected frame-securing interventions and interventions of this kind offered to frame-sensitive patients may cause temporary periods of symptomatic regression. In most instances, however, frame-securing interventions ultimately lead to cure rather than regression.

(11) It is important to remember that with respect to alterations in the ground rules, *both interpretation and rectification are necessary.* All such work should be done at the behest of the patient's derivatives. Interpretations without rectification will generally not obtain derivative validation, and rectification without interpretation will lead to a split image of a therapist—capable in one sense, and incapable in another.

(12) Anticipating current and future clinical research, we may think of the *secure frame* as those conditions under which *catastrophe* will be anticipated and experienced by both patient

and therapist. The *deviant frame* confronts the patient with chaos. It can be shown clinically that chaos is a major defense against catastrophe. In general, the communicative approach is essentially nonchaotic, thereby exposing both patient and therapist to issues of catastrophe—of death and death anxiety—which are key factors in madness. Noncommunicative therapy fails to correctly identify the organizing factors in the patient's material—the adaptive contexts. As a result, it is not possible to synthesize the patient's material in a way that defines the actual patterns of unconscious meaning in the hour. As a consequence, such therapies deal in chaos, thereby providing major defenses agianst catastrophe. For some patients, chaos may well be the only source of relief from madness. The problem then becomes one of creating forms of chaos that are more constructive and relief-giving than destructive and damaging.

(13) As our final precept, we may be reminded that errors are inevitable in the work of any psychotherapist. Indeed, we all retain a core of madness, of vulnerability to expressed madness, and a measure of unresolved emotional conflict. The goal is to make as few errors as possible, and in addition, to be able to detect these errors—at best, within the session in which they have occurred. Quite often, the therapist will intervene verbally with what he or she considers to be the best intervention available, only to discover flaws as soon as the intervention has been completed. The patient's derivative material will often facilitate a subsequent corrective intervention.

In other instances, it is the presence of negative interpersonal images, specific allusions to a failure to understand or to unavailability, and the absence of cognitive validation that will alert the therapist to an error. In these situations, it is important to review the material that has served as the trigger for the error, and to engage in a very brief period of self-analysis in an effort to determine the unconscious basis of the mistake. In addition, the therapist should attend to the patient's continuing material and endeavor to reformulate, turning most often to the search for a trigger that has been missed. Next, the quest should be for overlooked derivative perceptions, and for an opportunity to intervene correctly. The primary issue is the original material that has been erroneously formulated, but a secondary issue that may require interpretation is the parient's encoded perceptions of the actual mistake.

The detection of errors relies on the therapist's *monitoring function*. It is not uncommon after intervening to have a lapse and to fail to monitor the patient's mateial as encoded perceptions and validating or invalidating commentaries on the therapist's effort. Nor is it uncommon to become fixated on a particular adaptive context to a point where other significant contexts are overlooked and with them encoded perceptions that are critical to the unconscious basis of the patient's madness. Then, too, it is often difficult for therapists to accept a patient's telling encoded perceptions of his or her madness and to work fairly and meaningfully with such material.

Although arduous and painful, there can be no substitute for a commitment to the truth as it exists within patient and therapist, and in the therapeutic interaction. It is only through truth that we may grow and flourish. And in psychotherapy, the pursuit of truth is, in the long run, well worth the pain.

RECOMMENDED READINGS

Freud. S. (1926). Inhibitions, symptoms, and anxiety. *SE* 20:77–178.

Langs, R. (1982). *The Psychotherapeutic Conspiracy*. New York: Aronson.

Langs, R. (1985). *Workbooks for Psychotherapists: Vol. III, Intervening and Validating*. Emerson, NJ: Newconcept Press.

Langs, R. (1985). *Workbooks for Psychotherapists: Vol. II, Listening and Formulating*. Emerson, NJ: Newconcept Press.

Langs, R. (1985). *Workbooks for Psychotherapists: Vol. I, Understanding Unconscious Communication*. Emerson, NJ: Newconcept Press.

Langs, R. (1985). *Madness and Cure*. Emerson, NJ: Newconcept Press.

Index

ABOUT THE AUTHOR

Robert Langs, M.D. is Executive Director, The Program for Psychoanalytic Psychotherapy and Chief, Center for Communicative Research — Beth Israel Medical Center in New York City. He is Research Professor of Psychology in the Derner Institute at Adelphi University, Garden City, N.Y. A classically trained psychoanalyst, Dr. Langs has practiced psychoanalysis and psychotherapy for over 25 years. He has written more than 20 books on psychoanalysis, psychotherapeutic technique, and the therapeutic interaction.